ADVICE

for an

imperfect

MARRIED

WORLD

I0022208

ADVICE

for an

imperfect

MARRIED

WORLD

Wisdom and Wit
from Friends & Lovers'
Queen of Hearts

PAT GAUDETTE

Founder, Friends & Lovers the Relationships Guide
www.FriendsandLovers.com

Home & Leisure Publishing, Inc.

Advice for an Imperfect Married World:
Wisdom and Wit from Friends & Lovers' Queen of Hearts

Published by Home & Leisure Publishing, Inc.
P. O. Box 968
Lecanto, FL 34460-0968
USA

Copyright © 2004 Pat Gaudette.
All rights reserved. No part of this book may be used or reproduced in any manner whatsoever without written permission, except in the case of brief quotations embodied in critical articles or reviews.

Published 2004

Printed in the United States of America.

ISBN 0-9761210-2-6 (Paperback)
ISBN 0-9761210-3-4 (e-book)

Nearly all marriages, even happy ones, are mistakes: in the sense that almost certainly (in a more perfect world, or even with a little more care in this very imperfect one) both partners might be found more suitable mates. But the real soul-mate is the one you are actually married to. -- J.R.R. Tolkien (1892 - 1973)

Contents

Since 1996, people have been pouring out their relationship woes via email to "Queenie," the very opinionated and no-nonsense online advice columnist for *Friends & Lovers the Relationships Guide* (www.FriendsandLovers.com). ***Advice for an Imperfect Married World*** is compiled from Queenie's columns dealing with problems facing marriages and what could be considered "seriously committed" relationships. Her first book of columns, ***Advice for an Imperfect Single World,*** was published September 2004.

Letters have been edited as needed for clarity, to correct errors in grammar, and to delete or change names, places, dates, locations, and/or other identifying information in order to preserve the anonymity of the writers and those with whom they are involved. Any similarity to persons living or dead is purely coincidental.

Queenie's comments both online and in this book are provided as entertainment only and are not meant to substitute for relationships counseling or other professional and/or medical services or treatments.

Pat Gaudette
Founder, Friends & Lovers the Relationships Guide

Trouble Between the Sheets

Trouble Between the Sheets

*"My husband has a very high sex drive. It seems like every
time he gets near me he wants sex and I want to sleep."*

Let's face it, in olden times people got married so they could have sex without getting in trouble with their family, church, and society in general. Of course they were probably already having sex but they were sneaking around, catching it as they could, and even though it made the sexual experience more thrilling due to the "putting one over" aspect, it also made unmarried sex hazardous when an unexpected pregnancy was the outcome.

"We" have evolved over the decades so that for many people the sin of sex without marriage no longer terrifies them. Just as all pendulums swing far to the left, the sexual pendulum has been swinging back to the right since the super sexy Sixties.

Living together isn't a big deal and for highly enlightened younger generations, sex has become just another exercise to keep trim. In the United States, a president who convinced many (but not all) that oral sex isn't really "sex" has helped to shed the sin aspect of that intimate encounter which may explain why such a high percentage of young people casually engage in oral sex or essentially any type of sex as long as it doesn't include vaginal penetration with ejaculation.

So it's been a wild and sexually crazy time and adding to the mix has been a dramatic increase in AIDS and other sexually transmitted diseases. Remember when only gay men were dying of AIDS? Straight women are another increasing statistic brought about by unprotected sex, sometimes due to a straying spouse.

There's no doubt that sexual intimacy is extremely important within a marriage or a committed relationship. Couples should be on the same "page" as far as sexual needs and performance or trouble is not far away.

Statistics are no guide when it comes to sex. Surveys sample a small amount of people and even then, when talking about sex, the results aren't necessarily accurate. Each couple must find their own satisfying and acceptable frequency and methods.

♥

Dear Queenie, I met and married my soul mate 4 years ago. We have our share of difficulties, some worse than the average couple, but we work through them well. The major problem? He loses his erection as soon as he gets near me. We can kiss, hug, and it'll be raging, but as soon as my hand goes near it, it'll soften. Oral sex has never been a problem, just intercourse. This has been happening for almost a year now.

I can understand the occasional impotency problem related to stress, financial problems, the use of stimulants or depressants, but those excuses don't cut it when he's sober. An "other woman" has been ruled out due to his work schedule, and also the fact that he doesn't go out, ever, without the family.

I've gained weight since we've met, and lost my job and don't current work. My own self-esteem is at an all-time low because I'm no longer that successful, independent woman he met and fell in love with. When he can't perform, I feel even worse.

It's to the point where he doesn't even try anymore. Last time I made a very suggestive move, he decided to play with the puppy instead. It's been months since we've had intercourse, and probably a year since he's actually been hard enough to penetrate and last over 4 minutes.

I am desperate. We have no insurance to pay for counseling, and I'm becoming very frustrated. I have even told him that he's pushing me into the arms of another man. Right now, anyone who even speaks to me like a woman is attractive to me. — Laura

Laura, the more you try the more stress there is on him to perform. Stress will make him less able to perform making you feel as though he finds you unattractive sexually. It's a vicious circle and some of it is no doubt due to the change in how you see yourself — no longer the svelte successful woman that you were just a few years ago. What happened?

I certainly hope you're going to use all your efforts to get your marriage back on track instead of taking the easy way out and trying to find sexual fulfillment with anyone who happens along who knows you're available for a few well chosen words.

You don't say why you have changed so much in such a short period of time but it's certainly time for you to work on your self-esteem so that you're not a loser magnet and you make a mistake that could be fatal to your marriage.

Perhaps it's some of those "other problems" that are causing problems in the bedroom for the two of you particularly if this is a new problem in your relationship.

Put some time and energy into really looking at the interaction between the two of you and be honest about what might be the problem(s) that are causing this to happen. —Queenie

♥

Dear Queenie, my husband and I have been married for 10 years and have probably made love less than 10 times. This is a problem in our marriage. He has no desire and has been impotent for quite some time.

He has been to the doctor and gotten help with pills twice and still no attempt to make love to me. He says he loves me and that there is no one else. This I believe because he is with me all the time.

I feel worthless and my self esteem is way low. This has affected our marriage for years and I'm about to end it. It seems crazy to end a marriage because of this. My gosh we're in our forties. I might add that the doctor told him nothing is wrong with him. Please help me. — Char

Char, have you tried couples counseling? How about sex therapy? Do you love this man enough to try whatever it takes? Does he love you enough? How much lovemaking did you do before marriage? Did you have passionless dating or did things change after marriage?

To end a sexless marriage is not so wrong if one partner is extremely unhappy and the other makes no effort to change. Life is way too short to spend it being sexually frustrated. — Queenie

♥

Dear Queenie, my husband has been involved with phone sex (900 numbers) and porn. He says he is "clean" and has been for a while. The problem is that he also lies. I think I have caught him but naturally he denies everything.

Does this qualify in the "cheating" department and if so, how many times does one give "second chances"? What about our kids? What effect will this have on them? — Ashley

Ashley, everyone at one time or another has lustful thoughts about someone they perhaps shouldn't. Should that be considered "cheating"? If so, everyone has cheated. For simplicity's sake let's say cheating is having intimate relations, either sexual or emotional, with a real, live person. That would exclude phone sex and porn. Now, if his activities are causing you distress, then there is a problem.

If you can learn to accept that he will occasionally need this type of stimulation and relax about it, then the problem is resolved. If you cannot accept it, then the problem remains and you have to decide if this is bad enough for you to consider ending your marriage. If this is all, I wouldn't think it would be.

If he is doing these activities in front of the children, then their perspective regarding acceptable sexual activities will be influenced. Personally, I think most people would agree these are activities that are best done in private, without children around.

Counseling for the both of you is much less traumatic and expensive than divorce. Please consider it. —Queenie

♥

Dear Queenie, my husband and I have been married for 20 years. He is faithful and loyal, but there is has been very little sex in our relationship. I have become obese, and no longer feel feminine. Lately I have been noticing that I avoid looking at men. I am on anti-depressants and do not feel healthy or good about myself. I have tried repeatedly to communicate my needs to my husband, but have had no sustainable change in intimacy.

I believe that I use my weight as a sexual deterrant, so that I will not be tempted by other men. I also see myself dressing in gender-less clothes to further camoflage myself. How can I change this? I want to feel like a woman again, but don't want to hurt or abandon the man I am married to. I feel like disappearing. — Ursula

Ursula, you have to feel good about yourself but being depressed won't get you to that place. If you are on anti-depressants then you must be under the care of a professional. Hopefully you are in counseling or going to get counseling to deal with your low self-esteem and depression. You and your husband might also benefit from couples counseling.–Queenie

♥

Queenie, my husband and I have been together for 10 years. Now he's confessing that he has been having homosexual feelings for some time now. He told me that he had been molested as a youth. Could all of this hve stemmed from that? We have always had a very open and loving relationship. Although he tells me he would never act on these feelings I just don't know how to react to it all and it seems as if my life is on hold. — Natalie

Natalie, what is he asking you to do? If he wants the freedom to explore his feelings, then there's a problem, the same as if he said he wanted the freedom to date other women.

As far as why, this would best be answered by a counselor or other trained professional. — Queenie

♥

Dear Queenie, my husband tells that he has been masturbating right from his seventh grade. He also has the habbit of looking into swimsuit

magazines. He also keeps giving looks to other beautiful married women and expects them to do the same. Is this normal? — Marnie

Marnie, I'm not qualified to say what's normal for your husband but it sounds normal for men in general. If he gets angry that women don't respond then there's probably a problem. — Queenie

♥

Dear Queenie, I still have sex with my ex-husband. I've been divorced from him for 2 years. We have children who live with me, he sees them but they don't know I see him too. The only time he and I get along is between the sheets, otherwise we disagree on almost everything which is why we split. This can't be healthy, I feel like we never got divorced. We even talked about moving back in together so we wouldn't have to sneak around, but not getting back together.

Is he just using me? I know there's no more love on either side. This is a bizarre situation, how do I get out of it before someone gets hurt? — Ann

Ann, you can't emotionally divorce him until you stop the physical intimacy. Yes, it's certainly convenient for him to be able to have sex when he wants it with someone he isn't legally bound to, and that he doesn't have to pay for. This sounds like a perfect situation for him but not so perfect for you.

With no love between you, how can you feel good about yourself during these physical encounters? You also don't give yourself a chance to meet someone who would give you the true love, friendship and companionship that you deserve.

If he were my ex, I'd tell him the bedroom is closed. — Queenie

♥

Dear Queenie, I am married to one of the best human beings any person can meet. He is well liked by everyone he comes across. We have been married for a little over a decade. The one problem we have is in the romance department. He seems very uncomfortable in that area. There is no doubt that he loves me very much.

I on the other hand love him but find that I need someone to be there for me romantically as well as all the other areas of love. I have made many failed attempts discussing this problem with him. He does not view it as a problem. So, for the last several years our marriage it is basically nothing more than "very best friends." I cannot describe it any better than that.

This is very scary for me because I had only two relationships prior to my marriage. Those two relationships were very good in many ways. So, I was not prepared for what I am experiencing now.

If he was a mean-spirited person, abusive, selfish, a cheater and all the other poor traits usually associated with one's demeanor that wrecks relationship, I would not be so confused on how to handle the matter. It would be a pity to divorce on what it appears to be such a petty issue but is in fact very important. I can not imagine what you could suggest that has not already been tried. — Carol

Carol, what type of relationship did you have when you were first married? If things have changed since then, when did they first start to change? If he never was on the same track as you in this matter, why did you decide to marry? If you can find the beginnings of the problem, you'll be closer to reaching a solution.

Once again approach him to discuss the situation. Since he doesn't see it as a problem, it may not be one for him even though it is for you. You must not make it appear to be his problem or it may create a "performance" problem to add to the current situation. Tell him that the physical thought of him makes you want him so much and you'd like the two of you to set aside some special time for intimacy. Don't discuss how it used to be or make comparisons.

Reach for him in bed. Be the aggressor. If he draws away or wants to stop, make every attempt to not take it personally.

If you husband truly does not have an interest in sex, there may be a physical or psychological reason that a doctor or properly trained counselor could determine. Perhaps something in his past is hindering his enjoyment. Or perhaps he has an undiagnosed disease or illness that is a factor.

Is there stress from his work or other areas in his life that would inhibit him sexually? While some men might find a release through the sex act, stress kills the desire and libido of many others. Are you succeeding in your career while his is on hold?

This is not a minor issue and I can understand why you would not want to remain in a marriage that was not sexually fulfilling. It is, however, worth trying every possible avenue, including pleasuring yourself, before dumping such a good man for this reason alone.

Whatever you do, do not discuss the matter with family or friends. And do not compound the problem by seeking the intimacy you need outside of your marriage. — Queenie

♥

Queenie, Let me know if I'm overreacting in this scenario. I'm a happily man who has a young female friend that is like a younger sister to my wife and myself. Recently, she was telling me about a rough period she went through during her college years. She frankly told me that she was happy she never got AIDS or got pregnant as she had been promiscuous during that time frame. When I asked her how many men she had been with during that era, and she replied "ten"!

I am in no way naive, but this young woman is smart, talented, and ultra-beautiful and I really felt sorry that a young lady of her caliber was sucked into that type of 'cheap' lifestyle. She's OK now, but I can't help but look at her differently.

So, my questions are: 1) Am I overreacting? Is having relations with 10 guys the norm with college female Gen-Xers? 2) How is it that a young lady can have everything going for her, but she somehow develops a low-self esteem posture that allows her to be basically used and abused by low-life guys?

It just seems so tragic. What are your comments? — Stan

Stan, let me see if I understand this. Before this little talk you had the highest regard for this smart, talented, ultra-beautiful young lady and now you think she's a slut? How many guys could she have slept with and still been a "nice" girl in your morality code? One? Three? Five?

I suspect that you're of the old school that believes "nice" girls don't give "it" up until their wedding night. Good theory but who is in the back seat with all the healthy young men who aren't expected to wait? Or are those virile young men supposed to have two girlfriends: one for fun and the other for marriage?

Of course you're overreacting!! You were completely out of line to get into a discussion of her sex life in the first place, regardless of who started the discussion. Even further out of line to ask how many men she'd been with, and then use your personal value system to judge her. — Queenie

♥

Queenie, I got married in my early 30s, so I was single for quite a while. As a single guy 'with a conscience,' I used to watch time and time again as young women would allow themselves to get 'used' by guys who basically would brag that they 'dogged' women. This cycle was repeated over and over, and even then I couldn't understand the motivation of the otherwise 'together' women who weakened and got involved with dominant knuckleheads who had NO conscience whatsoever.

And no, for these women, it was NOT just a mutual 'roll in the back seat;' invariably, they willingly got involved with the wrong guys for the wrong reasons, and ended up with hurt feelings (at best) or pregnant/ diseased (at worst). Ivy Leaguers, grocery store clerks, school teachers... the background didn't matter, the scenario was inexplicably the same.

Which brings us to my friend. What truly shocked me is that, during her 'rough era,' she was not just 'mutually rolling in the back seat.' She explained to me that, time and time again, she would jump into relationships (always with dominant boorish types), and for 3 or 4 weeks they'd 'go at it,' then she'd be unceremoniously dumped by the guy as he'd sprint off looking for new conquests. This sad situation was repeated again and again, until she finally woke up one day and called a halt to this behavior, before she could "get pregnant, or even worse, AIDS."

So again, I am not 1) sexist...I don't believe in the double standard, and have never condoned what might be considered 'typical' male behavior, and 2) naive, because I know that this type of thing happens over and over. But I have to ask a version of my original question: "why do you think that a young woman with her looks, talent and intelligence, found comfort and risked her future by meeting strange guys (her words) and worse (married guy) and ultimately letting them use her for nothing other than sex?"

Believe me, I am not trying to judge this person...I'm just trying to understand how someone so talented could have so little control over her emotions and could essentially 'reward' the 'less-than-good' guys over and over, while stripping layers off her self-esteem at each turn? I must admit, to me it is heartbreaking. Now that I've given you a (rather lengthy) more detailed explanation, what do you think? And, how can other young women prevent this from happening to them? — Stan

Stan, I don't believe any of these relationships started with a guy walking up to the female in question and indicating that he wanted to have sleazy sex with her so he could add her to his list of conquests. They probably started with soft words and promises, spoken by the guys with one goal in mind and believed by the women with another goal in mind. Some men like to brag about their "conquests", it makes them feel more macho. Unfortunately, it doesn't help the reputation of the women involved, particularly when the guys probably exaggerate about their successes and sometimes lie just to save face.

Inside every adult is a frightened little child seeking comfort. That little child does not know it is beautiful or talented, it knows that it needs a hug. That little child takes comfort in the touch of strangers who say they are friends. The child believes. And the child gets hurt, over and over again. If the child is lucky, at some point the "adult" steps in and says, "this isn't working, there's more pain than comfort coming out of these relationships. We must do something differently." Then the adult takes charge for a while. The adult teaches the child and the child develops a different set of needs. Sometimes those needs are worse than the prior needs, sometimes they are better.

Your friend believed these men cared for her. Perhaps some of them did. Not all relationships work out; nor do all relationships last for a lifetime. It is not possible to tell someone else how to live their life, nor to guide them so they learn from the experience of others. We humans are headstrong creatures, believing we know all the answers. If we live long enough, we learn just how little we truly know.

It sounds as though your friend is maturing well. She cannot change history, only learn from it.— Queenie

♥

Dear Queenie, my wife and I have been married for 18 yrs. We have two sons in their teens. Even though our marriage has the usual problems, I still love my wife very much and she claims she loves me. We are currently in a rough spot in our relationship, but neither of us wants a split and divorce.

Recently my wife admitted that she was sexually abused by two older boys when she was a young teen. This explained why she has never been very fond of sex and intimacy. I have asked her to see a therapist, but she refuses. My question is, can the emotional damage from the childhood abuse cause lifelong problems with her relating to me as her husband and lover?

I love my wife very much and want to help her confront her fears, so she can be a happier person. If she refuses professional help, what can I do to strenghten our marriage? — Ray

Ray, your wife's early abuse could certainly color her perception of the sexual act. But, just as two boys influenced her sexual attitude, so can you influence it. Without pressuring her, without being aggressive, without making this your number one goal in life, you can slowly, gently, teach her about the pleasures of physical intimacy. That means very long foreplay, and not necessarily bringing it to conclusion through penetration.

That means emotional intimacy and sharing of thoughts and feelings outside of the bedroom completely unrelated to sex. That means slowing down to a pace with which she is comfortable. And that means having much more empathy for your wife's feelings about this most intimate of acts.

I can understand her reluctance to see a therapist even if it would be in her best interest. That is another stranger who would be told about this degrading experience, another person to judge her (her thoughts) for something that was not her fault. As a matter of fact, the more people who know about this early abuse, the more her embarrassment, so please do not talk about it to family or friends. Therapy for the both of you would probably be a good investment for your marriage. — Queenie

♥

Dear Queenie, I have been with this man for 10 years. We have not had sex for a year and a half. He said it wasn't me, but that he had no sex-drive. Well he seems to have a sex-drive when he thinks I am asleep or when I leave the house!

The relationship has been steadily declining for awhile, and at this point it's like living with my brother, but I don't know how to end it! He's a good man but we obviously just don't do it for each other anymore. He has had some terrible luck over the past few months, and I feel guilty about wanting to split up, when he's down on his luck but I am miserable!!

Any suggestions on how to break it off, and get my guts up to do it? — Lucy

Lucy, if having sex with him is the only reason you're still together, then I doubt you could leave soon enough. If, however, you love him, then wouldn't you rather empathize with his situation and be an understanding partner?

I suspect his terrible luck has driven his confidence into the dumpster and perhaps he just doesn't have enough confidence to believe he could please you. If he were to try and fail, it would only be that much worse. Pressuring him for physical intimacy can only add more stress.

He knows you're upset, and he knows he's not making you happy in this very important area of your relationship. So take the pressure off. There are other ways you can get the physical relief you need by yourself. Perhaps with a new, caring, no pressure attitude, he'll relax and respond. For that matter, show him what you do to please yourself — it might inspire him. — Queenie

♥

Dear Queen of Hearts, I am 32 years, married with a young son. I never knew if I had any problem with sex but we could never have a normal or happy sexual relationship. It is not that we can't perform but there is less wish, the frequency is maybe 2 or 4 times a month.

Counseling didn't help much so we tried to accept it as part of destiny and concentrated on other aspects of life. But as the intimacy was never developed thru love making our other efforts do not help. We both know something is missing and is needed. We have tried all other resources but don't see any solution.

Now there is another lady in his life, with whom he has a very intimate, satisfying and happy sexual relationship. My morals and ethics and heart do not allow me to accept her in his life and be happy. I trusted him, I had never dreamed of him doing something like this.

I don't see any life beyond him or our family. He feels responsible for us but does not want to give up on this other lady.

Am I in a helpless situation? In our society and by law it is immoral to have this kind of a relationship and we may end up in bigger mess.

What is the amicable solution in this situation for we three involved. I desperately need visition to see things and decide priorities and get out of this situation with less pain to me and my dear husband as well. If not happiness at least I want some peace in life. Please help me! — Mir

Mir, I don't know the customs of your country so I cannot make suggestions as to how you should handle this situation.

Is divorce allowed? Does he wish divorce? If he doesn't wish divorce then he must end his relationship with this other woman in order to remain with you and so that he does not violate the customs of your law and society.

You should not have to accept your husband with another woman as part of your life. I hope that you are able to achieve the peace and happiness you deserve. Good luck. I wish I knew enough about your custom to be able to help more. — Queenie

♥

Queenie, my husband of 6 months seems to have lost interest in a sexual relationship with me. After numerous discussions, I have learned that he feels uncomfortable about himself physically. How can I be supportive and increase the intimacy in our relationship? — Dora

Dora, how did he feel about you before you were married? Did you date long enough to really get to know each other or was there no actual sexual intimacy until you were married?

If the two of you were sexually active, without problem, before you married then there may be some other reasons that he is having difficulty now. If his current difficulty is the only experience the two of you have, then there could be other reasons for it.

Counseling could be a good start for him and for the both of you. As far as trying to "stimulate" his interest, there are numerous magazines and books that should give you some ideas. I also suggest that you try to focus on cuddling, tenderness, and romance.

If he has a problem with the sex act itself (thinking of it as "dirty," for example) counseling may be very necessary to get to the root of the problem. If the problem is physical, a trip to the doctor to rule out any illness, diseases, or other physical problems, is in order.

Above all, don't take his rejection personally although it can be very difficult not to. — Queenie

♥

Dear Queenie, a widower from church, almost 74, has approached me stating he wants to have a relationship. I consent to get acquainted, I know he has just lost his wife a few months ago, so I figure he needs a friend. But he says he wants a long term relationship complete with SEX.

He claims to be very healthy, he acts younger than he is. He gives me gifts, takes me to dinner, we've see each other every day for the past two weeks. We talk a lot, tell each other a lot about our past. We hug and kiss and he of course enjoys petting.

He says he wants more than sex and he doesn't expect me to marry him. (I'm almost 30 years younger.) He was almost angry when I finally told him we weren't going to have sex, and he left immediately. I did not intend to "play games" although I will admit to leading him on. The complete truth is I was uncomfortable with the age difference. I suppose it would be salt in the wound if I returned his gifts, right? — Donna

Donna, you probably salted the wounds already by giving him the impression that you were physically attracted to him and then telling him "no way!" when it came time to pay up for his attention and gifts. Depending upon the type of gifts, I think it might be appropriate that you return them. — Queenie

♥

Queenie, I am a 25 year old mother of 2 young children. My husband has a very high sex drive. It seems like everytime he gets near me he wants sex and I want to sleep.

It's not that he is dull in bed. He isn't at all. I just don't want to have sex. This usually ends in one of two ways, we either fight about it and

he accuses me of infidelity or I give in. When I give in, he still satisfies me but I just don't seem to crave sex like I did a few years ago. He's not open to counseling or anything of that nature. He isn't very easy to talk to either. He gets very defensive and standoffish. What is wrong with us? — Ellie

Ellie, there isn't much communication between the two of you, for one thing. For another, taking care of two young children would wear out most anybody. And knowing that you are going to end up in a fight about sex, which will then lead to giving in to sex, certainly isn't very romantic.

If he won't change, then you'll have to make an attitude adjustment on yourself. The fights and the accusations of infidelity will eventually cause major damage to your marriage. Counseling could certainly help the two of you although it could help you, too, if he won't go with you. — Queenie

♥

Dear Queenie, I have been married for 10 years to a man I thought was wonderful. He adopted my two sons and has 2 children from a previous marriage although only his oldest child lives with us.

Our sex life has never been right since we said, "I do." He acts so different now too. He is grouchy and works an off shift. I am very unhappy and when I try to explain it to him he tells me I am ridiculous and I should see what all goes on around us.

The kids keep us busy but marriage shouldn't be put on hold until the kids grow up. I need more. He puts blame back on me for everything. Nothing is ever his fault. I think I am seriously falling out of love. — Barbara

Barbara, the responsibility for a wife and four kids may be getting to him. It takes a lot to keep a family going, and the financial burden falls mainly on his shoulders. If you're unhappy with him, he doesn't have too many reasons to be glad to be home when he does get off work.

With three young children at home I have to think yours is a hectic household much of the time. Add a man who is tired from work, and a wife who is angry, and there are not a lot of reasons anyone would enjoy coming home to this household.

Unfortunately, no matter how unfair it may seem, the woman usually has the power to make or break a relationship of this type. Put his feelings first, as you did before you were married, and treat him as you did before you said "I do" and I'll bet he might be more romantic and a happier husband. — Queenie

♥

Dear Queenie, I've been married for almost 5 years, and I want to be married. I also want kids. My spouse and I agreed on the kid thing before getting married, but up until recently, he was unsure about having kids. We've finally progressed on that front, agreeing to have kids.

Here's the trouble - I've lost my passion for him. I question if I ever had passion with him enough to get married. I've never enjoyed our sex. I feel mean saying this, but I've definitely had better sex when I was single. We seem to be without common goals, and we lack passion. I feel he's lifeless and I find this less than exciting. He likely has the same comments about me. I'm bored, and yet I do think my husband has lots of great qualities I'd want in a husband, but I feel like he's my brother. How can I be responsible and move past this? — Zoey

Zoey, feeling as you do, there's really no foundation to build a happy family. Couples counseling might be the best investment the two of you will ever make. Either you'll get the passion and excitement back into your marriage or you'll have a better understanding of why it just may be best to call it quits. Please don't make any quick moves without lots of discussion. –Queenie

♥

Queenie, my friend from high scool came for a visit. My wife and I have talked in the past about adding a third person to our bedroom fun, and as you probaly guessed it did happen with my friend. My question is, since we did have a good time should we do it again or could it cause probems in our relationship? We have been married for fifteen years and until last night my wife has never been with anyone else but me. Now I'm afraid she is going to want to experience even more men, and maybe without me knowing.

Did I open a big can of worms by allowing this to happen? She says it won't, but since she's reached her thirties she has been hard to satisfy and she wants sex all the time. What should I do? — Joe

Joe, threesomes are dumb. It's also adultery by the dictionary definition: a married person who has sex with someone who isn't their spouse. Yes, this is a big can of worms and no excuse is good enough even if you think you need help satisfying your wife. In the future, instead of adding a third person to your sex play, I'd suggest some sexy videos and lots of battery-operated bedroom toys. — Queenie

♥

Abusive Relationships

Abusive Relationships

*"The last time I saw him, he called me a 2-cent whore and told
me he hopes I drop dead. For some reason he hates me now and
I wonder if it's just so he'll feel better about his affairs."*

Abuse isn't just being a punching bag when your spouse is
in a bad mood. While black eyes, bruises and broken bones are the
most obvious signs of abusive relationships, verbal and emotional
abuse can be just as damaging and sometimes even worse.

No one gets into a relationship because they enjoy being
beaten and abused. Some relationships start without any outward
clues that abuse will develop and it may develop so slowly and
insidiously that the person being abused isn't aware that the
relationship has turned into an abusive one.

Many abusers are kind and loving outside the home to
everyone except the person or persons they have singled out to
abuse. In any neighborhood, in any social class, families live with
terrible secrets of what goes on behind closed doors, a husband and
father who emotionally brutalizes, a wife and mother whose sharp
tongue leaves lasting scars, a child who traumatizes another.

An adult abuser may have been abused as a child. Children
who grow up in homes where their mother or father is the one being
abused will have nothing else to guide them when it comes to their
own adult relationships and the cycle will continue.

There is no excuse for abuse, nor any reason to remain in an
abusive relationship. Identifying the abuse, getting help, and getting
away if necessary, isn't easy. Counseling may be the first step for
someone being abused to gain enough strength to get away from
their abuser and to understand that they do not deserve the abuse.

The National Domestic Violence Hotline Website is at
www.ndvh.org and it has a comprehensive information about all
forms of abuse. If you are in an abusive situation and need help
NOW, dial them at 1-800-799-7233 or 1-800-787-3224 (TTY). An
excellent book for abused women is *It's My Life Now: Starting Over
After an Abusive Relationship or Domestic Violence* written by Meg
Kennedy Dugan, M.A., and Roger R. Hock, Ph.D.

♥

*Dear Queenie, my husband is verbally and emotionally abusive.
He is clinically depressed with sleep problems, and refuses to admit it and
get regular treatment. When I went on antidepressants, my moods and
demeanor improved, but I gained lots of weight, so I think he's worried the*

same will happen to him if he does it. My weight is a big deal to him, and it seems he can't stop talking about it. I am middle-aged, menopausal and on HRT. I am a size 12 (used to be an 8/10), look good, have a good job and am raising two gorgeous girls.

He says he's not happy, and that my weight is a major problem. He's threatening to leave if I don't lose 20 pounds in the next two months. He tells me I look bad, even though I know I don't, and he criticizes the food I eat, all the while stuffing himself.

Counseling has not worked for him; it seems I have to do all the changes. I have made changes for the better but I still have trouble with my weight. He did not like the first counselor because she sometimes saw my point of view (who also told me privately that he was really into "midlife" as in crisis). -- Sheila

Sheila, you have too many issues for me to comment although I will say that a size 12 is not overweight. It sounds as though your husband is searching hard to find fault and your weight gain is the only area he can successfully attack. Again, size 12 is not overweight. The both of you need to continue counseling and I hope each of you can get through your personal problems and then work on your marriage. —Queenie

♥

Hello Queenie, I thought I found Mr. Right. We have a child together. We had a issue of domestic violence, the first (and only) time it happened I called the police. He is in jail and has been for almost six months. Now I have found out about some infidelity in our relationship. He wants to be back with me for our son. I'm not ready, I can't get the truth from him.

It seems everyday I found out something new. I have been there fincially, mentally, and emotionaly for him through the whole ordeal. But I want to know am I wrong (selfish as he says) for not wanting to be with him. There are a lot of separated parents out there, and sometimes it makes us better parents. Everyone is against me on this, they say I should give him one more chance. — Melanie

Melanie, it's your life, you must do what you feel is best for you and your child. "Everyone" can have an opinion, but it's not their life, it's yours, they have nothing at stake. It is always easy to tell someone else what they should do and to make them feel that they are the reason a relationship is dysfunctional. I don't know if this relationship is worth saving. You must make this decision because it's your life. —Queenie

♥

Dear Queenie, my husband and I can not seem to get along at all. The main reason we got married was because I got pregnant again and felt like I couldn't make it on my own. There have been times when we would break up over stupid things and he came back crying because he spent the night with one of the girls he was friends with at work. He says he was so hurt he had to talk to somebody but, nothing happened, he slept on the floor even though she had a nice couch. He took me to her house and she said nothing happened, but if it did, it wouldn't matter cause we weren't together. I haven't trusted him since and never would have taken him back if it wasn't for the fact he got saved and was the perfect Christian for a little while.

We've had terrible problems since her, and recently he told me that he would pay for me and the kids a place to stay until I get on my feet. He has been perfectly content with the fact we're gone and I drive by his house every night and early in the morning and for the past two nights he hasn't come home at all. The last time I saw him, he called me a 2-cent whore and told me he hopes I drop dead. For some reason he hates me now and I wonder if it's just so he'll feel better about his affairs.

I know he'll come back in a few weeks, being the sweetest most loving man you've ever seen, wanting his family back. I have two small children and I can't stay out all night to catch him in the act. Should I go with my gut instinct and believe that he is cheating? What would you think? — Heather

Heather, this is no way for a marriage to be. There's no trust and there's abuse. Is this the way you want to live the rest of your life? If not, do something about it. Get counseling, a divorce, or whatever will make this life better for you. —Queenie

♥

Dear Queenie, my husband and I argue all the time. I feel like just calling it quits sometimes. We argue for no reason over the stupidest things. He can just have a bad day at work and come home and take it out on us. Please tell me what to do. I hope it is not to late. — Tammy

Tammy, I can't tell you what to do because I don't know what's wrong. Even if I knew what was wrong, I couldn't tell you what to do because it's your life not mine. I will say this: it takes two people to make an argument. You don't have to keep an argument going. —Queenie

♥

Queenie, I am going to be brief. I am a married woman, I've known this man since I was 15 years old (I am 25) and now we have a child together. I can't stand him anymore but sometimes he's getting on my nerves, I must tell you he's very violent (never beat me) but he is very violent and doesn't have any patience. And at my work, I am in love with my boss. He's single, no children, and we seem to match together; we love each other very much. I asking for your help! what can I do? — Connie

Connie, I don't have any advice other than you need to either stop seeing your boss and repair your marriage or get a divorce and perhaps your boss will turn this into a legitimate relationship once you are legally single. If your husband is abusive and you fear for your safety or the safety of your child you should contact a shelter in your area. — Queenie

♥

Dear Queenie, how in the world do I tell my husband of 15 years that I want out?? We have 2 children, and each time I suggest or bring up the topic he goes on about what a lousy mother and wife I have been, how I've never tried to make this work, that I never listen. He has been verbally abusive and can manipulate me out of my own thoughts.

I want out. I want to leave. He can have the house, I just want joint custody of the kids, and to be left alone. What can I say to him that won't cause another horrible shouting match? I don't want to be a coward and leave a note, I want to tell him to his face. I respect him enough for that. But I don't want to live through the period of time it takes to tell him and get out. -- Dara

Dara, making the decision to leave and then acting upon it is the hardest part of all. Once you decide you'd rather live without him than with him, and do whatever it takes to get out, you'll be amazed at how free you feel and how wonderful life is outside of an abusive relationship. As you're well aware, abuse comes in many forms and not all leaves visible bruises.

Every day you remain is another day you've lost. If today was the last day of your life, is this how you'd want to live it? -- Queenie

♥

Dear Queenie, I was in an auto accident several years ago. I was left with injuries which are still unsolved at this time. I was rewarded a settlement. My husband has no regard to the way in which this money was recieved. He just wants to spend "My blood, bones, teeth, and other injuries

32

money" that I recieved; on things that would benefit him. When I did recieve my settlement, I paid off everyone we owed, I also set him up in business and he refuses to replace this money.

I am looking for another opinion/outlook on this. As I have suffered, and I'm still suffering from this tragedy, and I feel as if I'm being taken advantage of. I would never of touched any of his money if it was him that laid on that highway not knowing if he was going to live or die.

P. S. To add insult to injury...he had the nerve to stop for a burger on the way to the hospital while I was in route from one emergency room to another for a life threating injury. I've not been able to drive since. I'm a prisoner in my own home, and I have to take this inconsideration from my own husband. — Tanya

Tanya, when two people marry there no longer is "my" money and "your" money but rather "our" money. It is a shame that you were so severely injured and that you still are hurting from this accident but your husband has been a victim of this accident also. If your marriage was a good one prior to this and the accident has turned your relationship into what it has become, then both of you have lost a great deal. Do you feel that he deserves to be in as much misery as you? Do you want him to suffer also?

The money received from the settlement belongs to the both of you. If the accident had occurred to him instead the money would still belong to the both of you even if he was the one who had the pain and the injuries.

Was he driving you to the emergency room when he stopped for a burger? If so, then he was inconsiderate and putting your life in danger. If you were being transported in an ambulance (that he wasn't driving) and he could do nothing with regard to your immediate medical needs, then what is the problem with him making a quick stop to get some food?

My personal opinion is that you need to spend some of that money on counseling to get your anger under control or this marriage is going to blow completely apart. —Queenie

♥

Dear Queenie, three years ago I started dating a man I thought was quite nice and we seemed to get along rather well. He was also very good to my little boy. My parents thought the world of him and several months into our relationship decided to help us buy a house by lending us some money for a down payment. I was a little weary at first but I dream of happy endings and soon jumped into this with both feet.

I found out I was pregnant and was thrilled. I always wanted to have two children. He was alright about the pregnancy when I told him but he was a total bastard while I was pregnant. He was violent and attacked me and threw things at my son. I could not bear the thought of packing up my things once again and moving so I just let these things slide. After our daughter was born things seemed to be better for a while.

We lead two separate lives. I have gone back to work P/T and when I am out he is home and vice versa. He has not said he loves me since before I can remember and he has started telling me that I am stupid and other not so nice things. Sex is mean and the things he calls me and tells me during sex are things that I don't like. He belittles my parents all the time and I feel very unhappy all the time. He yells in front of the kids and then makes me think it is my fault for pushing him.

To make a long story short, I need to figure out what I am doing and how to make this insanity stop. He refuses counciling and I am afraid to leave with two children from different men. I have no desire to be on welfare. How do I support two kids by myself and where do I find the strength to start to pack? I feel like I am in a catch 22 and can't get out! -- Jenny

Jenny, I don't know what happened to change him from the man you thought he was to the man he is, or if your initial need for him blinded you to his faults. Whatever has happened, this man is certainly too mean-spirited to stay in your life any longer without undergoing a major personality implant.

You are not a failure for leaving this loser. Nor are you a failure if you leave and use welfare to get your life back on track. You are an intelligent, hardworking lady who has fallen on bad times due to a couple of poor choices. That happens. You just have to use what you've learned to avoid the same mistakes in the future.

He is abusive and demeaning to you, disrespectful to you and your parents, and your children are witnesses to this terrible behavior plus they are learning by example that this is the way husband and wives interact. If not out of respect for yourself, for love of them, you should walk away from him. Do you have a women's shelter in your area? Could your parents provide temporary lodging for you and the children? You'll find the strength, because you want to survive. Good luck. -- Queenie

❤

Midlife Issues

Midlife Issues

*"I feel my 51 year old father, who has been married to my
mother for 31 years, is going through a midlife crisis and
possibly preparing to cheat."*

Growing old is the pits! But, as the saying goes, the
alternative is even worse. Aging issues can cause even the sanest of
people to act foolish and make choices that wreak havoc upon the
people who care the most for them.

It happens when the face in the mirror is your mother's or
your father's, when you look down and see an old person's hands,
when you keep outgrowing your clothes despite exercising more
and eating much less.

Sags, bags, wrinkles, gray hair or falling hair are all part of
the aging process and while Botox, liposuction, facelifts and other
surgeries and techniques may remove a few years from your outer
appearance, there's sometimes very little that can make the inner
you feel young again.

Middle-aged men may find temporary "youth" with a
younger woman, just as may middle-aged women find it with a
younger man or another man. Midlife betrayal is probably the
number one reason for long-term marriages failing.

The "nest" empties at midlife leaving some women
questioning their usefulness or deciding the time is finally right to
leave a less than perfect marriage. Men who have felt obligated to
remain in an unhappy marriage because of their family
responsibilities may leave home when the last child is no longer
dependent for support.

Regardless of the issues, midlife can be an extremely chaotic
and rocky time for relationships and many of them won't survive.

♥

*Dear Queenie, I am 18 years old and I have a big problem I cannot
handle: My mother moved out two days ago, left my father and could not
give us any reason for that. My father offered her anything: to change his
life, to not go to work that long, to go out with her more often but she would
not accept any of these ideas.*

*She says it is too late without having ever complained before; he
should have made these suggestione earlier and not after she told him about
these problems. I think she's getting ideas from some guys she's had contact
with on the Internet. I tried to talk to her but she does not speak about that,
neither with me nor with anybody.*

My parents were together now 26 years, we have no financial problems, my parents have never argued, never cheated. And just recently they were planning on renovating the house.

My mother suffers from panic attacks and takes very strong pills and a doctor said it could be that they changed her so much because you must not take them longer than 2 years. She is not willing to see a shrink or have a counselor. Can give me any tips on how we can treat her right and maybe make her come back to us. — Sara

Sara, I know you want to help your mother and father get back together but this is between the two of them and it isn't your responsibility to get your mother back home. You can tell her how much you miss her but trying to act as intermediary between your mother and your father is the place for a counselor not you, their daughter.

Of course you want to help your father. Of course you want to help your mother. Yes you want the home restored to the way it used to be. But there were things there, between your mother and your father that made her unhappy enough to leave. You cannot know these things because you aren't inside your mother's head, you don't know what she has needed over these years that your father was too busy or otherwise unable to provide.

There comes a time in everyone's life when they either know that the life they have is the one that satisfies them or that somewhere there is a better life and they must go in search of it. Occasionally they will return home, having discovered that what they sought was right there all the time. Perhaps your mother will do exactly that.

You can't force your mother to return to a home that makes her unhappy. Life is way too short for that. Let her know that you love her and that you hope she finds what she's looking for. And tell your father that he needs to talk to a counselor about his marital problems, not his daughter. —Queenie

♥

Dear Queenie, I'd like to know what the heck is going through my wife's head. We've been happily married (I thought). We have 2 beautiful girls, we live in a beautiful house, don't have any money worries, drive new cars and everyone is heathly.

Three months ago we had a little argument, nothing out of the ordinary, and she totally went off the deep end. She said she's not happy. She is cold and distant one minute and sweet the next. She totally ignores

me sometime and has a different personality with different people. She has started smoking, drinking beer, and wearing clothes styled for high school girls.

She feels the need to gossip all the time and is happy when she talks to her girlfriends. She's cold toward me, selfish and self centered and only cares about herself. She's alienated herself from her those of us who love her.

Her pregnancies were difficult and after the second child was born she lost a lot of weight. Now she has become obsessed with her looks and I also found she has "a friend" at work. She just turned 36 and claims "She's found herself" and said she isn't letting anyone control her anymore. (No one ever did) Nice huh?

She went for a physical and we're waiting to see if there might be some kind of physical problem; she's also going to therapy although she says it isn't doing her any good.

What do I do? How do I get my loving wife back. Hormones, midlife crisis, or mental breakdown? I need some input. Help! — *Rocky*

Rocky, hopefully the therapy is going to uncover some answers or perhaps the physical will turn up something. Midlife can be a very difficult time for some people and it would seem that your wife is working through a lot of aging related issues at this time. Hopefully your marriage will survive although some don't. Take care of yourself and don't take her actions personally, which is easier for me to say than it will be for you to do. —Queenie

♥

Dear Queenie, do you have any articles or know where I can find out about female midlife crisis. I believe my wife is having one. She recently lost her job which was everything to her and all of a sudden she does not love me anymore. She is acting similarly to the male mid-life crisis described in the article on the web. -- *Neal*

Neal, there are all types of self-help books available at your local book stores or online through Amazon.com and other booksellers.

If a person ties their personal value to the job they do, and the rewards (bonus, salary, etc) they receive, when the job is gone, they believe themselves to have lost value. It can be as traumatic as divorce or death of a spouse.

Your understanding of the situation is important, and it may mean that you'll have to spend a lot of time just listening to her say the same things over and over. Many people just need a sounding board, "someone who cares," not necessarily someone who says "look, just go out and get another job if it's so important!". You can help by being supportive and letting her find the answers instead of trying to find the answers for her. -- Queenie

♥

Dear Queenie, do you have any advice for a wife whose husband is going through what I consider a midlife crisis? After 20 years of what I thought was a great marriage, he says he is no longer in love with me. He wants us to continue living under the same roof for the kids (17 and 14). -- Stella

Stella, this is not going to be easy. Take some comfort from the fact that you have just been given a ticket to ride the same roller coaster many other women have ridden and survived.

Since he wants to continue living at home, does that mean he wants the freedom of doing as he pleases at the same time? (Dating, acting single, etc.) There need to be some rules, particularly since the kids are going to be impacted by everything that happens between the two of you. You cannot keep your sanity or your own self-esteem if he starts acting single but expects married privileges.

Every man has his own personal agenda at this time. You will have to develop your own also. Counseling for yourself might be a good start, counseling for the two of you an even better option. I recommend counseling for you because if he doesn't want to go, you could use all the moral support you can get at this time. You might also want to consider counseling for the kids. Good luck! -- Queenie

♥

Dear Queenie, can women have the same kind of midlife crisis as men? I read the "My mid life crisis" story and by substituting she for he and her for him it was almost what it happening to my wife. Is this a common thing? -- Dale

Dale, sure they can, and it's probably more common than you'd expect. Of course, sometimes they're so busy coping with their man's midlife crisis that theirs just gets overlooked. -- Queenie

♥

Dear Queenie, I feel my 51 year old father who has been married to my mother for 31 years is going through a midlife crisis and possibly preparing to cheat. His father died a few months ago and since, he has been

responding to internet personals and looking for the lost passion he no longer gets from my mother.

Do you know of any good advice, or books that deal with this subject? I do know he has cheated in the past, but has been true to the marriage for the past few years. Any help would be great! -- Melanie

Melanie, midlife is a bad time for all family members. Each person makes the passage in their own way and their passage may wreak havoc on all fronts. If your father is starting into a rocky midlife crisis there is very little you can do other than to be there for your mother's comfort and support. At the same time, please try not to take sides. It may be as difficult for him, particularly with the recent loss of his father, as it is for the rest of the family. A good book for your mother would be *How to Survive Your Husband's Midlife Crisis*. She can get online support by joining The Midlife Club at www.midlifeclub.com. -- Queenie

♥

Hello Queenie, my wife and I have known each other for 14 years and have been married for 5. This summer, my quiet, conservative wife became increasingly outgoing. She couldn't stay home and was always going out with her friends. Also, she has become obsessed with work. She has a very good job and does well and is a workaholic. She just got a promotion and had people fighting over her for her to work for them.

Everything has changed about her, her looks, her clothes, her taste in music, her social habits. I am no slouch myself but now there is no intimacy in our relationship. Naturally, she was receiving a tremendous amount of attention from everyone at work and then a man swept her off her feet. She went to dinner a couple of times and she said he made her feel special. I don't think that they slept together.

She doesn't know what she wants right now. She says part of her wants to be single and see other people and she says another part of her knows that that would be a huge mistake. She says all of her dreams of a family are with me but that she is not physically attracted to me right now. The famous "I love you but I'm not in love with you."

She is going to see a counselor and I have resigned myself to the fact that I cannot worry about things I cannot control. It is hard though because she works incessantly. So I am rolling with it, doing little things to let her know that I love her but not smothering her, and not interfering with what she wants to do.

I think this is some kind of crisis or phase and that she will come out of it but how long do I wait, and am I doing the right thing? -- Lonnie

Lonnie, it does indeed sound as though she is going through a crisis of her own, redefining what she needs to make herself happy. She is in counseling but you should also get counseling so that you can get a grip on what is happening, learn how to handle it (even though you are doing quite well), and get in touch with your personal needs and goals.

She is changing. If you don't, there will be no common ground between the two of you and your marriage won't stand a chance. The possibility exists that she may not want to remain married. If so, you need to be able to accept and handle such a decision. Your independence might also cause her to look at you in a new light. Independence is a very admirable quality. -- Queenie

♥

Dear Queenie, help me please. I feel my wife is going through her midlife crisis at 40. She tells me she needs space, she feels like everything around her is choking her. She tells me she loves me but she has to be on her own to work this out.

She is letting our 11-year old son live with me, because she said that I can care for him better because we can do father and son things together. She wants me to date her while she lives on her own and insists that we will work this out only if she leaves. But what do I do about my son? What do I tell him about why his mother is leaving? He already knows she is leaving and he is very hurt by this and is beginning to hate her..

I think she is having an affair. Everything she is doing now is on the sneak and I don't know if I can trust her anymore. I love her with all my heart and soul, and when I tell her she says that I am mentally abusing her. She says that she might be gone for a month maybe a couple of months or a year. She doesn't know how she will feel, but she has to be on her own.

What do I do? She won't admit she is going through her Mid-life Crisis and she won't go to counseling. She tells me that I'm the one that is crazy. -- Darryl

Darryl, by now you must know that you cannot control what she's doing or how she feels. You cannot control anyone but yourself.

Regardless of whether she'll go to counseling why don't you consider counseling for yourself so you can get the help you need in order to make the decisions that are right for you in this situation?

It might be that starting divorce proceedings would be appropriate. I don't like to suggest this but your life now is a series of unanswered questions and the only way for you to gain control is to make some decisions.

Your decision could be as simple as setting a deadline for her to return after which you will take step 2 (which could be legal separation) and then step 3, etc. Any deadlines could be adjusted as you feel they need to be based upon your current situation.

Even if she admitted to going through midlife crisis it would mean nothing other than you would have a name for the situation your marriage is currently facing. That wouldn't solve the problem.

There are situations within the marriage and within her life that she needs to work through. How she works them though and what the end result will be are unknowns at this time.

You cannot count on her returning to the marriage, nor can you be certain that she will leave it. Given that uncertainty you must do whatever is necessary to get yourself and your son on emotionally healthy ground. Look out for yourself and look out for him. Your wife is already looking out for herself so it won't do any good to worry about her at this point.

It is extremely important that you don't talk badly about your wife in front of your son. He already knows there are problems but she's his mother and it is unfair to him to draw him into this situation over which he has no control (just as you don't). -- Queenie

♥

Dear Queenie, I am at my wits end! My husband needed some time to think and went away for the weekend. He came back and announced he doesn't love me anymore! He says he has been unhappy for several years.

We have been married 24 years, happily I thought! He stayed and we are in separate rooms. We have talked and I am trying to find out what the reason is. He's been to the doctor and he's not depressed.

He has agreed to go to marriage counseling. I think probably he may have had an affair or fling and is feeling overwhelming guilt! He is convinced he does not love me anymore and I honestly don't believe him. He thinks the relationship has run its course. What do you think? — Sue

Sue, I think marriage counseling is a good first step for the two of you. Be prepared to hear things that may hurt you, and be prepared to accept that this marriage may be over. It takes two people to make a marriage and if he's not willing, you won't be able to hold it together on your own. Middle age is a very difficult time for many marriages and not all of them survive the stresses. Above all, don't take his actions personally. —Queenie

♥

Stay or Go?

Stay or Go?

"What would you do if your man is never home and never takes you out anywhere? Even for your birthday and comes home accusing you of sleeping around?"

Not all relationships are meant to last a lifetime. Despite marriage vows of "until death do us part" there are situations that justify divorce. Violence and abuse, infidelity, addictive behaviors can all lead to relationship breakdowns.

When is a marriage or serious relationship bad enough to leave? Abuse in any form should never be tolerated; if an abuser isn't willing to change, the one being abused has the responsibility to themself and, to any dependent children in the relationship, to get away from the abuse and the abuser.

If a partner is a cheat, the one who is being cheated on can either learn to live with betrayal or end the relationship. If they stay they face the possibility of the cheater leaving when he or she meets the one person they can't live without as well as the potential of being infected with sexually transmitted diseases.

Addictive behaviors can be controlled but only if the person with the addiction is willing. Co-dependency is a problem in addictive relationships, and counseling may help someone drawn to addictive personalities to understand why they feel so "comfortable" in these types of behaviors. Just as children of alcoholics will seek out alcoholic partners because their "comfort level" is with this type of behavior, so will children who grew up in abusive homes feel more comfortable in abusive relationships.

So, stay or go? There are no easy answers. Are the issues petty and easily resolved or too bad to overcome? Some relationships are strong enough to survive the worst behaviors, some aren't strong enough to get past even the petty ones.

♥

Dear Queenie, I am a 51 year old woman involved in a long distance relationship. We didn't get married, but I left the state with him and took along my two girls, pre-teens at the time. He got a great job and took care of us. Of course, there were problems from the beginning. My girls didn't want to respect him or obey him at first.

The children are the product of my third marriage. Since their birth, I had basically sworn off men and actually was a bit of a "Feminazi" for the first ten years of their lives, and it rubbed off on them. My man came into my house knowing that we had these attitudes. I worked hard to show them that not all men were bad, as I had previously taught them, that he was a good man. They balked whenever he attempted to establish order with them. But it did get better. He worked; I didn't have to. I lived the life I'd always fantasized about—the stay-at-home mom.

Then he lost his job. He had problems collecting unemployment. We got behind on rent and utilities. We packed what we owned into the car and moved in with his cousin and her husband. That was a big mistake because his cousin began disciplining my girls and letting her kids do as they pleased.

One night turned into a complete brawl with my kids hitting her, and me and them going to the police and staying the night in a shelter. The next day, when I called the house, I found that my boyfriend had bagged up our stuff. In other words, put the garbage out!

Friends have told me that if he were any kind of man, he would have left with us. But he did not. I didn't have the opportunity to discuss this with my so-called partner. Right now, I feel so hurt, and so foolish— because I knew better than to trust a man, yet that's what I did.

And now, we have a government apartment with no furniture, no cookware, no tv, no nothing but ourselves and the clothes on our backs. I am starting a graveyard shift job hopefully soon. My feelings are ambivilant: Half of me says "you go, girl—you CAN do this—you've done it before"! The other half, the half that has lived with and loved this man for over a year, cries out "WHY?!" -- Gayle

Gayle, of course you knew better than to "trust a man" yet you've trusted three of them enough to marry them. And you trusted this man enough while he was able to provide you and your girls with the life you'd always dreamed of. And you trust the opinion of "friends" who tell you what "any kind of man" would have done.

At this point it becomes a question of whether you retreat back into your prior mode of thinking all men are bad and continue to instill that belief in your daughters so that they can have the same kind of life you have chosen for yourself or do you seek counseling and learn what's driving you in this direction.

I'm also concerned about the physical violence from your daughters; they may be mirroring what they've seen in your past relationships. Kids learn from experience, what they see at home, and they take those behaviors into their own relationships.

There may be too many issues to put that relationship back on track so that answers the "why". So how do you want to live the rest of your life? You have the power, do you have the ability to find the answers and live the rest of your life wisely?—Queenie

♥

Dear Queen of Hearts, once upon a time two kids (both only 18) met eyes and gave into their great physical attraction and got involved. Things happened too fast and before really getting to know one another they had a physical relationship that lead to a baby. They did the right thing and got married and became a family and things worked. Until Mom (me) admitted that she was left feeling empty and unloved.

I don't think that I am in love, I doubt that I ever was. It seems that I am in this relationship for my child. I don't feel like my husband loves me for who I am, rather he loves the role that I play: caretaker, maid, cook. I don't feel like we connect, we merely exist.

Can I make myself love him, should I just focus on our family and try to be content with making a good home life? Is the idea of finding the one, a soul mate, a fairy tale? Is it worth wrecking this little thing we have going? I am unhappy, but maybe there is something I can do to fix how I feel. Like accepting my life as mother and wife and quit dreaming of a love that doesn't exist. Other than the not connecting I have nothing to complain about of my husband he is a good guy. I should love him, shouldn't I? —Tammy

Tammy, you have a child and a husband who is a "good guy." For some women, that *would* be a fairy tale life. Maybe you did move into motherhood and marriage too quickly but now that you're there, you have responsibilities to your child and to your husband.

There is no reason that this man who caused you such great lust (yes, that's what you'd have to call a physical attraction such as yours when love wasn't a part of it) shouldn't become your lover and your soul mate. It's really in your court to find those things that are good within your relationship and accent those.

Tell your husband how you feel. Don't whine or make him feel at fault or put him on the defensive. Simply tell him that you're not feeling very special and that the two of you need to spend more time getting to become friends and lovers. Plan some private time, get involved with activities that the both of you enjoy. Maybe he's not feeling quite so special either.

Letting go of a "good guy" in order to find an elusive "soul mate" can be a major mistake particularly if that good guy is soul mate material. —Queenie

♥

Hey Queenie, I'm 23 my girlfriend is 27, and we have two wonderful young girls. We have been together for most of 5 years, been kinda rocky though. We don't drink, or have never cheated. The problem is that she is so set in the way she does things that any compromise is out of the question.

We have money problems mostly, but we are never without. The apt. we now live in she had before we met. I understand it's "her" home but she makes me feel like I don't belong.

We have child topics too, like if I'm in the right for trying to get some sort of obeideince in order. The oldest child is not mine, but I have always treated her as if she were. She can say some really heartbreaking words to me, and I to her also. She has recently kicked me out several times, only for us to get back in a few days.

We always say we'll do better, for us, for the girls, but it never happens. I have really treated her good, I don't know what to do for her to make it good again. I think she really does love me, but she just wants it "all" her way, hey it's a 2 way road right? Please help if you can, I hate it for the girls. — Bobby

Bobby, someone has to be in control of a relationship when children are involved. Since the oldest child isn't yours and since she, as the mother, is most dominant in the kids' day to day care, it is most natural for her to be in charge at this point since there are no legal obligations in place which would be if the two of you were married and if you adopted the oldest child.

Now, having said that, only the two of you know whether or not you should get married since it appears there is a lot of turbulence in your relationship. Of course, that might be due to her wanting more of a commitment from you and you not willing to make the step to make this relationship permanent. What do you think? —Queenie

❤

Dear Queenie, is it worthing trying to save a marriage in which there is a double standard for the woman? My husband is currently out somewhere drinking and did the same last night because he is mad that I did not tell him I was changing jobs.

By the way, about 4 months ago he chased and got a job that requires him to travel, and took it without us discussing it. This is the kind of behavior he exhibits when he is not in on the decisions I make even though he doesn't include me in his. He is almost 41 and I am his fourth marriage. How do I resolve this? — Ellen

Ellen, you already know the answer to your question. What I'm wondering is why the two of you are playing so many games with each other. Neither of you talks to the other about things that are important to the both of you. Changing jobs is no minor deal in a marital relationship, not your job change nor his.

Do you make decisions without letting him know so that he will see how you feel when he does the same? Or does he make decisions without letting you know so you'll see how he feels? If there's any love here the two of you need to get some counseling to develop it to its full potential. –Queenie

♥

Dear Queenie, I have been married to my wife for about seven years. We dated before for about two years and were mutually compatible. She started a new job about 9 months ago and her attitude towards home changed drastically. She started complaining that marriage and marital responsibilities are too much for her to handle.

As we have a 6-year old daughter besides our jobs we were unable to have romantic times together very often and this bothered her. Recently she complained of my not being very grateful to her parents and her parents do not like me any more. Based upon our discussion about this she moved out to her parents' home a month ago.

I have attempted to reconcile with my wife but she is determined to try out separation. Her response to my attempts are that if she finds herself to be unhappy then perhaps we will get back together. Is it possible or it is more likely an excuse? Is it worth my while to reconcile with her? I still love her a lot.

She likes to only visit our daughter almost every other day at my home for 1-2 hours. My daughter is growing to dislike her and avoids being with her alone, wanting me to be there as well. This behavior bothers her and she has begin to say that since our daughter does not really miss her she has made the right decision moving out.

She says that her parents do not like our daughter to stay at their home and thus she prefers she (our daughter) stays at my home. She does not want to share the expenses of child care although our incomes are equal. She claims there is no other person that she is dating. I don't know if I should believe her. Thanks for your opinion and suggestion. -- Ed

Ed, seven years seems to be a critical point in many marriages. Almost as though a switch is thrown and one partner decides that they made a bad decision seven years before. The same spark isn't there that drew them into the relationship or they have more responsibility than they want, and they just decide to throw everything away, hurting a lot of people in the process.

I don't know if you are the type of husband who shares in the household responsibilities or the type who considers that the wife should be able to go to work, come home and keep the house, and be a good parent, all without assistance. Each of those is a full time job if done well. A woman carrying too heavy a burden of responsibility might want to run away from it all if she feels that is all her life was ever going to offer.

Romance is very important to any relationship and having jobs and the other responsibilities of a marriage should not eliminate romance — schedules have to be adjusted to include time for the two of you, time to renew the romantic side of your relationship. Without that if someone comes along who appears sympathetic, a romance-starved husband or wife is an easy conquest.

Simple things like bouquets of flowers (or even one elegant rose) for no occasion, romantic cards left on the pillow or tucked in a briefcase, or the words "Do you know how much I love you?" will add romance to a busy life. If you have to schedule a "date" every week, do it! It's much better than having to schedule visiting hours.

What a sad situation for your daughter, particularly if the grandparents don't want to have their granddaughter around. Is your daughter that ill-behaved that she isn't welcome in her grandparent's home? Or is there something else that would make her unwelcome?

You have several things that need to be resolved: the relationship you have with your wife, the relationship you have with your in-laws, the relationship your wife has with your daughter — you need to talk to a clergyman or a counselor and try to make some sense in this marriage. Don't throw in the towel yet! Good luck. -- Queenie

♥

Dear Queenie, I have been married for 17 years. About 5 years ago, my husband had an affair to which he has admitted after the woman called and told me about it. Before that affair, however, there was some evidence that he may have had other extramarital relationships (condoms, early morning calls to women, staying out 'til dawn, and a call from a former girlfriend apologizing for having messed with my husband.) He has denied having any other affairs but the one.

For the past couple of years, our relationship has been strained, with us barely speaking to each other. Then a few months ago, my husband

started wanting to have sex all of the time. This made me suspicious that something was going on or had just ended. Since this started, I have found a suspicious phone call he made back to someone in our home state while he was on a one-day business trip (I believe it is a woman.). Also, I have evidence that he intentionally hid one of our phone bills from me.

I'm not sure what to do. I don't love my husband any more but for some reason, I'm afraid to get out of this situation. I have a good job and can support myself, so this isn't it. What should I do? -- Tammy

Tammy, your husband has lost your trust. You don't love him any more. Your relationship has deteriorated to more pain than pleasure. You have a good job and can support yourself. You know what you should do. Must I say it?

Fear of the unknown is holding you back. This is the only life you have. Make the best of it. Dump the guy. Now — before he gives you AIDS or some other gift you can live without. Please, you deserve better. --Queenie

♥

Dear Queenie, I am in an unhappy marrage. I have met someone that I fell in love with and I'm considering leaving this situation. I have been unhappy for about 2 years now. Talking hasn't changed my feelings at all. Should I just end this or stick it out? Many people in my family will be disapointed in me. When is it time to stop thinking about other people and start thinking about me. Many people will be hurt by this and I don't know what to do. Please help!! -- Arnie

Arnie, people will always be hurt when a relationship ends. What is important is to make certain that ending the relationship is the right thing to do. If it isn't, you could end up hurting yourself in addition to everyone else.

You don't give enough information for me to know if you've been married for a long time and have just in the past two years begun being unhappy, or if you've only been married for two years and unhappily the entire time. My response will consider both of these possibilities.

If you have been married for many years, can you remember when you truly loved your wife? If you can, has she changed so much that you should end the marriage? Or are you fighting the boredom that comes from marriages that don't challenge each partner? If that's the case, you should do everything in your power to make it work before deciding to end it.

If you've always been unhappily married, I question why you married your wife at all. If you didn't marry for love, and if the reason(s) you did marry are no longer important, then it would seem there are no reasons to remain in the relationship.

Either way, you should not be involved with someone else while you sort out this situation. If you decide that you want to save your marriage, you will only hurt the other person waiting for your marriage to end.

Ending a marriage because someone else waits is not the best way to keep family relationships cordial — toward yourself or toward the person for whom you break up your marriage to be with. If ending your marriage seems to be the right thing to do, try to do it as honorably and as gently as possible. -- Queenie

♥

Queenie, what would you do if your man is never home and never takes you out anywhere? Even for your birthday and comes home accusing you of sleeping around?-- Crystal

Crystal, I'd ask him whose bed he was keeping his shoes under, and then I'd stop waiting for him to take me out or come home. I would ask myself if I wanted the rest of my life to be the same or if I wanted to change it for the better. That means *you* take control of your life, with him or without him. It's your choice. -- Queenie

♥

Dear Queenie, eight years ago I met a man with whom I fell deeply in love. At the time, both of us were single parents trying to establish ourselves in our careers. We spent two intense months together and then our paths took us to opposite sides of the country. He married and had a child shortly after we separated. I became involved with a man a few years later and we lived together for about five years.

Last year, I received a phone call from "Tom." It took me by complete surprise. He was in the midst of a divorce and I was in the process of ending the relationship I was in. We began corresponding through email, phone calls and letters. Eventually we arranged a meeting. I found that I was still in love with him after all those years. It was like a fairy tale. He invited my daughter and I to come visit him and his children for the summer.

It was a difficult decision, but I left everything and drove to the other coast. It was to be a trial period that would last through the summer and then we would decide if we would become a family.

We had our share of good times and we had more than our share of rough times. The main thing that we have in common is our love for each other. Otherwise, we are complete opposites from parenting to politics. We don't even argue constructively.

At the end of the summer I was not prepared to give him an answer. Eventually, my lack of decision caused a decision by default. Simply put, I stayed because I did not decide to leave. I have continued in this manner ever since and it has taken its toll on both of us and put great strains on our relationship.

I have not made any effort to make this place my home. I have not taken the intiative to look for a job. I have not met anyone with whom I can talk to or share with. In seven months I have not made one friendship outside of Tom and the children. It's been difficult to live without the support of my friends back home.

I am afraid of doing anything that will further my commitment to stay here and cut my ties back home. It's not that I don't love him. I'm mad about him. I am just having an incredibly huge adjustment problem. I know this isn't healthy for me or anyone else. I know I need to make a decision. I just can't seem to take the first step.

Tom is getting tired of wondering whether I'm staying or going. I am becoming increasingly depressed. If you can help me please respond as soon as you are able. I am afraid that this long period of indecision may end with a rash and hastey resolution that might prove to be a grand mistake. At any rate, I would like to quite living out of a suitcase and make a home for myself and my daughter. Thank you for listening. -- Dana

Dana, it sounds as though you're depressed about the relationship in which you're involved. Something is just not filling all of your needs, is it? It would be foolish for you to stay just for the sake of not wanting to live out of a suitcase.

As far as a home for your daughter, she'll be happiest when you are happy, whether or not you're involved with someone.

Those first two months were not enough to make a relationship that would last or the two of you would have combined paths instead of separating.

How has your relationship changed so that you would think it was better than it was then? Or is it? Perhaps "love" was actually "need" and now your needs are different?

I think any action at this point is better than the situation in which you find yourself. Action will at least start dialogue and either further expand the relationship or end it so you'll be free to grow some more. -- Queenie

♥

Dear Queenie, I am a single woman with 3 children. My problem is I was married for 13 years when I left my husband who was cheating, addicted to alcohol and was verbally abusive to me and my teen son. I had to leave the marrige and try to get away to think straight. It wasn't easy on my own but I was much happier and at peace.

My husband shacked up right away with someone he had had an affair with while we were married and they lived together for a year. He left her because he said that he wanted to come back and that he still loved me and he wanted to be close to the kids. I said no and he kept asking, got the kids to ask me and finally I agreed to let him stay on weekends for a trial.

It didn't take long for him to get back into old habits. He started judging me and making comments and yelling at my son on a regular basis.

My two younger children love their Dad and look forward to the weekends but I dread them. I've become depressed and don't know what to do because I made the decision to let him stay with us and I don't want to hurt the kids.

He wants to get together more and is acting like we are still married and like nothing has changed. I want out. What do I do? I don't want to hurt my kids but I'm drowning. When he did live apart from us he did not see the kids on a regular basis so I am concerned that my children will suffer if he starts spending his weekends somewhere else. Any advice would sure be appreciated. -- Nora

Nora, I think your kids are going to suffer more if you are so unhappy. In my opinion, since you are divorced, I think you should get him out of your house and out of your life as quickly as you can.

You say he's back to the old habits. They don't sound like habits that are good for you or for your children. He wants back with you because you enable him to have a place to come home to even with his terrible treatment of you.

He's using the kids to force you into a life you don't want or need. That is unfair to you and to the children. They need to understand that you are very unhappy around their father and that there are many kids who have mothers and fathers who no longer are living together. Please visit the divorcesupport.about.com Web site and pay particular attention to the information relating to Alcoholism and Co-Dependency. You have to get yourself together in order to clear this man out of your life.

If you do what your kids want, what will ultimately happen? I think you know. You will lose yourself, and when your kids are grown they'll go out on their own and you'll be left with nothing but bad memories. Get some outside help and get this guy out of your life. -- Queenie

♥

Dear Queenie, I met my wife when she was 18 and I was 22. We were together the whole time she was in college and married shortly after she graduated. I felt the marriage was great, we never fought, got along great, it was all I ever wanted in a marriage.

The problem came about a year and a half into our marriage when she decided that she had married too young and never had a chance to be on her own. So, she moved out into her own apartment and totally cut our "relationship" off.

She said that she loved me and always would and that she couldn't have asked for a better husband, but she just didn't want to be married or in a relationship at this point in her life. Of course I was devastated because I really loved this woman and didn't expect this to happen.

We did the whole marriage counselor thing to no avail. The marriage counselor said she could tell that we really loved each other and that we were best friends, but best friends don't always make the best lovers.

My wife also discovered a "friend" on the internet around the same time. She would spend hours at night chatting with him. Anyway, it's been about 6 months since she moved out and nothing has changed. She still has her internet "friend" that she has been to see a couple of times, and I'm still wondering what the hell happened.

She says that he is only a friend and that she doesn't want a relationship with anyone right now. The problem is I know that she is lying. I read some of the e-mails at the beginning of their "friendship" and it was no friendly conversation. I would just love to hear it come out of her mouth. Is that too much to ask?

She is so confused, she has me confused. She says that she may want to work things out some day but she doesn't know when that will be. She is taking things "day by day" she says. Did I mention that her "friend" happens to be 17? (maybe 18 by now and she is 24) Apparently this kid knows how to say all the right things. This is killing me. I hope this resembles some sort of question. -- Don

Don, will it help to say that this is not an uncommon occurrence when someone doesn't have the chance to experience life on their own before they make a commitment such as marriage? I try to stress that early relationships are facing long term commitment problems but it doesn't mean that anyone will listen.

It means that people will continue to fall in love and believe that it will last forever even though they don't have the emotional experience to make such a commitment. Young lovers belive that "they" have a love that is "different" that can overcome all the obstacles that other young lovers have stumbled on.

Right now, you don't have a marriage. If she does "discover herself" perhaps you won't be the one she decides she needs for the rest of her life. If it were me, I would end this "marriage" and move on. It won't be easy but living this way is way too painful. -- Queenie

♥

Dear Queenie, my husband told me that he isn't sure if he still loves me. We have been married for 17 years. I am having a hard time living in a loveless marriage. I still love him very much.

He has changed into a cold hearted person, he is not the same wonderful guy I fell in love with. He is seeing a therapist to find out why his feelings have changed. As of now he really haven't told me much of anything regarding his feelings. Should I ask him to leave or just wait it out. How will I know when to ask him to leave? -- Deborah

Deborah, I'd opt for waiting it out if you love him. It might benefit you to also see a therapist to get a handle on your feelings. As long as he is in counseling there's hope that the man you fell in love with will return. You can't sit back expecting that to happen.

What if he decides he doesn't want to remain married? He's taking care of himself; you need to take care of yourself and be prepared for anything that may happen between the two of you.

Marriages end and it is not a disgrace when you've done your best. As far as knowing when, no one else can make that decision for you. Don't ask him to leave until you are ready and prepared for life without him. He may leave without a backward glance or it may shake him up enough to try harder. It's a gamble either way. -- Queenie

♥

Queenie, me and my husband just got back together. We was split up for 7 months. He caused me a lot of pain and hurt. I met this other man. He is so good to me but he wants no commitment. I can't get over this hurt and pain my husband caused me. He tells me it won't happen again. I took him back cause of the kids. I'm not sure what to do. Should I give one more try or not. I buried all my feelings toward him. I'm caught in the middle. He wants to control me again. I can't let him to that cause I like my freedom. Tell me what to do. -- Mavis

Mavis, I can't tell you what to do, it's your life and you have to decide what is best for you then make it happen. If you don't love your husband, get a divorce. *Then*, once you are divorced, and have your emotions back in line, start dating others. Right now, you are uncommitted, confused, and looking for someone to save you. You have to save yourself. Unfortunately, that's just the way life is. -- Queenie

♥

Hi Queenie, my husband recently told me that if he had it to do all over again, he would not have asked me to marry him. Yeah, the knife plunged right through my heart! He says he has not been happy for the last couple of months. I'm not ready to just let go. He says he is not at the point of wanting to seriously get a divorce yet. We can get along so well at times, and then he can make me so mad.

He has a friend at work who is a married female. I am so jealous of her I can't see straight. I've told him how upset I am with the relationship he has with her. He talks to her more then he talks to me. I've tried to explain to him that the closer he gets to her the farther he pushes me away. It just doesn't register in his head.

Sometimes I wonder if he is using that relationship to make me so mad that I will leave him so he doesn't have to feel bad for leaving me. What can I do to make this relationship work? How can I accept his friend as just that?-- Donna

Donna, what your husband doesn't understand is that he is getting his emotional needs filled by confiding in his coworker, while your emotional needs are screaming for attention. Men don't understand that emotional bonds with other women can be extremely threatening to a marriage; they think sex is the only way of being unfaithful but emotional infidelity can also destroy a marriage.

The two of you should be best friends as well as lovers. If this other woman is taking your place as his best friend then you have every reason to be jealous of that relationship and to worry about the damage this will cause to your marriage — particularly if he's now talking about divorce.

If you want to fight for your marriage, meet this coworker, go to lunch with her, get to be her friend and see if you can neutralize the bonding that is taking place between the two of them. Don't accuse her of trying to steal your husband, after all, she's married. Invite her and her husband over for dinner or out to dinner with you and your husband. If she and your husband are just good friends, this shouldn't pose a problem. This will also give you a chance to see how she and her husband relate to each other.

How your husband reacts to your contacting this woman will give you a lot of insight into the depth of his feelings for her. If there's more than friendship involved and if he wants you to do the dirty work of divorcing him, stand firm and make him take that step. You aren't the villain in this movie, you're the victim. —Queenie

♥

Dear Queen of Hearts, I am trolling the web looking for a friend. You see I am professional woman, mother of two, who has no friends. I have no one that I can call, no shoulder to cry on, and I have been in need of a friend lately.

I have tried the chat groups, tried to jump right in and find someone interested in listening, but that proved unsuccessful. I really don't know where else to turn.

I am married, but husband is very cold. He doesn't like it if I have any other emotion other than "happy." No complaints are heard, no ills are rectified. Every time I try to talk to him we end up in a huge fight and he threatens to leave. Every time I have a complaint, legitmate or otherwise, it is turned back to me--I have the problem, not him. He has no ability to feel empathy or concern regarding how I feel. The funny part is that he manages to give those qualities to others, but not me.

We never do anything together. We haven't ever been the type of couple that really went out, but now we do nothing.

I still hope against hope that he will one day realize that I am an important part of his life and that I am not replaceable, but it hasn't happened. That's how I feel, replaceable. How I feel, who I am, doesn't matter. In fact we would have a super marriage if I wasn't me.

He admits that I give him the very things that I ask from him, but I guess he has decided that what he gives, what he does is good enough-- equal or greater then what I give to him--so nothing changes.

As I said I am looking for a friend, not advice. I don't need someone telling me that I should leave or stay. I can't leave, not with my children, not now. But I can't hope anymore either. Maybe a friend to listen to me, to tell me everything will be all right. Maybe a mother to adopt me.

Thanks for reading if you got this far. -- Danielle

Danielle, you don't want advice so I won't give it. One day I hope you'll realize that there are only so many seconds, minutes, hours, and days allocated to each of us and wasting any of them is a very foolish expense. This is real life, right now, not a dress rehearsal. Your sadness over your life comes through loud and clear and if I could I'd adopt you. -- Queenie

♥

Dear Queenie, I have been married to my husband for 20 years. He's a good man, doesn't drink or smoke, never has hit me, but 5 years ago he became the biggest gripper about everything! If he sits at a traffic light too long the weekend is ruined. He never wants to go anywhere or do anything.

I am a very independent person and find this behavior frustrating. I have wondered since we seem to have very little in common and I have asked him to stop and he doesn't, what should be my next move? Stay or go? -- Jean

Jean, how can you be married for 20 years and have very little in common? I can understand how his behavior would frustrate you. If you want to save the marriage suggest to him that the two of you get counseling. If he doesn't want to go to counseling, you might want to give it a try so that you can learn to either adjust to his personality or make a decision about your future that doesn't include him.

What happened five years ago that may have caused your husband to lose interest in things around him? Has he had a physical check-up lately? There could be some treatable causes for this change in his personality and you would hate to give up on a marriage to a "good man" without looking for alternatives. -- Queenie

♥

Hello Queenie, my husband and I have been married for 20 years, and I have always felt something was lacking in our relationship. When I would mention this to him, he would blow it off and tell me that it was nothing or ignore me.

Recently I have found that what was lacking was my love for him. I like him well enough but I don't love him and don't think that I can find the love I had for him again.

I want out, I'm tired of carrying the load of the marriage, the house and the bills. the kids are older now, almost out of school, and I feel that I want to go on with my life from here alone. I'm 38 and I think I have alot more productive years ahead of me and can't stand the thought of living in a marriage that feels empty for me.

I have tried everything from plannning elaborate evenings with dinner, movies, sexy nities and wine to spending time just being with him, over the course of a year to see if I can rekindle the love I once had for him. It hasn't so far. He says he's more in love with me than ever, but I feel so empty inside that I'm hollow!

He says that I don't have to love him to have sex with him, and I feel that I can't because of my lack of feelings. He wants to take care of me even if I move out and wants to continure being my lover after I've started a new life. I feel like this is a strain on me, because I'm sure he wants to keep an eye on me to see if anyone visits me.

When I first told him that I may be moving out, he cried and was mean with words, and has since decided that this would not be a good approach if he wants to keep me around him. He has told me that he will help me any way he can, if he can just make love to me when he wants. I don't know what to do with this situation, I would like to stay friends because of the kids but I don't want him or this marriage anymore. What would you suggest? -- Janice

Janice, it sounds as though the marriage is over. My opinion is that you should do whatever it takes to get through the divorce and on with a life without him. His request for sex on demand is ridiculous and demeaning to you. Don't degrade yourself.

This isn't going to be easy but once you get past the decision making stage it should be all downhill. Good luck. -- Queenie

♥

Dear Queenie, I'm in a marriage and am not sure that my partner truly loves me. He's still here and taking care of me and my three children. I love him very much and am not sure what to do — do I let him go and try to make his life happier or do I wait it out and see if this is just a phase for him?

I know that in our marriage I have felt the same way at times, but my love for him never truly leaves me — do you think his love will come back? Sometimes just doing the normal daily things can overcome a person and that person can get lost in life — not always sure what they want in a marriage, work, family, love - I think that's where my husband is — I want to reach him but not sure how to go about doing it in a way that doesn't bring up divorce or separation. -- Angie

Angie, you don't say what he's doing to make you think about divorce. Obviously something is very wrong. What don't the two of you talk it out? Perhaps you need a marriage counselor? I just don't have enough to know what to suggest. -- Queenie

♥

Dear Queenie, my husband is an alcoholic. I wanted to have a birthday party for myself so I asked my husband what he wanted to do for the party, because our birthdays are pretty close so he says "I want to have a beer keg party". This is something I haven't done since I was in college.

Up until this point he had been handling the alcoholism really well. He hadn't had a drink, as far as I know, until about a week before the party. About 3 or 4 months had lapsed between the that point and his last drink.

He had been feeling real good about life. His logic in starting back to drinking was I am doing good in life. I think I can handle a few drinks. Well, needless to say the party was a failure. He got very drunk, insulted me several times, and made a move on my best friend! I saw this. He says he was "blacked out".

My question is, should saying he was "blacked out," make a difference on how I handle this situation? He has taken full responsibility for his actions, but this isn't the first time this has happened. (He use to "black out" a lot.) I realize this is one of the problems of alcoholism.

I have tried to get him to get help, but he says it won't do any good. I got him into AA once before, and he seemed to be doing very well, but he always slips. I know this man loves me. He has a serious problem with alcohol, and now it's even starting to affect his health, very badly. I don't know what to do. I've watched this problem get worse and worse. I just don't know what to do. -- Marilyn

Marilyn, knowing that he was an alcoholic, why did you go along with the idea of a beer party? You knew what would happen!

You both need to get involved with AA, him to get back on the wagon, and you through Al-Anon to learn how to live with and cope with an alcoholic without being a willing codependent. Your other alternative is to give him an ultimatum: get help or get out.

Living with an alcoholic, particularly one who has black outs and is abusive, is no way to live. Without him taking positive action to quit forever, and you using positive reinforcement instead of providing easy access to alcohol, it will only get worse. -- Queenie

♥

Dear Queenie, when I first met this guy, he was interested and I was not. He is 27 and I am 33. I have been married before and he has not. He's a smoker and a drinker. I am not. I drink a little, but I do not drink every weekend, nor do I drink to the point of where I am drunk. He does.

I've been in a similar relationship, and it ended with me being hurt very, very deeply. So deeply in fact, it took me two years just to be able to drive through his hometown without getting sick to my stomach.

I did not like this guy I've been seeing at first because I thought he was a lush. I've kept him at a distance, but now we've grown closer and I've let my guard down. I know in my heart of hearts that this guy is all wrong for me. Like most men, he doesn't express himself very well (except when he's drunk) and I am very expressive.

I slept with him for the first time this weekend. He didn't call last night and of course I feel hurt. I know there's no need for me to say anything to him about it because he won't understand why I feel bad. Besides, he's never pushed me or made me feel bad about waiting as long as I did.

I know this guy is all wrong for me, but I do care for him and I'm always hoping that he'll change. I know that the only way he can change is if he wants to. I'm finding myself conforming to his ways and I've got to stop or it'll be more heartache for me. I sit around with all his smoking, drinking, vulgar talking friends and I know I don't fit.

My question is, how do I go about getting out of this relationship without causing unwanted conflict for myself? This is the first guy that I've had feelings for in almost three years, and that makes it all the more difficult for me. I want to give him a chance, but how long should I put up with this stuff? Thanks for your help. -- Paula

Paula, you can put up with it for the rest of your life if you need this kind of pain. Or you can get counseling for yourself to find out what drives you to seek losers so that you can enable them to continue to be losers.

As far as this man is concerned, you already know the answers to your questions. Now it's time to seek the answers to why you need this pain. No matter what, you don't deserve this treatment, despite what that poor little inner child of yours believes. -- Queenie

♥

Dear Queen of Hearts, I have been with my partner for over thirty years and have 3 children. I am an ex addict and am hiv+. I know he is still drinking and drugging. I have talked to him on several occassions, but to no avail. I don't want to leave him because under all that he is a good guy. What would you do in this situatin? -- Norma

Norma, have you joined Al-Anon? Since you don't want to leave him you need to get as much emotional support as possible in order to handle your present situation. -- Queenie

♥

Dear Queenie, I have been married for three years! And my husband abused alchol for all of it. He has now stopped the alchol abuse and has cleaned up his act but my love for him seems to have gone and his touch repulses me sometimes.

Is there anyway for me to get thru this and love him again or should I end the marriage and just move on with my life. I have been feeling this way for 9 months now! Any advice would be helpful. — Brandy

Brandy, if he was an alcoholic when you married him, I suspect you are a co-dependent. What that means is you "need" to be in a relationship with someone who has a dependency problem such as alcoholism. When he cleaned up his act, it changed the relationship into one that you're not comfortable with. I suspect also that if you end the marriage that you'll move into a new relationship with another person with a similar problem.

It's only my opinion but that's what I think "might" be the problem in your marriage. I'd suggest that you seek counseling for yourself to learn why you need to be in these types of relationships. You might also get involved with your local Al-Anon group — you'll meet a lot of co-dependents who are trying to understand the same thing. If you don't get some help, you're going to continue this cycle throughout your life.

It's a shame that you married him "for better or for worse" and were happy when he was in his "worse" mode and now that he's "better" you can't stand him. Don't you see something wrong with this picture? -- Queenie

♥

Friends and Family

Friends and Family

*"My wife and I share an open relationship, but lately she
seems to be making me feel that my son is not welcome in our
home."*

Relationships are difficult enough when there are only two
people melding their individual personalities into a harmonious
unit. Add into the mix the many personalities among extended
family as well as friends and acquaintenances and life can turn into
a virtual soap opera.

Couples owe their primary loyalty to each other, and their
children, but that won't always stop family members from butting
in where they don't belong or from taking sides when they should
remain impartial during the stressful times which occur in all
relationships.

Friends, too, may get much too involved in situations that
are best left alone. Friendships can break from poor advice or too
much meddling. More than one friendship has ended when the
"friend in need" is seen as "the friend who knows too much about
our personal life" when a warring couple reconciles.

Nosy friends, meddling relations, snoopy co-workers, they're
all part of every day life. Most people mean well, some will always
try to cause trouble, and a few are just plain irritating regardless of
the situation. It requires good judgement to keep friends and family
with your best interests at heart close by and those who don't a safe
arm's length away. Knowing which is which can be the real trick.

Second and subsequent marriages can mean even more
problems as husbands and wives juggle their current responsibilities
and those still required to children, stepchildren, and exes plus
"baggage" from past relationships.

No one ever guaranteed life would get easier with
experience.

♥

*Dear Queenie, I am a life long friend of a "Joy," a gay woman; I'm
hetrosexual and have been married to a wonderful man for 25 years. Joy's
relationship with Liz of 17 years broke up recently and it was devastating
for Joy. She went into gay chat rooms and immediately met someone else
(Connie). Sparks between them ignited into a furious fire almost
immediately.*

*Joy and Connie simply cannot stay away from each other and their
affair has continued this way for 4 months now. Joy is an educated woman*

and has a good career while Connie has a blue collar job and virtually no education. There's not much in common between them except for the sex. Joy's professional and social obligations are suffering because of this new "obsession" but she doesn't seem to be able to resist this woman.

Clearly Joy is on the rebound and she's one of those people who can't be alone. She was ready to move in with Connie until I convinced her to speak with her therapist about the situation and the therapist agreed with me.

I am worried about Joy, she is juggling so much but still won't stop this breakneck pursuit of Connie, nor will she stop being at Connie's beck and call.

I need to know what to say to her, to say some words to her that would help restrain this fire in her blood. I am happy for her in that she has found someone who cares for her and I truly like Connie, but I am concerned about Connie's manipulation of Joy and the fact that Joy simply cannot stay away from Connie. Joy has always been the most responsible level headed person I've ever known, up until Connie came into her life. How do I help my dear friend? — Olivia

Olivia, has Joy asked for your advice? Joy is an adult not a child. Be there as a friend but step back from telling her how she should run her life or who she should love. I, personally, think you're stepping way over the line when you spend so much energy worrying about who Joy is or isn't sleeping with. You certainly are running the risk of her telling you to mind your own business and I think she'd be quite justified in doing so. —Queenie

♥

Dear Queenie, I have been happily married for 6 years. My wife and I share an open relationship, but lately she seems to be making me feel that my son is not welcome in our home. He has been in a lot of trouble but right now he is staying with her sister. Now all the two of them do is fight back and forth. I know deep inside they really love each other what can I do? — Bill

Bill, this sounds like family counseling would be a good investment for all of you. How about giving it a go? —Queenie

♥

Dear Queenie, I have been dating a guy on and off for almost 4 years. We have broke up last year. This year we decided to give it another try. My concern is about his children. He has two of them and the child support is taking alot of his money. I'm not sure if he will be able to provide

for me and our possible children if we get married some day. What advice do you have? You can be a brutal as you need to be. Thanks — Kelly

Kelly, I don't have to be brutal, just realistic. This man owes his children support until they reach legal age. That is the legally and morally correct thing for him to do.

When you fall in love (and marry) a divorced man with children, this is something that you have to work around if you love him. If you can't accept his responsibilities, please let him go so he can meet a woman who can. —Queenie

♥

Dear Queenie, my boyfriend is going to buy a house and wants me to move from my hometown to live in his house with him and his kids. My kids are grown and on their own, however, if I move in with him, it will mean taking care of his two kids and being out in the country, and financially we would be just getting by. I know from past experiences money can put a lot of stress and strain on a relationship.

I guess what I'm beating around the bush about is do I want to move away from my family not knowing what is going to happen with us, and do I want to take care of kids again. I've raised my kids and feel it is the time to live, right?

We have been dating 4 months and we both believe fate brought us together. He is younger than I and is very stubborn. I'll be able to put more money away there than I can here. I don't know what to do. If I stay I lose him. But, if I stay, I could meet someone here. Please help. — Beverly

Beverly, four months isn't long enough for you to pack up everything and move to the country to become this man's housekeeper and surrogate mom to his kids.

If you had absolutely no questions, if you adamantly knew this was the right thing to do, if you weren't writing for advice, if you weren't thinking about meeting someone else, that would be one thing. But you aren't absolutely sure this is the right thing to do and that should be your strongest clue to wait at least six months or more to see if the spark is still there. Nothing is so lonely as being somewhere you're desperately unhappy. —Queenie

♥

Dear Queenie, I am 27 and dating a man that is 41. We have a wonderful relationship together, but we do have some problems with his two daughters and their mother. The girls are in their teens and they have always liked me but every time the mother has any time with them it always

makes them despise me for a week or so when they get back. The mother has gotten married and moved on with her life, and she has already ruined one of my boyfriend's previous relationships by making him choose his daughters or the girlfriend.

They were never married and have been seperated for 11 years now. Am I over reacting when I get worried that she may do the same thing to our relationship? Is there anything you think I can do to help the situation? Is me speaking with the mother a bad idea? Please help with anything you have! Thanks — Nanci

Nanci, this woman cannot "make" your boyfriend do anything he doesn't want to do. If he loves you, nothing she does will affect that love. You can expect his daughters to want their father to remain unattached so that they have his undivided attention. That's normal. If you go into competition with them, you'll lose so don't even try. Speaking with their mother is a bad idea if you're trying to put some boundaries on what she says about you to her daughters or to their father.

If you think you can meet her in neutral territory and become friends, then you might accomplish something. It really depends upon how serious your relationship is with this man — if marriage is a possibility then you'll need to learn how to deal with "the baggage" of his life which will become a part of your life after marriage.

These girls have one mother and one father. They've had to adjust to their mother's new husband and their father's girlfriends over the years. They have learned not to blindly accept anyone their father starts dating — surely you can understand this.—Queenie

♥

Dear Queenie, my brother-in-law and his wife are going through a nasty divorce. It's my wife's brother, with whom she is very close. I used to be his friend years ago but got tired of his selfishness.

Now he wants a normal relationship with his new girlfriend with my wife and I. It is destroying my good marriage. Where can I get support? My wife and I can't talk about this. -- Dan

Dan, unfortunately, you can't choose your in-laws when you choose your marital partner. I would suggest that you try to learn to at least tolerate your brother-in-law for the sake of your wife and your marriage. Your wife loves her brother despite his faults and to keep peace you need to try to make peace with him. -- Queenie

♥

Dear Queenie, my older sister, who is 3 times divorced and who has been through an abusive relationship, lived with my wife and I for several months. Originally, she had come to stay with the agreement that she would stay for a few days at a time, between trips looking for a job.

After she arrived, she decided to work several part-time jobs and not look for steady work; we finally asked her to move out, since she was interfering in our relationship, and not contributing to the bills, even though she has thousands in savings.

My wife has always been very gullible, and is taken in by people like this; she feels sorry for my sister, and insists on involving her in our relationship. When I have tried to talk to either of them about this, my sister becomes very manipulative, and tries to pin the blame on me. My wife becomes very defensive, and runs back to my sister for advice.

My sister is 50 years old; why can't she get a life of her own, and quit wrecking mine? My wife and I are currently attending marital counseling, but my wife gets extremely defensive of my sister, saying she "has been through hard times." Any ideas, or am I better off in divorce court? -- Arnie

Arnie, only you can decide if divorce is better than your current situation. I don't know what the problems are between you and your wife and it isn't something I need to know.

You and your wife need to learn to communicate without shouting, becoming argumentative, or getting defensive about your actions. Your wife needs to leave your sister out of the role of counselor and confidant. Your sister needs to butt out when the conversation turns to the problems in your marriage.

Marital counseling is good and I hope that this issue is able to be resolved through the counseling so that you can take care of the other issues that are destroying your marriage. -- Queenie

♥

Dear Queenie, how do you get your child's father to back off and let you move on with your life but still be able to communicate for the child's sake? -- Mona

Mona, if he's trying to hold on to you using the child as an excuse, you have to be firm and tell him that the relationship is over. He still has legal rights regarding his child so you have to respect that. If he cares about his child, try to explain that it's important for his child's sake that the two of you maintain contact but that contact does not mean the two of you must be anything more than polite friends and caring parents. -- Queenie

♥

Dear Queenie, I have a 2-year old son and have separated from his mother after 3 years of living together. I've started a business that takes up much of my time. I want to meet someone, however, it kills me when I think about my son having two separate lifestyles, half brothers and sisters, stepmoms and dads, and splitting his time between his mom and a stepdad and then me. -- Steve

Steve, it's better for a child to be raised by loving parents who aren't living in the same house than to be raised by warring parents who stay together "for the child's sake." Your son is growing up in the type of household shared by more than 50% of the children in the U.S.; his and yours are not unique situations. It is the norm rather than the exception.

You don't say why this relationship ended. History is a clue to the future. Try to learn from your past experiences. -- Queenie

♥

Dear Queeneie, four months ago I visited my best friend at her family's home in our home town. We have been sisterly close for most of our lives. We are both in our early twenties. She has a two year old son, and is married with minimal complaints about her husband.

The second day of the visit we have a heart to heart talk. That evening we hit the nightclub for a girls' night out. Early into the night she spots my first love who I had an on and off relationship with in my teens. She was always a good friend of his for much of that time too. I still have an attraction to him.

We spend the entire evening talking, dancing and drinking together. Towards the end of the evening, while dancing, he kisses me then her very passionatly.

The next morning I am still bothered by this and tell her how I am feeling. She says I have nothing to worry about but when I asked her not to go out with him if he should call she got furious! Later, she cooled off and apologized. I left that afternoon as planned.

Later that week I get a phone call from my first love, and elated I tell my friend who reminds me of his past untrustworthiness, and says to play hard to get which I do. I begin to hear less from my friend, and when we do talk it's short conversations. One day I just flat out ask if they're dating. After a little beating around the bush she confesses. I am first stunned then hurt, and finally concerned. This man has been known to lie and cheat.

Within two weeks time my friend leaves her husband and her child to move into an apartment with him. Meanwhile, his divorce is being finalized at the same time — he married the girl he was cheating on with me, and had a child with her. So she is avoiding me and our friendship and living off credit cards, partying with him.

I'm over being envious and hurt, but I am truly concerned for my friend. How can I offer her any support if she blocks me out? I have told her that our friendship is the most important thing to me in this situation. It's been three weeks since I last called. Do I let this go altogether or hope she comes around? Help. -- Sue

Sue, you and your married best girlfriend go out on the town, make out with your married ex-boyfriend, you want to date him again but your married friend beats you to it, he leaves his wife (who he left you for), she leaves her husband (and child) so they can party together, but you're not upset with her, you want to help her only she won't talk to you. Is that about it?

There's no friendship here. This is a soap opera. Let go. Get out of this mess and get on with your life! -- Queenie

♥

Dear Queenie, I have a baby from an ex-boyfriend whom I was very in love with. He left me just before my baby was born. He never wanted to marry me. He's 20 and said he was not financially stable. He has not come to my house in over 2 weeks. Last time he came my baby started crying when he carried her and maybe that's why.

When I was in labor I called him at 2:00am and he showed up five hours later. I know he is very bad for me but sometimes I think about the old times and start to cry. Is that normal? -- Wanda

Wanda, of course it's normal to feel bad about how you thought your life was going to be and feel overwhelmed about how your life is right now. But, the reality is, those good thoughts about him are in the past and you have a baby daughter that needs you right now and who will need you for a lot of years in the future.

He may not be financially stable but he needs to be legally obligated to provide financially for this child of his. If he isn't making child support payments contact your local legal aid or ask family or friends to help you get the legalities taken care of.

Not marrying you does not mean he isn't obligated to provide for her until she is at least 18-years old. If he doesn't know that, it's time he learned.

As much as you believe you love him, his actions are loud and clear that he doesn't love you. I suggest you write this loser off and concentrate on making a good life for yourself and your daughter. There's a good man out there for you, but you have to be ready for a new relationship when he shows up. -- Queenie

♥

Dear Queenie, I have a very good friend at work who I've known for about ten years. I'm not interested in him romantically — he really is just a friend. However, he's been having a problem that I find is having a strange effect on me.

Basically, his 20 year marriage ended last year when his wife left him for another man. She had been having an affair prior to the marriage ending. Her lover lives in another country so she only sees him every couple of months and in the meantime she leans on my friend for emotional support. There aren't any children involved.

My friend is suffering terribly over her. He's tried to cut her off several times, but she persists, phoning his friends and relatives when he doesn't respond. I haven't been openly critical of her—I've just been a sounding board—but I'm having a hard time watching him suffer.

I know he was a good husband to her, faithful and supportive. I always got the sense she was the dominant one in their relationship and I find myself becoming more and more disgusted by the things he tells me.

She's clearly enjoying having two men in her life. I think the shock of her affair, at least initially, weakened him so much that he now just doesn't have the gumption to stand up to her. Two of his close friends died around the same time and that's had an effect on him too.

I've always been the sort of person who believes Ann Landers when she says MYOB—you know, Mind Your Own Business. I've never, ever interfered in anyone's relationship, but this situation seems so unjust. I guess I should 'fess up and admit that a major relationship of mine ended a few years ago in a very similar way. I ended up moving to another city just to get the guy out of my life.

I'm thinking of writing a letter and having it forwarded to my friend's ex-wife to make her think her new relationship is in trouble due to the distance so she would move to where her boyfriend is if she wants to keep the relationship. If I do such a letter, I think she'll either leave or try to get back with my friend. Either way, she'll feel forced to make a decision.

I'm not really expecting support from anyone, however, I think this friend of mine is in desperate need of a guardian angel. I'm not confiding in anyone and, from an ethical standpoint, I'd like some guidance. Am I doing the right thing? -- Carol

Carol, in my opinion, no, you aren't doing the "right thing" by getting more involved in this situation than you already are. Quite frankly, this relationship could backfire on you if they ever did reconcile and if you care about your friendship you might want to start detaching and becoming less involved.

Much of what you see in him may actually be what you feel about yourself, feelings you have transferred to him. I think there is probably some major baggage you need to still dump from the relationship of yours that ended so badly.

I suggest you let things progress as they will without playing "guardian angel." No matter how much information you have about the relationship, there are doubtless major pieces to which you're not privileged. How will you feel if what you do causes him even more pain by the whole thing taking a twist you never anticipated? MYOB. -- Queenie

♥

Dear Queenie, I have been married for nine years to someone who is very loving and kind as well as a truly devoted father. The trouble is that the course of my life changed very drastically a few years ago due to an extremely serious accident which left me permanently disabled. While my family and close friends have come to accept me the way I am now, my husband's family acts as though nothing ever happened and we should just get on with our lives.

His parents and siblings still expect us to be able to drop everything and go visit them, even though I am quite limited in what I can do. Due to financial problems -- I haven't been able to work a day since my accident -- we have needed a lot of support, and all of it has had to come from my family and friends. His family just expects my husband and I to cope with the problems on our own and have never so much as cooked a meal for us or helped out with the care of my son on even one occasion, even during my numerous surgeries or hospitalizations.

I can't seem to help blaming my husband for his family's indifference. I feel they are like "fairweather friends" who only want to see us at their own convenience and in the good times and holidays but the rest of the time stay away so they won't be "roped-in." I don't really want a relationship on these terms. My husband, on the other hand, seems to be in denial. I suppose the behaviour of his family is very hurtful to him, but I feel he must accept them as they are and not expect that they will change, because people never really do.

I am afraid this is going to split us up, which would be disastrous for our little boy and the new baby I'm expecting this spring. But on the

other hand, I feel so angry at him I can hardly stand to be around him and our intimate life has all but stopped.

We have tried marital counseling, but my husband is also a very poor communicator and really refused to apply himself during the sessions, so the therapist had no choice but to discharge us and let us work things out for ourselves. All that's happening is we are growing more and more distant with every passing week and month. This is no way to live.

Is there any way I can deal with the anger I feel toward his family without taking it out on my husband? We have tried resolving it with them but without any success. They promise to try harder to spend time with us and their grandson, but they never keep the promise.

I feel they have absolutely no sensitivity to the terrible situation we are living with. On top of everything else, we are going through a very stressful and expensive litigation and the last thing we need is this sort of added stress with his family. I am beginning to think there is just no point keeping in touch with them at all, but am afraid this would be too much to ask of my husband. Any suggestions would be gratefully accepted. — Sally

Sally, your husband's family has no obligation to provide for you, no matter how needy you may be. Neither does your family but you have probably put a major guilt trip on them and rather than deal with your anger they're doing as much as they can even if it causes problems you probably could care less about because you feel your problems are greater than anyone else's because of your disability.

You are telling his family what you expect of them, and then when they don't meet those expectations you get angry all over again. Your husband is the most logical target for that anger you feel so you dump on him. What a happy household yours must be.

There are families throughout the world dealing with much more adversity than you are. How do I know? You're obviously healthy enough to be pregnant with a second child. You have enough money to afford an "expensive litigation" that I suspect may result in a major cash influx sometime in the future at which time you'll tell your in-laws to get lost. You aren't homeless.

Perhaps the marital counseling didn't work but that doesn't mean you shouldn't consider counseling for yourself to sort through all of the issues you're dealing with and to get a grip on the anger that's choking you. Most of the stresses you're dealing with apparently are those you have created. —Queenie

❤

Women Who Cheat

Women Who Cheat

"My problem is now I'm starting to get bored with my husband again and the man I work with is sparking up that flame with me."

Adultery: voluntary sexual intercourse between a married person and someone other than the spouse.

Affair: an amorous relationship.

Amour: a love affair, esp. an illicit one.

Betray: to be unfaithful or disloyal to.

Cheat: to be sexually unfaithful.

Infidelity: marital unfaithfulness.

Unfaithful: not faithful to duty, obligation, or promises; disloyal.

Those are definitions from the *Random House Webster's Dictionary*. They don't explain why women cheat, they define sexual cheating. But sex is not always the reason women cheat. Sex becomes the means to the end, the path to emotional intimacy that may be missing in their marriage.

Why do some women cheat? Because they have never learned to respect themselves or to say "no."

Why do some women cheat? Because they doubt their own ability to survive without a man so they make sure another man is waiting before they walk away from their current relationship.

Why do some women cheat? Because they are unable to be faithful to just one man.

Why do some women cheat? Because they want to put the burden of initiating a divorce on their husband and they believe that an affair will make him angry enough to file for divorce.

Why do women cheat? Would having a suitable answer make the cheating less painful or more understandable? How could it?

♥

Dear Queenie, why would a happily married woman look to have an affair? -- Tom

Tom, a happily married woman wouldn't. -- Queenie

♥

Dear Queenie, my wife cheated on me with my best friend for over two years and by the time it ended she had pushed me to bankruptcy and I almost lost my house because of the money she spent on this guy. She also walked out on me and the children for this guy. The only reason I am still in the relationship is because of our children.

I don't trust her at all, I don't think I could ever trust her again. The only reason she gives me is "I was young and did not know what I was doing" Not good enough for me? Should I stay for the children? Yes I still love her but not like I did before. I never show emotion, but on the inside I am crushed. Should I leave? I will never leave my children, I think that's why I'm still here. — Chad

Chad, if being young was an acceptable excuse for cheating then no marriage would be safe. Your wife's reason was poor and the pain she caused is tremendous. There isn't anything anyone can say that is going to make the pain any less for you.

If she wants the marriage to work and you want the marriage to work then the two of you need to get couples counseling. And you could benefit from individual counseling to get more of a grip on the anger you're feeling. Anger is okay but at some point you have to let it go or it will eat you up inside. — Queenie

♥

Hello Queenie, I have a question. I recently cheated on my hubby. I didn't want to, it just happened. Now I'm in trouble, he knows and I don't know what to do. I love my hubby dearly and the 3rd party is definitely out of the picture. My hubby doesn't think the other guy is gone and he's pretty upset about this whole thing. So, what is the best way to explain to him that it will never happen again?

Some people say "once a cheater always a cheater," I don't agree with that, believe me, I learned my lesson big time and it will never happen again. You can stake your life on it. I guess my question is can he trust me ever again? If you don't answer this, I will understand, at least I got stuff off my chest. — Lisa

Lisa, answer me this: if your husband cheated on you and he told you he didn't want to cheat on you "it just happened" would you be pretty upset and have a hard time trusting him or would you forgive, forget and let bygones be bygones? Think about it before you think he's making too big a deal about your betrayal.

As far as explaining to your husband that it will never happen again, he never thought it would happen the first time so he's not apt to believe you at this point. Regaining his trust is going to take a long, long time. You'll never hurt as much as you've hurt him, no matter how long it takes him to forgive you. — Queenie

♥

Dear Queenie, I need some advice on how to cope with this situation. My wife of 7 years has just informed me of an affair that she had about 1 year ago. Why did she wait so long to tell me? How could she go on for so long without telling me?

When she told me I was crushed, all I can think about is the graphic details that my wife will not tell me about. Why do I want to know such details, where they did it, how many times, what exactly they did sexually in detail? These mental pictures haunt and hurt so bad. I know that this person works with my wife and I also know that this person is married and has children.

I have repeatedly asked my wife to tell me his name so I can contact this person and tell him that he needs to tell his wife or I will, but my wife says that it would not help our situation. Late wake-up call I guess. I wonder if other people in my situation would also want to tell this person's spouse and if it would serve any purpose.

I am so confused and I am so in love with my wife. I have spent the last 5 days crying on and off, feeling sick to my stomach, and my body feels broken literally. I want this to work out, she is my everything, my soul mate, my friend and lover. Can we fix this, will the pain ever go away? We have agreed to get counseling and I have apologized for anything that I may have done to cause this to happen. I need to know if I should pursue getting details. — Dell

Dell, more details will not help you get over being hurt by this betrayal. More details will just add to the pain you already feel. Only time and forgiveness will do that. Please pursue the counseling.

Identifying who the man is and telling his wife is only hurtful to his wife and cannot help you heal. It is part of your need for revenge. She probably already knows about or suspects there was an affair and is in her own anguish. You should not add more pain to her life by contacting her with details of this affair.

If you love your wife you will forgive and try to forget instead of tormenting yourself. And stop blaming yourself. You didn't cause your wife to cheat. Regardless of any problems within your marriage, cheating was her choice. — Queenie

♥

Queenie, I have been married for 11 years and I have been seeing another man for the past 5 years. I love my husband but I also love this other guy. This other guy hasn't mentioned anything about me leaving my

husband or anything. I don't know whether I should leave my husband for this other guy or just break it off with the other guy. What should I do? — Pam

Pam, I suggest you leave your husband for the other guy. Your husband deserves a wife who understands what marriage vows mean, which you very obviously don't.—Queenie

♥

Dear Queenie, I am in desperate need of some advice. I have been married for 11 years and have two children. I have always considered our marriage to be good. Not perfect, but not bad either. The sparks haven't been there in quite some time, but he is pretty good to me. He isn't physically abusive and is very good to our children.

I have recently met someone that I think I am falling in love with. I can't believe it's happening, but it is. I am scared to death and don't know what to do! This person makes me so happy and I love to be with him. There has been no sexual contact at this time. Please help! — Kelly

Kelly, to believe that a marriage will always be full of sparks is to believe in Santa Claus or the Easter Bunny. Marriage has its ups and downs, its good days and its bad ones. Affairs are full of sparks and all good days. Then you get married and the 24/7 brings the ups and downs and the sparks get fewer and farther apart.

If you're married to a man who treats you and your children well don't throw him away because there aren't any sparks. However, if you're determined to get together with this new man then at least do the honorable and decent thing and get a divorce first.

Okay, so maybe this new guy won't stick around if you're free and available, maybe he only wants to play with a married woman, or maybe he will stick around but maybe he'll have second thoughts about getting serious with someone who would break her marriage vows. Do you see how tangled this can get? You have two children. Set a good example for them.— Queenie

♥

Dear Queenie, I met my future wife while I was in college and she was a junior in high school. She was so shy, that her friend had to introduce her. After one year of uncontested love for one another, I popped the question. Six months later, we had the biggest wedding in town. I joined the Army for financial problems and was deployed a lot, but always came home to my loving wife.

It was picture perfect on the surface and we had a beautiful baby. Two months later our baby was born I was stationed overseas for a year, it's where I am now. My wife seemed to be stressing out over living with her parents again. Her mother would always criticize her for everything she did for the baby. I tried to pay attention and listen. There was little else I could do. I tried to be supportive and know when to give advice and when to be a listener.

She started to hang out with her friends and then she got into a cyber relationship with a guy. I found out about it because I checked her email account and found his emails to her. I know I shouldn't have done it but I did and I gave her several chances to tell me about it, whether or not she was lying to me, she kept insisting she wasn't though I knew she was.

We had a long conversation and I confronted her and told her to break it off with him, and she said she did. I believed her until today when I saw she was in contact with another guy from the same town. I don't know if I can ever trust her again.

We always said that if one ever cheats on the other, it's a divorce, no questions asked. I don't know if I can be with her any more. A passionate moment might remind me of her doing the same thing with someone else. I love my wife more than anything in this world. I know we've had it rough, but I have never cheated, flirted, hugged, kissed, or danced with another woman since day one. I want to believe her, I just can't yet. There is no trust in me for her. I just want to know what to do. Should I leave her? Should I not go home? What should I do? — Tom

Tom, so far you have a lot of suspicions but no physical evidence that your wife has cheated. Nothing that you have found supports a sexual affair unless you left out some details in what you've written. She spends her free time with her single friends and online and you spend your free time worrying that she's being unfaithful and searching for every clue you can find to back up your fears.

One thing you learn if you really do love someone, you don't put "set-in-stone" rules into your relationship with them unless you want a way out of the relationship. I'm not saying that an affair isn't bad but there are many marriages that have been made even stronger because both people loved each other enough to really work on putting the marriage back together after an affair.

You say you're scared of losing your wife but you also say that no matter what she says about this other guy the marriage will be over. You say the trust is gone. You wonder if you should leave her, if you should not go home.

I can't tell you what to do but I can certainly recommend that you stop thinking your wife is the town tramp — that's what you're implying. The two of you need to talk and you need to listen without judging. You've already found her guilty of the one crime you feel is not repairable. I don't know if it's too late for the two of you to repair your marriage. Are you willing to try?— Queenie

♥

Dear Queenie, I am married, but not happily. My husband is chronically ill, but not terminally ill, and has been for all 12 years of our marriage. He wasn't ill when we were dating and those were some of the best years of my life. Since marriage, I have no real relationship with him other than caretaker/patient.

Is it moral to have an outside relationship for my own sanity? If I were to walk out on the situation, he would likely die, most literally, of a broken heart because he does not realize I am this unhappy.

It is a moral dilemma to me since I was taught to accept traditional marriage vows as sacred things. I feel as though I will have a nervous breakdown if I continue as I have, being "single" yet not able to find a partner. -- Betty

Betty, there are no reasons that make adultery an option in a marriage. Is it "moral" to cheat for your "sanity"? Would you buy it as an excuse if your roles were reversed? If you were chronically ill and your husband needed more than you could provide?

How much of a "broken heart" do you think your husband will have when he finds out you have cheated on him? Whether you leave him now in a search for sexual fulfillment or commit adultery, he's going to be hurt. You can either leave the marriage as a lady or as a tramp. Which way makes you happier?—Queenie

♥

Dear Queenie, I'm a newlywed of 6 months. I had previously cheated while engaged with a man I work with, but my fiance forgave me and we got married. My problem is now I'm starting to get bored with my husband again and the man I work with is sparking up that flame with me.

I don't know what to do anymore! I love my husband and don't want to hurt him but then I get advice that what he doesn't know won't hurt him. I can't get this other man out of my head and sometimes he is all I can think about. Sometimes I think I have this problem because I only dated a few men in my life before I got married! Please give me some advice, good or bad I will take it! — Liz

Liz, some women only date one man before they get married — and they are very capable of remaining faithful during their marriage. You're looking for an excuse to cheat, any excuse will do. Don't worry, you'll find one.

If you think that your husband won't be hurt by your cheating if he doesn't know, your thinking is flawed. He will find out, he will be hurt, and then what? You'll be sorry and beg him to forgive you. How much forgiveness do you think a two-time cheater deserves?

Look at yourself through this other guy's eyes. If you sleep with him now, you're a married woman with loose morals who is an easy lay. You're safe too because you won't be demanding commitment from him. Is that the image you want of yourself? If not, figure ways to make bedtime with your husband more interesting and exciting and keep your sexual escapades in your own bedroom. — Queenie

♥

Dear Queenie, what should I do about my wife who is always chatting and sending greeting cards to another guy? She also defends him at social events (he is a celebrity that she went to school with). She does this when I am in the same room with her but says it doesn't mean anything. She is always instant messaging him. — Tab

Tab, tell her that her attention to this guy is making you jealous and you'd appreciate it if she wouldn't spend so much time chatting with him, sending him cards or spending time with him. If she can't understand this, ask her how she'd feel if you had a woman friend that you treated the same way she's treating this man friend of hers. — Queenie

♥

Dear Queenie, I am in a horrible relationship that should have been over years ago but because of guilt and a child, I have stayed for all the wrong reasons. This has made me stray, and regardless of wrong or right, I found someone who made me feel everything in life can be good. He made me feel emotion again, something I have lacked for far too long.

We have been seeing each other for only about a month and one night we went out with a friend of his. We were drinking and me and my lover's friend kissed. I blacked out and can't remember what happened but I have to believe it did happen because they said it did. Anyway now my new love is so disappointed with me particularly since his last girlfriend cheated on him.

This man is worth my life changing, getting my divorce final and doing what ever I can to make things right. I want to prove to my lover that I am really not the person that would just go around kissing his friends.

His friend also admitted to me when I confronted him the next day that he was the one to initiate this, then proceeds to ask me what my plans are for the night. The nerve after the disaster that has already been caused and he didn't even care about his friend.

I don't know what to say or if I should say anything about his friend's part in this although my lover did tell me that he knew it was mainly him. I never wanted to kiss this guy, this is the worst hurt that I feel I have ever caused anyone and all I want to do is make it right. Please share some wisdom with me. -- Veronica

Veronica, you are a married woman with a boyfriend. You, also, apparently have a drinking problem. In the eyes of most men that would make you fair game for whatever they might propose. If you want to gain respect, you will forget about your lover until you are legally divorced, and you will get some help for your blackout drinking. You have a child that deserves better, and you deserve better than what you're currently giving yourself. —Queenie

❤

Dear Queenie, I have a question, that pertains to someone I know. This person has been married for about 6 years, and is bored and dissatisfied with her marriage.

She took a night school class, and developed a crush on her teacher. The course is finished and she wants to see the teacher again. She has no idea if the teacher likes her, she never revealed her feelings to him but she thinks that he's attracted to her. She can't stop thinking about him. They met one time, outside of class to drop off an assignment. What should she do? Is it possible that she can see this person as a friend since she is married?

Is it ever possible to meet the person of your dreams even though you are already married and be just their friend? — Confused

Confused, let's unconfuse this: no! it's not possible. If this friend wants to dishonor her marriage vows she will continue mooning over the fantasy of love with this man. Friendship with him is not possible. Lust and adultery is. —Queenie

❤

Dear Queenie, my wife had an affair for the past year and a half. I found out about it when she became pregnant (I had a vasectomy over a year ago). She was pregnant once before by her lover but at the time I did

not want to believe that she was having an affair so I dismissed it because she had a miscarriage. Two months after the miscarriage she was again pregnant and it was then that I went back to my urologist to confirm I was indeed sterile.

When I confronted her she admitted she was seeing someone else and that they had suddenly decided to call it quits (how convenient). She told me most of the details that dreary day and more as time went by. Since confronting her I discovered a lot of things that were not apparent to me at the time. I never knew, never had a clue or any idea what was going on. I felt and still do feel like a fool. She of course said she never wanted to leave me and that it was a big mistake but most of all that she loves me? It's very hard trusting her today considering all the lies and deceit.

The other man was an old high school friend she saw frequently due to work. They would comfort one another when things went bad at home (he too is married). The conversations eventually lead to a planned evening and then into a more casual fling. During the whole time I was completely oblivious to the affair and I wonder if it was not for the pregnancy would she and he still be in the affair. I will never know. We have not told him about the pregnancy or his wife about the affair. I did not want to ruin her family because mine was ruined.

My questions are: Should I tell the other man about the pregnancy? Should I inform the wife about the affair? Should I have the biological father sign papers relinquishing all rights to the child? Should I adopt the child? Should I trust her or am I just kidding myself into believing a lie that will come back to haunt me? I know I am a fool but I do love my wife and as professing Christians I would like to forgive her and move on. — Thomas

Thomas, I'm not a lawyer so I don't know the legal ramifications here but I believe that when a woman is married and she has a baby, that the man to whom she is married is considered the legal father unless she says otherwise at the time the child is born and another man's name is put on the birth certificate. If that's the case (and you'd have to check with a lawyer to confirm it) then you don't have to adopt this child and you don't have to have this man sign over anything.

There are a lot of issues here and I'd certainly suggest that you consider joint counseling before making any long term decisions. If you decide to end your marriage due to this affair and pregnancy, the unborn child needs some protection whether you're named as the father or this other man is. —Queenie

❤

Dear Queenie, I left my husband of 6 years and my 5-year old daughter to be with my lover of just 10 days. I know this may sound stupid but something clicked inside both of us and I truly believed I was in love. I subsequently hurt my child and my husband who was and still is a good friend to me.

I was in the relationship for six months until, after a lot of arguing and falling out, I decided that we should call it a day. We have broken up and gotten back together several times and I am sure that we would not have as secure a future as I had before and I believe that this is the real way I have to go. I am now obviously thinking I threw away a good relationship for a bad one although we have had really good times as well.

My ex-husband would still have me back I think but I don't think I want him back. I am very confused and not sure which turn to take. I may have ruined mine and my child's lives for nothing. I miss my boyfriend although I know it wouldn't probably be a good relationship in the long term. Please, any advice would help. - Sunny

Sunny, it sounds as though "lust" is what clicked between the two of you and when reality set in, lust didn't turn to love. You need counseling to figure out why you are so confused. As for your ex-husband, don't do him any favors — if he loves you enough to forgive you and take you back, don't go back unless you can return this unconditional love unconditionally. He'll get over you. — Queenie

❤

Dear Queenie, me and my wife have been together for 5 years and we have 2 kids. We met at work, lived and worked together 24/7 and then got married. Then I got a job on the third shift and we spent less time together but we got used to it. Then I went to second shift so that we would not need full time child care since we could not afford it. We have spent even less time together.

About a month ago I found a love letter from her to a guy eight years younger she works with. I finally got her to admit it and now she says she does not know what she wants. She wants to separate and I know she'll probably keep seeing him and even if she stays she still could anyway because I am not home.

It seems like a no win deal. Should I just give up or should I fight? I love her so much and I know she still loves me. What should I do? -- Ben

Ben, the two of you haven't been able to spend much quality time together and that has made a mess of your relationship. That's too bad because you have kids who need both parents and there's probably some love left if the two of you could talk it out.

Don't give up without trying everything you can to get the love back you once had. Maybe all it will take is romancing her like you did when the two of you first met.

Is there any chance you can get another shift so the two of you could spend more time together? Don't you think child care would be a better expense than a divorce and then child support payments? -- Queenie

♥

Dear Queenie, I have been married for four years to a wonderful man. Lately, however, I have had a wandering eye. I work with a guy that I have become friendly with. He would like to have more of a physical relationship, I keep reminding him that I am married. It doesn't stop him from making advances.

He is so sweet and intriguing, I melt even when he touches my shoulder or gives me a pat on the back. I want to be with him, but know that I can't, however I am afraid of losing him altogether if I push him away.

He has a very jealous girlfriend who he has a child and lives with. She suspects him of "cheating" on her with someone from work. I don't want any harm to come to me or him, but I can't stop thinking about him, day and night.

I am afraid my husband will suspect something, even though nothing has happened. How can we remain friends? I try not to get too personal with questions about his relationship with his girlfriend because it is none of my business, and it doesn't matter anyway if he were single.

I am falling for him big time. I think of all kinds of excuses to go to his department to see him. This is not good for my marriage and I am afraid something will happen. -- Trixie

Trixie, apparently his girlfriend has every reason to be suspicious and it wouldn't be surprising if your husband already suspects something is going on although he may not have zeroed in on exactly what. You are primed and ripe to commit adultery. You are married to "a wonderful man." This other guy will take whatever he can get because he can, not because he really cares. Push him away. Lose him. Or would you rather lose your husband?

You are being big time dumb playing such a stupid game. I can just about guarantee that if your husband dumps you, so will Mr. Wonderful. -- Queenie

♥

Dear Queenie, I've been a married woman for almost 15 years. We've had the good times and bad ones. Sometimes I've felt dissatisfied in my marriage, but I have never ever thought of having an affair. I'm a Christian and think it's just awful for anyone to be unfaithful to their spouse. I think it's messed up our children in America.

I have basically everything I want. Most women would kill to be in my position. My husband isn't too bad looking. Sex is good. Notice I said good. Not excellent. He is not romantic at all. Can even get mad at me at times if he wants sex and I don't. I tell him that's not the way to get it. My friend told me that's abuse.

I've been going to the gym for the last four years. I'm not sure when this started but this guy just started talking to me one day. I thought he was nice, good looking too. He started saying hi to me every day. Some days that would be it, once in a while we would get in a good conversation. He seemed so easy to talk to. Put me at ease. Really seemed to listen to what I said. He has a good sense of humor and can make me laugh.

Recently I lost some weight and it seemed that he noticed me a little more. I've had a crush on him but it's just gotten worse. He's said a few things that make me think he may like me too. I can't be totally sure. He's married too. I just get these vibes from him.

I didn't see him for about two weeks. He must have been on vacation or something. Anyway, when I walked to the club the first day he was back, our eyes met and I just about died right there. They seemed to be telling me that he missed me. We then looked away, but I can still see those eyes. He always looks at me. I get shy and nervous and look away.

His eyes always meet mine. I feel so drawn to him. I think about him all the time. I feel like I'm a teenager again. He hasn't said anything too personal. I will think to myself that he's just a nice guy or maybe he does this to all the girls. I don't see that happening anyway. He seems to show off a bit when I'm around. It just seems like he feels the same way.

My husband is suspicious. I stare off into space a lot. I feel so different. I don't feel myself. I'm really nervous. I want to go somewhere all the time. I always hope I will see him. Never really do. All I want to do is listen to music and dance when nobody's around. I don't want to do my housework. I can't think about it.

I tell myself that it's stupid and to get over it. It's not right. If anything came of it, it would mess up my life. My friend told me that I can't help how I feel. I feel like I've never really been in love before in my life. I also keep telling myself that I could get hurt big time.

I just don't know what to do. I feel confused. How could this happen? I don't want to stop going to the gym. Our town is small and that's the only good one in the area. I really enjoy going there, and have made lots of *friends. I guess I don't know how to handle this. I'm going crazy! Thanks for any advice you can give me. -- Cora*

Cora, now you know how easy it is for someone to commit adultery. You haven't actually done it yet, but you are giving it serious consideration.

Do you really think the lust you feel for this man is going to justify the pain and sorrow you will cause your husband, your children, your family (mother, father, brothers, sisters, in-laws?), your friends, and yourself? Make no mistake, if you cheat with this man, you will get caught and you will get hurt.

One thing that makes affairs so exciting is that you can make the other person into a fantasy lover. They become what you want them to be not what they actually are. You see him as a very dashing and romantic person but in reality he, also, is thinking of or is already a cheat. How romantic is that? Ask his wife.

Affairs provide excitement. There is a thrill of stolen meetings, getting away with something, being secretive. And, you see each other at your best times. You prepare for the meeting, and it's over before you have time to get bored with each other. The anticipation of the next meeting keeps you going. You have a lovely secret, it fills your thoughts and keeps you warm. It's not reality.

You are bored. You need some activities that will enhance your marriage and the lives of your children, as well as your own life. Getting involved with this man won't accomplish this.

Here is what I think and let me say that it's up to you to make decisions as to what you must or need to do. I think you should stop going to the gym or at least stop going when you know he's going to be there. I think you need to put him out of your mind and focus on your husband and your marriage. Perhaps, to make sex better than good will only take some creativity on your part.

You're getting ready to blow a really good marriage for what may turn out to be even less than good sex. Some guys are all show and nothing more. Wouldn't it be a shame if this guy was?

Wouldn't it be a shame to destroy your marriage and your reputation for a guy who came on to every bored housewife he met? Believe what you will, bored housewives make easy targets for guys who want sex without commitment. -- Queenie

♥

Dear Queenie, I have been married for 16 years to a man much older than myself. It has been a successful marriage, and we are very well

off financially, but I now find myself looking at men my own age and wanting a "soulmate." I found one 18 months ago, and we fell in love. We had an affair for 6 months, but I wouldn't leave my marriage so he finally left me for a very young girl with small children. He is now living with her.

The problem is, that, after a whole year of not even seeing him, I still love him with all my heart. I had to see him recently because of work and the pull was still there. I found myself drawn to him like always, and felt exactly the same way about him that I did a year ago! I think of him many times a day, and cry every night because I miss him so. He was my best friend as well as my lover, and I can't seem to get over him!

I had my chance, and didn't take it, so what can I do to make all the pain go away? The girl he is with is such a bimbo, I can't stand to see him with her. I don't know if he still loves me, even if he did, I don't think he would tell me because he doesn't want to be the cause of my marriage failing. Also, he has nothing and I have a lot of money and a good career. -- Connie

Connie, you call his girlfriend a "bimbo"? What do you think a wife who cheats is called? Adultress is one word that comes quickly to mind.

You obviously didn't want to give up your security to take a chance on love with this man. So much for loving him "with all your heart."

He isn't the reason for your marriage failing, you are. A wife who cheats is not the benchmark of a successful marriage, unless you're relating success to the size of your bank account.

Do him a favor. Forget him. He deserves better. So does your husband. -- Queenie

♥

Dear Queenie, all of my relationships are currently familiar with my partner and love him to death and can't imagine how I could ever consider anyone else. I also love him to death as he is the hardest working and most pleasant man I have ever known.

We are not only live-in lovers, we are in business together. The problem is that I am having a hard time separating being in love with loving him for all that he does. Although we have been involved with the business for several years, we have have made very little money so far though the potential is there. The finances have put a strain on our relationship with me being resentful because I feel I am doing all of the work to push the business to its potential and he is busy making money for us to live.

I am very frustrated that he doesn't just say "tough, the bills are late" and concentrate on our business and so that it can finally make money.

The real dilema is that I have recently met someone who is a friend of a friend. He flirted and I told him I was in a committed relationship. Since then, we have spent time together in a group setting and it is undeniable that there is an attraction between us. People around me have asked me if I am aware of the obvious. I tell them yes I am but I am an adult and I can handle it.

I have been married, divorced, and lived with someone else for a few years and now live with my partner although we are not formally engaged. I am college educated and I am not the flighty type. I feel like there is a foreign being in my body. Who is this person that is undeniably attracted to this man?

I have never before met someone that I trusted immediately. This is a man that if I wasn't committed could ask me to run off and get married without knowing each other well and I think I would say yes.

My partner is aware of our friendship and since most of my friends are men, he is ok with a new friendship. He does not know that we have spent some time together discussing our feelings besides friendship. We have kissed very shyly and when together it is as if we have known each other and been together for years.

This is one of those moments in your life where you just know you are at a crossroads and you need to make some hard decisions but if you don't you will regret it for the rest of your life. Thank you for listening and I would appreciate any advice that you feel is relevant. -- Lilly

Lilly, this is your journey and your crossroads. No one else can make it for you or smooth the bumps along the way. Maybe I can help with a few comments and questions to move your decision process along.

There is nothing wrong with feeling the way you do. Perhaps you have finally found your soul mate. Perhaps you're so close to commitment with your partner that you're searching for a way out.

Working together will strain even the best of relationships. You are resentful that he does not work on the same aspects of the business as you, nor in the same manner as you. Saying "tough the bills" will do much to destroy your credit rating and the way that potential investors, creditors and business associates would view your business. That's bad for any business.

He isn't the same person as you and he needs to provide the stability and security for himself (and you) that comes from taking care of today's business. You should be happy that he is so conscientious although I suspect you find this boring since you want the business to take off and apparently feel that without the two of you on the same exact course it will take longer than you wish to wait.

Your involvement with this new man is going to cause a lot of problems — but you already know that. Your partner may already suspect that you have more than a casual interest in this new friend. Is now a time for the two of you to talk in open honesty about the situation? Are you ready for whatever reaction he might have to your interest in this man?

How much are you willing to lose? How much do you think you love this man? How much do you think this man loves you? Is your interest in this man worth losing everything you have with your partner? If your partner walked out of your life today, how would you feel? If your partner told you he had fallen in love with someone else, how would you feel? If this new man said he wasn't sure just how he felt and he wasn't ready to commit to something long term, how would you feel? Do you think your business arrangement with your partner could survive if you left him for this man?

Honesty is critical to the success of a love relationship as well as a business relationship. So is being true to yourself. Unfortunately, when three people are involved in a relationship meant for two, someone is always going to get hurt. -- Queenie

♥

Queenie, I am 43 having an affair with a man 20 years younger who I love dearly. I've left home but my husband wants me back. I don't trust myself at ths point, always wanting to be with the other man. I want to go, want to stay, and have been unhappy lots of years. I have a young son who hates me and doesn't want to see me. I started seeeing a therapist who is not much help yet. Help. -- Alma

Alma, you need much more help than I can even begin to give. Stick with the therapy, it will probably take a while to work through all the issues that have caused your life to be so unhappy. The affair is wrong as long as you are married. My suggestion? Stay in therapy and stay away from the guy who is young enough to be your son. -- Queenie

♥

Dear Queenie, I've really screwed up my marriage. I had a one night stand and this wasn't the first one. It seems that every time everything is wonderful and going well, I need to to screw it up. Why do I need to destroy my life this way and what can I do to stop it? -- Yvette

Yvette, I'll try to play mini-psychologist on this one but you really need to speak to a professional and get help to overcome this terribly damaging problem. It's not something that can be easily resolved without getting to the underlying causes for your actions.

I think that somewhere in your past is a reason that you feel you don't deserve to be happy. Every time your life gets "too good for someone like you" you do something to insure that you'll earn the punishment that a bad person such as yourself deserves.

We're all born good people. Most of us live our lives as good people and we deserve the best. You deserve a good life. You deserve to be happy. Breaking your marriage vows is a foolish thing to do morally and it endangers you and your husband with the threat of AIDS and other STDs.

Please get some help. I hope that your husband is the kind of good man who will stand by you as you rebuild your negative self-image and not take your actions personally. You're hurting him immeasurably. -- Queenie

♥

Dear Queenie, I am 23, married, and have a child. I love my husband and child very much, but I'm having an affair with another man. This affair has been 4 out of the 6 years I've been married and has been very exciting for me, helping me relieve my everyday stress. It started out as something I did when my husband and I split up for a few months and I needed someone and this man was willing to be with me for support.

After two months of him being there whenever I needed anything, and not trying to take advantage of my relationship being broken, I fell into lust with this man. We have awesome sex and we care deeply about each other and how the other one is feeling! He is a great friend (with benefits). These are things I don't get from my marriage.

My husband is a "party" kinda person, and a flirt with every girl but me. I need advice on what to do because I want my child to have a good life with both parents, but I feel like I could go on with this affair for a long time. How can you beat sex with two men that you love? I truly believe I am in love with both of them. I can't help it that one of them sends me into a world I've never known before sexually and he is not my husband. I feel very guilty everytime I talk to my lover.

What do I do? Leave my lover and be miserable? Keep up what I'm doing? -- Tonya

Tonya, why don't you divorce your husband and marry your lover? "Awesome sex" and deep feelings for each other would be a strong foundation for a long term relationship. Unless, of course, he is also married and cheating on his wife.

Does your husband have the same "open marriage" philosophy and rights? Are you agreeable to him getting "awesome sex" from someone who cares?

This is a poor excuse of a marriage and you are a very poor role model for your daughter. You already know what you *should* do, you don't need my advice. -- Queenie

♥

Dear Queenie, my problem is my ex! We split up because she was messing around. I took that bad, did quite a bit of stupid stuff and to avoid my temper she started lying about everything.

We went to counseling, she would tell me that we were doing fine, and all would work out so I would drop all my defenses, and she would get me again, with that guy. It hurt that much worse again!

I got pretty violent with the guy. That was after I was man enough to try to talk to him, let him know what was going on. I have been involved, with a few women since, at first I would just dump them and take her back.

We recently were at a family event and now she keeping calling wanting to meet and talk about reconciliation. I have refused, I can't not handle, emotionally, or physically, another let down like that. Plus I understand from outside sources, that she is living with the guy. I told her the last time we spoke that I would not even consider, anything, unless she went on her own, to counseling, for at least 3 months without me. Of course she hasn't. So I am still declining the meeting she requests.

The major problem is I still love her. But don't believe I can trust her, and it also has made me awfully untrusting, to others.

I have tried so hard, not to go out and replace, her with someone else, I have been involved, but never serious. My fears won't let me drop my guard, too easily, anyway. In your opinion, should I have this meeting with her? Or should I just continue to tell her no! I am afraid that if I get into a situation where she can get to me that I would take her back. -- Darryl

Darryl, it's so difficult to let go of the past. There's warmth and comfort and the memories of good times. So, too, does the past hold the memories of betrayal and hurt — not once but many times. Can a person change? Yes. Will your wife cheat on you again? If you take her back, you'll learn the answer. Will she hurt you again? Probably. Should you take her back? That must be your decision.

If you take her back you will have to learn to trust her again. That will be very difficult given the past. She will say something and you will believe she's lying. She will go someplace and you will believe she is meeting a lover. When the phone rings and it is a wrong number, you will believe her lover is calling. She will tell you she loves you and you will wonder if she's saying it to you or to someone else. Not trusting her will put a terrific strain on your relationship.

She must be prepared to deal with you questioning her every move — she has, after all, not been trustworthy for quite a long time. She hasn't sought counciling, she still has a live-in lover. How much more do you want to hurt?

Somewhere there is a woman who has a parallel life such as yours with a husband who has betrayed her. She is getting her life back together. She is trustworthy and in need of a good man in her life. She could be your soul mate. Too bad you're still hung up with a woman who doesn't know a good man when she's married to him! -- Queenie

♥

Dear Queenie, I suspected that my wife of 12 years was having an affair, so I started tapping our phone. After about a week, I taped a conversation between her and a man she used to live with before we were married. She was telling him how much she loved him and wished she had married him and had his babies.

When I confronted her, she told me that it was all just a game to her and that she hadn't done anything but talk. She said she hasn't seen him and wants to stay married to me.

This was two months ago. Now she tells me that she is really in love with him and still talks to him, but is still in love with me and wants to stay married.

I do love her, but I don't know if I can ever trust her again. Any advice? Should I keep working on this marriage or do you think it's a lost cause? There are also two kids involved. I'm a mess! Help. -- John

John, I can't say that this is a "lost cause" but it certainly doesn't look good. Loving wives don't play games with other men, certainly not games like these and this is not the way a wife treats her husband if she truly loves and respects him.

If she decides that she doesn't want to stay married, there is very little you'll be able to do to change her mind. Frankly, at that point, you would be better off letting her go. As far as the children are concerned, they're far better off in a home with one stable parent, than in a home with two parents who dislike and distrust each other.

You can't control her but you can control yourself. Take hold of your inner strength and don't let her tear you apart. -- Queenie

❤

Queenie, is it right for my wife to be having conversations with another man whom I really don't know? He only calls when I am at work, and she only talks to him when I am at work. This man is a friend of a friend and they've only known each other for two months yet she is telling him our martial problems. -- Walt

Walt, it's as right as you having conversations with another woman and telling her your marital problems. What do you think? -- Queenie

❤

Dear Queenie, I am happily married and have been for almost thirteen years. My husband loves me deeply, and is good at showing it. We are both very busy with our jobs, so there is very little attention between us during the week, but we try to make up for it on at least a couple weekends a month. Things are great between us, we don't argue or fight, we will talk things out if there is a problem, we ask each other's advice on big descisions, we are very compatible.

He has never cheated on me, that I know of, and I have never cheated on him. I love him, but he knows that I have never loved him as deeply as he loves me. I guess that is why he gets jealous of my male friends, even though they are simply friends, and they are friends of both of ours.

I have been going to night school and I have made friends with a man who is following the same curriculum as I am, so we had many classes together as well as an interest in the same subject. We talk to each other during breaks about the subject, and about school in general. We e-mail each other jokes and we talk on the phone occasionally. He is married, with a son.

Here's the problem: I have fallen hopelessly in love with this friend. No doubt, the symptoms are all there. Big time, head-over-heals in love. And we have never even as much as touched each other. I keep trying to convince myself that it can't be possible, that it couldn't be true, but it is.

I may have been trying to avoid it, but it hit me like a ton of bricks all of a sudden one day. I was trying to figure out what was wrong with me, why I get terribly nervous when I know I'm going to see him: sweaty palms, racing heart beat, thinking about him all the time. And it suddenly hit me, a little voice in my head said "You're in love, sweatheart," and my world came crashing down on me because at the same instant I realized I had to get him out of my life.

Any suggestions on how to get over this, how to get through until the hurt isn't so bad? Naturally, I can't even talk to anyone I know about this, the results could be devastating. -- Lisa

Lisa, you should be able to see why your husband is jealous of the men with whom you spend time. He has a very valid reason. The two of you aren't spending enough quality time together, and you are now in "emotional love" with someone else. If you don't think your husband knows, think again. You'd know if he had something else on his mind, even if you weren't sure what.

You're trying to figure out how to tell this guy how you feel and testing to see if there's enough going for the two of you so that he might bail out of his marriage and into your arms. That's why you're doing all the comparisons between the two of you.

I suggest that you just back up on the contacts with him and get busy at home trying to keep your marriage strong. Telling him that you're in love with him and your heart is breaking is dangling the invitation to join you. If you're serious about keeping your marriage together, you won't do this. You have an awful lot to lose and so far nothing substantial to gain. -- Queenie

♥

Queenie, help! I have recently decided to get a divorce because I was in love with my best friend more than with my husband. When I was still living with my husband, my friend flirted with me non-stop, invited me to spend the night, and often invited me over or out on dates.

Now that I am getting a divorce and living separate from my husband this friend has backed away. I barely ever hear from him. When I was living with my husband he told me he could see himself married to me. I'm trying to give him some distance now that he says he only wants to be friends. But it is really hard. Any advice? -- Wendy

Wendy, no advice from me. You've just learned that flirting isn't the same thing as commitment. Now you know this "best friend" wasn't as serious as you about a committed relationship. He liked you better when you were married and cheating. No heavy commitment requirements, a nice "no strings" relationship for him. Too bad you took him seriously. Better write this friendship off. -- Queenie

♥

Dear Queenie, we met through the Internet and have been dating for a couple of months. Things like her coming to my house and both

preparing dinner, then going out to have a good time and waking up the next morning, or me staying for the weekend at her house.

I've been divorced for 2 years and she's been separated for 1 year, and getting her divorce. From the beginning, she let me know that she's not interested in a serious commitment, saying "I don't want to jump from the pan to the fire" but saying that she was a "one man woman" and that it wouldn't be long until she settles down.

The problem is that from the beginning, she told me about a man out of state with whom she's been chatting and e-mailing since before we met, and she was curious about meeting him. I let her know several times that I didn't feel okay about it at all.

The last time we talked was two days before she flew out to see him. Her excuse was that she already had the plane ticket and couldn't get a refund so she had to use it. She called the night before she left but I wouldn't talk to her. I emailed her and told her that I thought we had something better and I basically terminated our relationship.

She emailed me back before leaving for the airport and asked that I reconsider and give her a chance. She's with him now and I haven't replied to her last e-mail. Can you give me some advice, please? -- Mike

Mike, she's a "one man woman" who's married (getting a divorce doesn't mean single), dating two guys? What kind of advice would you like? I think you should cool down as far as a relationship with her is concerned. Wait until she's divorced and stops playing the two of you against each other. I think you deserve better than this. -- Queenie

❤

Queenie, I am a 29 year old man who was divorced earlier this year after an 11 year bad marriage. I met a girl who was still married and we started having an affair. She left her husband which she intended to do anyway, not because of me. The relationship was great, and after about three months we moved in together. I treated her son like he was my own, she got pregnant and then had a miscarriage. She moved out and said she was confused, that she still had feelings for her husband but she loved me.

We kept seeing each other until two weeks ago when she told me she loved me but was tired of working on our relationship. I found out she has been sleeping with her ex and trying to work things out with him so I called him and told him everything about us. Now they're split, and she hates me for calling him. I love this girl with all my heart and want her back. I didn't hurt this bad when my wife and I divorced. What can I do to get her back? How do I get her to love me again? -- Jay

Jay, this was a bad relationship from the start. You were just divorced, you met a married woman with a small child who got careless, got pregnant (by you or by her husband?) and then miscarried, then couldn't decide if she wanted you or her husband so she moved out and now she won't speak to you because you told her husband what was going on.

She's married. Why would you want to waste your time on a woman who would cheat on her husband? And don't give me the old "but with us it was different" routine. She left you for him, didn't she? After she left him for you? You can't rekindle what's not there. Forget this instant wife and child and find yourself a woman who doesn't belong to someone else. —Queenie

♥

Dear Queenie, I have been going through a divorce for over a year and have a toddler. Shortly after separating from my husband I met a man who and began seeing him exclusively. Now after almost a year I have met another man who is everything I have ever wanted in a man.

My problem is that the first guy is not aware of this new guy. I know it is wrong but I have pushed the old guy away and begun focusing on the new guy. I have fallen so deeply in love with this man but when I am with him I think about the the first guy and how much he loves me. It is almost like I miss him. We still see each other and he begs me to come back to him. My child has grown quite attached to both of them.

In my past it seems as if I love the "chase." When I finally get a man to fall for me I tend to get bored and move on, breaking another man's heart. This is no joking matter and I feel ashamed.

What is wrong with me? Why can't I be content with who I am with? Both of these men give me everything I want. Love, support, passion, respect. I am so confused that I will lose them both at this rate and my fear is that maybe perhaps neither are good for me. I fear that in time with this new man I will be looking again to move on out of boredom.

I don't want my child to go through this and my heart can't handle this even though I know that it is my fault for this pain.

Now this new guy and I basically live together. The old guy calls every day and I keep saying that I need time to think and I care for him just give me some time and don't crowd me. Part of me realizes that I will never return to him.

I know that what I am doing with these men is wrong but for some reason I can't stop. I have fallen in love with the both of them for different reasons. One is out of emotional and physical attraction the other is out of emotional attraction. What do I do? -- Lulu

Lulu, apparently you have unresolved needs that will keep you hopping from man to man looking for something that they really don't have. You must search deep within yourself, find that neediness, examine and cure it, and then when you've grown up inside you'll be ready to meet the man who will make the mature you happy.

It's easy to blame everything on "childhood" occurrences, but the truth is, there is much within our childhood that determines how we will live our adult lives. Go back, search through those dark closets of your mind and find out what you've been seeking in your relationships that you didn't get when you were a child.

When you understand, you can put those things to rest. In the meantime, be honest with the first guy. You're leading him on, giving him hope, perhaps keeping him handy in case things don't work out with the new guy. That's not fair to him.

Someone is going to get hurt. There's no way it can be any other way. When three people are involved in a relationship meant for two, someone will get hurt! You have your entire life ahead of you. You owe it to yourself and your child to get some counseling to get your life together and stop hurting yourself as well as these men who fall in love with you. -- Queenie

♥

Dear Queenie, I'm 49, divorced and have been dating the woman of my dreams, who is only 26, for a month now. Although we are having sex, which she says has been great, I find myself falling in love too quickly.

She said from the beginning that she is not ready for a committed relationship. She says she is not seeing anyone else, yet I found out that she is. No big deal to me at this point. I told her I would give her the space she needs. She doesn't know that I know about the other man.

My question is: how can a woman be so turned on to me sexually and not begin to feel some kind of love. Our sex life keeps getting better and better with each time.

I have expressed my feelings for her with flowers and gifts, and at the same time, I have told her for her sake, that I am trying real hard not to fall in love with her. What can I do to show her that I will be the best man she could ever hope to find? How can I make her truly fall in love with me? Is there some secret potion?

She is absolutely the most beautiful woman in the world. She treats me like no other woman has ever treated me, and yet, she is seeing someone else at the same time, and tells me she enjoys my company, and loves it when we make love, but, she is not ready for a relationship. -- Stan

Stan, she may be almost half your physical age but she's way older than you when it comes to relationships. Sorry, I think her involvement with another man is a "big" deal, particularly in this day of sexual diseases! She's cheating on you.

Let her know you know and that you don't find her misrepresentation of the truth to be a particularly attractive quality. I doubt you'll do this because you're afraid you'd lose her. And you might. But right now, I don't think you "have" her.

Yes, there is a way for her to see how attractive you are and for her to learn how much she needs you. Stop being so serious. Stop dating her exclusively. Date others. Give her plenty of space. Forget the flowers and gifts.

When she knows you're not hers alone (she isn't yours alone now, is she?), and when she sees you out and about with some other beautiful woman on your arm, she'll feel the pangs of jealousy. If she doesn't, there isn't anything going in your relationship in the first place other than some nice bedroom moves.

You need to make her work for your attention. Be cool, be independent, be the man you used to be before you fell head over heels for her. Get back in control of the situation. She isn't the only beautiful, hot, young woman in the world. -- Queenie

♥

Queenie, I don't know what to do! I live with the father of my children but I don't love him any more. I'm so in love with this male friend of mine! I have told this friend that I love him and he said I love you too. And when I asked if he really meant it he said "yes, as a friend for now."

What does that mean? Should I back off and let him make the next move or should I try and find out what he meant by that? -- Nina

Nina, the first thing to do is make yourself free to enter into another relationship should one be available. Right now you live with someone, whether you love him or not. Doesn't it seem a little complicated to you?

Perhaps this is what your male friend meant when he said he loved you as a friend for now. Perhaps he is waiting for you to be unattached because he doesn't want to get any more involved with a woman who is already living with someone else. -- Queenie

♥

Queenie, I had been involved with someone for over 4 years. We were first friends at work and both married. My marriage had deteriorated and my husband and I divorced. My "friend" was also married with children.

His relationship also deteriorated to divorce. He had been separated for over 2 years and we had been seeing each other steadily. We had arguments mostly related to the slowness of his divorce coming through.

Earlier this year, I purchased a home and we moved in together. At the same time, a close family member became ill and I spent much of the time with her. At the same time, my friend's divorce came through.

He became very withdrawn, angry, and was feeling like a failure. He was not supportive during the time that I was dealing with this illness in my family. He became nasty and put me down. We had a terrible fight and I asked him to leave. He moved out with barely a struggle.

We have not seen each other in over two months. I have tried to have a conversation via phone and he has totally withdrawn, almost to the point of being paranoid with me. Is there any hope with this? I do love him, but the pressure of my life's challenges and his life's challenges seem to make it very difficult.

I love him dearly, but we both need to work at this. I'm not sure he can. He has told me to "stay away from him." It's hurting me tremendously but I'm doing my best. I've begun dating, but it's difficult. Should I wait longer and then contact him, or just say that it's over and move on completely? Help! -- Joan

Joan, there were so many issues that confronted the two of you in such a short period of time, and each of you had to deal with the stresses in your own ways. Sometimes this can bring a couple even closer together. And sometimes it can blow a relationship to smithereens.

Time is the only thing that will provide the answer to your relationship's longevity with him. For now, your attempts to get on with your life are probably the best move. Contacting him hasn't worked. He knows you're still interested, and with all the two of you have shared, if there is still some potential of a future together, I think he will have to make the next move.

Each of you has a lot of "personal history" to get cleared up and this is a good time to do that. Get yourself back in top mental, emotional, and physical shape and by that time either he will be back or you won't care if he ever returns. -- Queenie

❤

Queenie, my husband and I have been together for a total of 20 years. We have 2 children and he is a good father and husband. The problem is me. I was involved with someone else (my husband did not and does not know) who I have known all my life. This man is a family friend and he is

married. We started sleeping together before I got married, but the thing is I never really knew why I was sleeping with him, yes I did and do love him, but I've always known there was no future.

We stopped our affair but remained friends and once in awhile he would hit on me and I would refuse. His wife and I are quite close, yeah, I know, some friend I am. He and I have started again because the sex is incredible, and his wife is not sleeping with him and my husband is not the best lover.

I am trying to end it because I do have some morals believe it or not. If my husband found out he would divorce me and I don't think this man is capable or real love or respect for a woman. Why am I drawn to him? -- Monica

Monica, only you know why you remain in this adulterous situation. There is nothing good to be gained and everything good to be lost. You already know that.

There are many people who will be hurt when this affair becomes known: your husband, your children, his wife (your "friend"). Is the "incredible sex" worth it? Your husband may not be "the best lover" because you haven't given him the benefit of your knowledge to show him what you enjoy. It isn't necessary that he know how you know about this, you can tell him you read a lot of books.

It's not your job to supplant this man's sex life just because his wife may or may not be sleeping with him (most times the wife does indeed sleep with a cheating husband, it just makes for a suitable excuse when a guy wants outside sex).

If you really want to change your life, start now by being a devoted wife and mother. Now, today, is the beginning of the rest of your life. Perhaps, if you try hard enough, the past will not destroy your future. -- Queenie

♥

Dear Queenie, this is hard for me, because I think I already know how you will answer my problem. I am nearly 25 years old and have been married for 3 years. I think I married my best friend and not my lover. This is not necessarily bad — my husband (call him John) is a wonderful man and I know that I can live with him for the rest of my life and be happy.

The problem is that I have found a lover in another man (call him Bob). Bob, who is older than me, and I also started out as good friends, but after some time he confessed his attraction to me and we have engaged in some "heavy petting." What complicates matters even more is that Bob is

also married. He does not feel much for his wife, but thinks he is trapped because of his two children.

I believe that you will tell me to stay away from having an affair, but that is so hard to do. I find that I think about Bob more than my husband and that has caused enough guilt that I have confessed this to John. He loves me completely and wants me to decide what I want for myself, even though his own desire is for me to stay.

I am so confused because I love both men in different ways. Part of me feels that I have a responsibility to keep the marriage vows I made three years ago. But another part of me thinks it is doing a greater disservice to myself to stay in a marriage with someone that I am not attracted to.

I feel that I have gotten myself into a no-win situation — when I think about leaving John or staying with him, both options carry a lot of pain. What advice can you give? -- Laura

Laura, you are physically attracted to a man who cheats on his wife. You are willing to ruin marriage to a good man in exchange for what with Bob? John is long term whereas Bob is a man who cheats. However, that might not be a bad match in this case as you are extremely close to cheating on John.

The losers here are John, Bob's wife and kids. There is no reason to stay in a marriage because of the kids. Many men use this excuse if they want the freedom of other women without the responsibility of a committed relationship.

You are lucky that John is still willing to stay married to you and wants to give you time to sort this out. Other men would have shut the door on you a long time ago. -- Queenie

♥

Queenie, I am married and have been in a relationship with another man for the past five years. He was in the process of divorce when we first met, and since then has remarried. I have tried many, many, many times to end this relationship, but to no avail. We are bound to each other by some undescribable ties.

He was just married again in a few months ago, and has continued this relationship with me, physically and mentally. The reason we aren't married now is because for the past 5 years I would not leave my husband for him. He told me he married this woman just to show me that someone could love him. I want to end this, but we have tried so many times to stay away from each other that I am at a loss.

I deeply love this man, I would die for him, but he makes me miserable otherwise. He even says that he can't and won't stay away from

me. And I can't stay away from him. But the irony is neither of us wants our marriages to end because it would mean hurting two very fine people.

How can I find the strength to end this once and for all. Both of us have said that it is far more painful to be apart, than any pain we inflict on each other when we are together. I am at a loss.

What do we do? How can we end it and not die from the pain of being separated. I can't do it and neither can he. What is it going to take? Please help me. I want my life back without him in it, and without wanting to die because he is gone. -- Norma

Norma, neither of you wants to end your marriages because it would hurt two very fine people (I assume you mean your spouses). You don't think adultery hurts them? If you are so in love then be courageous enough to get divorced and marry each other! Your spouses will get over the pain. -- Queenie

♥

Dear Queenie, I am a 28-year old married woman. I got married last year, but we have been together for eight years. I work in a company where I have met a very intelligent person, married with three children. We worked very well together, and we felt very good together, but that's all.

After a year he left to work at another company but then we realized how much we missed each other. We started to meet and finally we made love. Everything is perfect between us. I like him for what kind of man and professional he is, and I like him because he makes me feel I am a woman.

My husband never was the romantic type, and we always had discussions about this. Sometimes we made love one time per month. I need to feel protected and to feel loved.

The problem is that he has three children. Do I have the right to take the father of three children? I love him as I love my life, but I don't want to make so many people suffer. On the other hand I know I can't live without him. He is all I wanted for my whole life. I'm so sorry I hurt his wife, I like her very much, she is a very good mother, and a nice person.

The last time we met he asked me to move together because we both feel we can't live one without the other any more. I didn't accept yet. But I love him so much, so much, what do I have to do? -- Amanda

Amanda, you don't have the "right" to take another woman's husband, much less to take a father away from his children. Any relationship such as this takes two people, so unless you drugged him, kidnapped him and forced him to cheat with you, he was as much a willing participant as you were in this affair.

Since both of you are married to other people, the only thing I can suggest is that you either divorce your current mates and then get married, or the both of you return to your current marriages and try to repair the damage your cheating has caused.

As far as pain, the pain is already there, the damage has already been done. What do you want to do with the rest of your life? What does he want to do with his? If the two of you did get married, would you really ever trust him, knowing that what he is doing to his wife -- "a very good mother, and a nice person"-- he could just as easily also do to you? -- Queenie

♥

Dear Queenie, I have been married for 9 years and have a 3 year old daughter. My husband and I have been having problems for the last two years and we can't seem to work them out. I have recommended counseling but he won't go.

About 4 months ago, I met a man that is also very unhappy with his marriage. We talk a lot and spend time together and we enjoy a lot of the same things and seem to be looking for the same things in a relationship/ marriage. I'm not sure what the next step is in our relationship. I know what we are doing isn't right but I can't stand the thought of losing him. Any suggestions? — Darcy

Darcy, unless the two of you want to make adultery the next step, you will decide if saving your marriage is a priority and if it is, you will forget about this other man and work on your relationship with your husband. If your marriage no longer matters, you will begin divorce proceedings.

If you choose divorce, and if this wonderful man chooses divorce, when the two of you are legally divorced then, and only then, would it be proper for you to take the next step that you now contemplate. I'm betting this unhappy man wouldn't be so eager to continue a relationship if it meant divorcing his wife first. I could be wrong, of course, and that's the gamble for you. How much are you willing to risk? —Queenie

♥

Queenie, my boyfriend and I have been dating for 6 months. We both left our spouses for each other. His wife was pregnant at the time and she just had the baby a month ago. She lives in another state. My boyfriend wants to fly up there every other month to visit the baby. I know I am being selfish, but I am having a hard time coping with all of this. What should I do? — Donna

Donna, did you really think this man's child was going to magically disappear from his life? You better develop some coping skills and be prepared to shell out some of the household money in order to support HIS child for the next 18 years. That's after you learn to share him with his wife and child when he gets the paternal urge. It's the chance you take when you mess with a married man — particularly one who has a pregnant wife. —Queenie

♥

Dear Queenie, I don't know if I can really, ever stay in love. Or maybe I have never found real love. I am married and have childern, we are not happy and have not been for some time. I think I have found the one. Except he is also married. It feels so much like nothing I have ever felt, almost like we were meant for each other.

I have been trying to leave my husband for a while, but I am too much of a coward to leave. My husband loves me I know and I do care for him deeply. I am being selfish and petty.

I have never felt this way about a man in my life. I don't even know if my lover would want me for life. Or if I could love any man for life. I need to know what real love is, or feels like, and if I am just being foolish -- Anne

Anne, real love does not cheat on another. If you want to test the love you think you have for this man be brave enough to leave your marriage and hope that he loves you enough to leave his. Anything less is not real love. -- Queenie

♥

Queenie, maybe you can advise me. I been with this guy who is 13 years older than I. Recently he decided that we need to be friends instead of lovers because he is married and so am I. He feels he needs to get his life in order, before that big day, so it would be best that we stop being sexually involved and just be friends. How do you handle this? Please I am lost — Sara

Sara, use his example as a guide. Get your life in order as well so that if there is a chance the two of you might have a future together you won't have a husband who will be in your way.— Queenie

♥

Men Who Cheat

Men Who Cheat

*"My husband cheated on me with his best friend's wife. He
confessed this to me because his friend found a naked picture
of my husband in his wife's coat pocket."*

A man knows if he is caught having sex with someone other
than his wife he will probably pay an enormous price. Even knowing
that his marriage is at stake, he will still risk it all to sample sex with
others. Just as participating in a dangerous sport can be extremely
exhilirating due to the risk, adultery can provide the same type of
exhiliration as the adulterer weaves a double life designed to keep
his spouse clueless and his lover grateful.

Even if a man is having an exit affair, a painful and cowardly
way out of a marriage, he must orchestrate it so that his wife picks
up on the clues that leave no doubt he is being unfaithful. In twisted
logic, he would rather be known as an adulterer than as the "bad
guy" who initiated a divorce. He may not expect or be prepared for
the devastation that follows.

If he isn't looking for a way out of his marriage, a man's
biggest fear when he starts a long term affair may be that his wife
will become suspicious of his activities and the time he spends away
from home. As the affair progresses, he may find he has even more
to worry about from his lover as she starts pressing for commitment
and makes threats to bring the affair into the open.

No matter what she agreed to when the affair began, most
women aren't happy being the woman of convenience; they want
to be the wife. No matter what promises he made in order to get her
to bed, the truth may be that he never intended her to be any more
than a "booty call," not a permanent fixture in his life.

Regardless of the odds, some men will take the gamble and
cheat. Some will get away with it. Some will not.

♥

*Dear Queenie, years ago I met my first love, we will call her "Jane."
We went out for a few months and when she went back to her ex-boyfriend
it broke my heart and it took me a very long time to get over her. Then I met
my wife "June" with whom I have had a good marriage.*

*There have been times I have run into "Jane." We have just been
drawn to each other. My wife is uneasy about me hanging out with "Jane"
and I suppose she's had reason but now here's the problem, "Jane's" husband,
the same guy she left me for, has walked out on her and their kids and I want
to be there for her but I have to do it behind my wife's back.*

Do I love "Jane"? No. Could I love her? Maybe if I could trust her again. But then there's the fact I have two kids of my own that I'm close to and I love my wife, but I am so unhappy at times with my marraige. What do I do? -- Brandon

Brandon, you have a wife and two children. If you love your wife, you will stay away from Jane. She dumped you long ago and you were able to find someone else to love. Do you really want to hurt your wife and children by getting involved again with Jane? That is what is happening.

When you are married, if you are committed to your marriage, you do not help an old girlfriend behind your wife's back. You're asking for trouble in the worst way.

Everyone has days when they wonder if they really want to be married to their current wife or husband. You see your wife every day, her good moods, her bad ones. You don't see just her best side. With Jane you see only what she wants you to see, her best image. And, you remember only the good times, not the bad times, that you had with Jane.

You asked what to do. Here it is: Get away from Jane. Let her solve her own problems. Take care of your wife and children. They need you. They love you.

It would be too bad if you left your wife for Jane, and you wife made a new life for herself, one that didn't have a place for you even if it didn't work out with Jane. And, just between us, I have a feeling Jane would probably dump you again once she got back on her feet. -- Queenie

♥

Dear Queenie, I am in love with a man who happens to be in love with me. He was divorced because his wife cheated on him but he never dated while he was single, and when she asked him to come home, he did, mainly because he missed his kids. They haven't gotten along well at all.

I've known him for a year, and we talk every day. We work at the same place but we're on different shifts. We started off as friends, but about six months ago, we both started feeling more than that. It seems that every weekend is going to be the weekend that it's over, but he doesn't want to lose his kids, and I don't want to be the reason that he leaves his home. He really is a wonderful person.

We have kissed, but that's as far as it has gone, and I respect him so much for that, because I know I would give in if he tried to take it farther. Both of us hate the situation we're in. I have never been married, and I

don't have any children, because I've never met Mr. Right, but I feel in my heart that this man is it, and I don't know if I should push him a little, or leave it all to him.

They never did get remarried. Whenever one suggested it, the other said "no way. " I feel that it is over with them and so does he, but neither he nor she nor I for that matter, want to be the one at fault when everyone asks why they broke up, especially when children are involved.

Is there a better way to deal with this situation? I doubt is is a "right way." -- Missy

Missy, what you're caught in is a triangle with a man who thinks he's married, and acts married, even though he isn't legally married. Since they never did get remarried, they're just in a "living together" situation, even if there are kids involved.

If he loves you, he'll make a clean break, and you'll stop worrying what others will think as far as who broke up their family. What difference is it going to make in the long term? There are thousands of breakups every day. And there are hundreds of thousands of kids living in single family homes or who share time between mom's home and dad's home.

I just don't see any justification for him staying with her if he is so in love with you, kids or no kids. The "right " way is to end it with her. They're already divorced. The only thing left to do is to say goodbye. If he can't do it, and if you can't say goodbye to him, prepare yourself for a very lonely life. -- Queenie

♥

Dear Queenie, married men in their forties tend to canvass for some good friendships or rather relationships with younger women. But married women after being married for a number of years do that too. Is this normal or a trend in this new age society now?

My good friend in his late forties, married for many years, is having a good contact with another younger married woman even though they're now in separate countries.

This seems to be quite common nowadays and I've heard many stories which make me a bit confused over marriages or relationships somehow. Is it right to be secretly in love with another man/woman even when both are married? Of course both parties have no intention to leave their spouse/family at all. -- John

John, you're making a lot of generalities here, branding a whole age group based upon the actions of a few people. Too bad your focus group isn't the segment of the population that believes in monogamy and the sweetness of caring and sharing despite temptation.

Your "good friend" cheats his wife and family, as does the married woman with whom he is "having a good contact." Just as some people are unable to cheat, some people are unable to remain faithful. He may not intend to leave his spouse but that doesn't mean his spouse may not get wind of what is going on and dump him. The same could happen to her. People who cheat don't usually think about the right of the wronged spouse to take control and cut the cheating spouse out of their life.

No, it isn't right to be married and secretly in love with someone else. You hurt the one you're married to as well as the one you believe you truly love. And, at some point, you even hurt yourself. -- Queenie

❤

Dear Queenie, can you help me? I'm a married man who has fallen in love with a married woman. We work at the same company but in different departments. She is a very attractive woman. We started out just casually talking, but now it has grown into something more than just friendship.

We both know what we feel for one another, but we are limited as to what we can do about it. We have not had sex, but we have had a few intimate moments.

As far as our mates are concerned, hers is very involved in his career, and mine has a lot of insecurities about herself. When my friend and I are together the chemistry is so strong that we just can't deny it.

What should I do? I love my wife, we have our problems as all couples do, however, I just can't seem to get my friend off my mind. She fits the mold of the type of woman that I've always wanted to be with. Help if you can. -- Randy

Randy, this is adultery times two! Are you going to let this woman's boredom with a busy mate ruin your marriage? It's no wonder your wife has a lot of insecurities about herself. Do you really think she's blind to your involvement?

You may think you can hide your feelings for this woman from your wife but you're only fooling yourself. You're in lust and it isn't pretty. I can assure you, this is one chemistry course in which you'll get a failing grade. Keep going with this and you can end up in divorce court and possibly even in the unemployment line. -- Queenie

♥

Dear Queenie, I am thinking of getting involved with a co-worker. We have been working closely together for the past 3 years, but I have known her for the past 5. When I first met her, I was attracted to her. Now that I have been working with her, I have grown very attracted to who she is, her values, her way of thinking.

We are both married, and, we are both in marriage counseling trying to resolve issues with our marriages. Her marriage problems started just after she got married and have slowly gotten worse. My marriage problems have begun recently and are totally separate from my feelings towards her.

We both consider our spouses our closest friends. We sometimes go out as a foursome and have a great time. Most often, I end up talking with her all night and my wife talks to her husband. The relationship between her husband and my wife is strictly platonic.

Recently, after some deep conversations, our spouses were out of the room and we kissed. Also, after one of our most recent talks, we hugged for the first time. We find that we miss each other over short periods of time, and enjoy each other's company when together at work or out.

We both feel that we can handle our work relationship okay. We also think we can separate our feelings from our current marriage problems. We have sort of agreed to try and keep it platonic, although it slowly seems to be getting harder in our minds. Neither of us have told our spouses of this, we think it would just make the current situation much worse.

Although we have the same educational background, work experience and some values, we grew up differently and have some pretty contrasting differences. We have already talked through all the cons of a relationship. We are different. It is not extremely severe and sort of exciting. It could work. What do you think about the whole situation? Forget it, or see where it goes? -- Ron

Ron, if your wife was writing to me instead of you, and she wanted my opinion because she was the woman in this situation, what would you want me to tell her? What has your marriage counselor advised about the situation? If you haven't brought this up in counseling, what is holding you back? If you're serious about your marriage, shouldn't you discuss this with your counselor? Even if you have to do it in a private session? What does your wife think?

Adultery hurts everyone involved. If it was just you and this woman to consider, it would be a simpler problem. Do you have children? Does she? What about your family and friends? How will they react? And co-workers and other business associates? Your social groups? There are so many people who will be affected by your actions. You may feel it isn't important what others think, but it will matter when it costs you the people and the relationships you hold dear.

Suppose you decide to keep your affair (it is quickly turning into one) a secret and then you decide it is a mistake and want to end it but she doesn't want to let you go. Suppose she tells your wife or her husband. Suppose she decides to tell the world about the great love the two of you share! Suppose you want it to go on forever but she decides she wants to stay with her husband? You think it is "sort of exciting" now?

Right now you have a chance to straighten out your marriage without causing irreparable damage. You haven't crossed the line to adultery yet.

If you feel the marriage isn't worth saving, be honorable and get a divorce. You will then be free to enter into other relationships although continuing on the honorable theme, those relationships should not be with married women.

You are quickly moving to a point of no return in this relationship. No matter how logical or intelligent you consider yourselves, it will still be adultery, and the cost will be tremendous.

My advice? Forget it. -- Queenie

♥

Dear Queenie, I am a small business man. There are only two of us. We are both married happily. My problem is that we started out as friends but we became close but not lovers. Our talks are about caring, family and life in general. Because of this I am in love with this woman.

I know she cares about me because I have contact with other women in the course of our business day. When I flirt with other women she is unsettling in looks and manner. She has said never to me while we work together. We enjoy each others company but I can't pass the last obstacle of making love to her, not sex mind you. Sex for me is only a physical thing. Making love comes from the heart. I wish I had meet her years ago.

How do we overcome this last hurdle? If it is not meant to be fine, but the ultimate giving of love is sharing of one's self. Any advice? -- Stanley

Stanley, you're knocking on the wrong door when you ask me for advice on how to get a woman to cheat on her husband. Since you're "married happily," why are you trying to "make love" with this woman? What do you hope to accomplish? Have her as a lover when it is convenient?

Have you ever considered that she is giving you those looks when you flirt with other women because she considers it inappropriate behavior for a married man?

My advice is to take a cold shower, and think about the expense of divorce if you push for this "ultimate giving of love" -- a real come-on line in my book. Dress it up all you want but sex is sex. At the very least you may end up with a sexual harrassment suit if this woman is one of your employees. -- Queenie

♥

Dear Queenie, I need help! My husband left me for this woman last year. I didn't want him to leave and begged him not to, but he did anyway, though he told me that he still loved me but that he loved her more. I tried to accept that even though I was very unhappy and had a hard time seeing them together.

Now he says he loves me and wants to be with me but he doesn't want to leave her because he says he still loves her but he loves me more. What should I do? -- Samantha

Samantha, do you live in a state that sanctions polygamy? If so, and if she (his current lover) is willing, your problem is solved.

Why would you even want to get back together with this man when he has hurt you so much already, and then is willing to continue the pain by remaining with her while professing his love for you? Does she know?

Are you seriously considering reconciling with him while he lives with someone else? Does he want you to keep it a secret? Not let anyone know that the two of you are sneaking around to have sex together? That's what it's all about isn't it? He wants sex with you now that he has grown bored with sex with just his other woman.

Maybe you feel this is justice, that this woman deserves whatever happens and you're happy to show her that he wants you more than he wants her. If he does, he'll leave her. He'll tell her that he loves you more. He'll do whatever it takes to earn your forgiveness. Your best bet is to cut yourself out of this equation.

It takes time to get over a failed love. The only way you'll get past this one and be able to meet someone with more integrity will be to just say bye to this guy and quit remembering the good times of a past that should be tucked away as a part of history. -- Queenie

♥

Queenie, we've been best friends with a couple for over 10 years and have done just about everything together including vacations and dealing with child raising issues. Then she walked out on him and two days later my husband left me. They split up two families to "see if we can find happiness together." They now share an apartment together. I was in total shock!

My husband told me up until the minute he walked out that he loved me. There was never any mention of not being happy. We have had the usual marital ups and downs, which I shared details of with my "best friend." How could they do this? Never have I felt this kind of pain. It's been three months and the divorce papers were filed last week.

I miss my husband but not the person he has become. I know I will never see those days again. There was a death the day he walked out, the death of our relationship. I feel like I'll be in the mourning phase forever. He was the love of my life, my everything. It was all taken away at the blink of an eye. How could I have loved someone that would do this to me? He couldn't have really loved me and that hurts. I guess there really isn't a specific question that I have, there are too many to mention. Any advice is appreciated. — Corey

Corey, the pain is too raw for you to feel comfort knowing that yours isn't the first marriage broken apart like this. Nor can you get much comfort knowing that he probably is in a relationship that will make him unhappy once the "glow" wears off and they get down to day-to-day 24/7 good days and bad days together. He just may decide you were the better choice and come running back.

Stop thinking he didn't love you during those years you were married. He did. Unfortunately, she and he had an attraction that neither of them was able to resist and so they put all of you into this ridiculous sideshow. Don't you think her husband feels as badly as you, just as betrayed?

Make sure you get everything you're entitled to in the divorce, that you and the children are more than adequately taken care of and don't feed the gossip mills by trying to give your version of what happened to anyone who asks. Be a lady, be silent and let those who want to know the juicy details get them somewhere else other than from you.

This is a terrible time but it will certainly get better and one day you'll look back and realize why this all happened. You have a lot of work to do, damage control with your kids and family, and making peace with yourself. Whatever you do, don't take his, or her, actions personally. —Queenie

♥

Dear Queenie, my husband cheated on me with his best friend's wife. He confessed this to me because his friend found a naked picture of my husband in his wife's coat pocket. My husband moved out that night.

When I first confronted him about it he lied about things saying that things did happen, then later he said that he did it because she made him feel like a man. He told me over and over how sorry he was and that he will do any and everything to make it up to me. He called and set up counseling for us.

After four visits, I told him that the counseling just wasn't working. The counselor was only working on my husband and I communicating better. All we worked on was me getting my children--his step-children--to do more around the house. The affair was swept under the carpet and we are supposed to talk about it.

I feel as if we need to talk about the problems between he and I, not about the children. Now that I have invited my husband back home things are totally different. Before he moved back in things were: "I'm sorry, I will do what ever it takes, I know that I don't have a leg to stand on now after what I did." Now things are: "I want this to change and that to change."

How do I go about finding a better counselor? Things are getting worse now that the counselor isn't in the picture. I fear he is with the other woman again. Help! — Sue

Sue, you are the one who decided that the counselor didn't know what he or she was doing while it is quite possible that the counselor was doing exactly what was necessary, trying to get to the root of the problems in your marriage. You don't walk into a counseling session and expect all the issues to be dealt with right up front. You peel off problems layer by layer and I suspect that the counselor was on the right track and you didn't want to hear about it or deal with what was being uncovered.

An affair is a symptom of other problems. That's what the counselor was trying to dig through to find. You're the one who called it off so why don't you talk with your family doctor and ask for his/her recommendation of a counselor. And then stick with it even when you hear things you don't want to hear.—Queenie

♥

Dear Queenie, last year "he" worked for a company and traveled out of state sometimes for days, sometimes weeks, 1 or 2 months at times. This relationship is in its 18th year. I missed him so much when he left, and at first I couldn't wait for him to come home. Then he started picking fights, arguing, lying. I heard him in the bathroom talking on his cell. He says he was just playing around to mess with me.

I jotted down my birthday on the calender to remind him. I see it whited out a few days later. Then I see "t's b-day" noted a few months later. He says he hadn't noticed. He sends for me while he's traveling to make up for all the trouble lately. When I get back a week later I call him and a woman answers. "You're not his girlfriend anymore I'm his new girlfriend now." He says he was in another room and that she was with someone else.

He always proved he loved me, always proved he was loyal. Now we're taking a nose dive and I've told him not to call me. He still calls. I've gone through lie after lie, disrespected, I've talked to her, still he denies everything.

He doesn't like confrontations yet doesn't avoid it, makes plans with me yet she shows up. Why not be slicker if he's just going to lie. I know if he cared he'd at least spare me and be more discreet but he's not too bright. But why keep me hanging on if he's got someone better or just new. I keep going back because I love him. What's his excuse for calling me and not letting me go? — Leslie

Leslie, he knows that no matter how badly he disrespects you, you're going to come right back to him. He doesn't need to be discreet or honest or respectful of your feelings. No matter what he does, you're going to take him back. Too bad you don't love yourself as much as you love him. If you did you'd tell him to take a hike. — Queenie

♥

Dear Queenie, I have been with my boyfriend for 6 years. We do consider ourselves a "married" couple because we both felt that since we have been together for so long, it was like we were already married -- but without a piece of paper to prove it. We had a great relationship and I had no complaints -- in any area. But he recently went out of state for business and left me in charge of our business.

During this time, I found out he had an affair with one of our employees. I don't know when exactly it started or for how long it lasted, but she recently turned up with a baby. He says it may or may not be his and plans to get a paternity test. He has not even seen the baby yet.

I am now pregnant. I desperately don't want this woman's baby to be his and don't know how I will handle him fathering a child with someone else.We do plan to stay together and probably get counseling, but I can't bear the thought of what he did and if it's his baby, how am I going to deal with it. Please help me. — Debra

Debra, I hope you now understand the importance of that "piece of paper to prove it." If I were to find myself in such a situation I'd get counseling to get my emotions under control so that I would have the strength to deal with this man and his problems. I would get legal assistance to protect my unborn child, my business interests, and my personal assets. I would have to forgive him and her even if I could not forget.

Whether you stay with him or decide to end the relationship, you have a lot of things to deal with all at one time. Please don't misplace your anger at the other woman — she may have been just as trusting as you and her baby has become the most innocent pawn in this whole mess. If the child does prove to be his, the baby will be a constant reminder of his affair and the two of them will become a part of his "baggage" to be accepted.—Queenie

♥

Queenie, I have been marrried for 7 years and recently found out that my hubby was having affair with a woman he used to know. When confronted, neither one denied it, so I gave him the ultimatum. He decided to end that relationship and keep his family. Now he has involved himself with work seven nights 5pm-5am and I don't feel this is a healthy choice for our relationship, nor our family.

When I talk to him about it he seems to think that I should not have a problem with what has gone on and that I keep living in the past. My feelings toward him are very mixed. I've done a lot of self help and know that I do not deserve a life of lies and cheating. I have asked him to go to counseling and he said that he doesn't need help, that we could go as a couple, but right know there is no time. I'm not sure what the next step is.
— Bev

Bev, don't wait for him to go to counseling with you, get into counseling by yourself so you can deal with the anger of his betrayal and then decide what kind of marriage you're willing to accept with this man. He ran from the marriage by having an affair and now he's running by working so many hours. You are right, it isn't a healthy choice for your marriage or your family.

He wants you to forget his affair because it's over. He thinks that's how easy it is. He doesn't understand that it takes time to work through the pain of betrayal.

If he's willing to go to couples counseling all the better but you need to get there for yourself either way and as quickly as possible.—Queenie

♥

Queenie, I have been married for almost 40 years. Before I left for a vacation, one that my husband didn't want to go on, he found an old girl friend's name on an internet classmates list, and asked if I wanted to talk to her since we were all friends when we were young. I said I had nothing to say to her, he could talk to her if he had something to say.

While I was gone boy did he have something to say to her. He was new with the computer and didn't type well so he called her up, and they talked to each other several times for hours at a time. Then I came home and he told me about the phone calls.

Now he will not talk to her with me present. He wants to go and see her and they made plans to meet without me knowing, but I found out. What do I do? He still wants to see her but without me. They secretly talk on the computer and he doesn't let me know what she says. — Cassie

Cassie, you're suspicious that there is something going on between the two of them and I'd be too, considering what you've said. Is your marriage worth saving? Has he ever cheated before? Frankly, I wouldn't care if he didn't want me along I'd be there anyway to see just how serious this new-old flirtation is.

If they haven't seen each other in thirty or forty years they may both be in for a shock when they do finally meet face to face and reality takes the place of fantasy. —Queenie

♥

Dear Queenie, I confronted my man on something his young son said to me that he'd seen him kissing another lady the way he kisses me. He said he hadn't kissed her that way and they're friends and she needed a kiss cause she was under a lot of stress by her ex and feeling low.

Why was I so insecure to let this send me into a hissy? He loves me and he has closed on a house and my name is to be on the title so neither one of us can move the other out when we get upset.

His sight is on the future with me not this female friend down the road. He's been going to the doctor a lot because his health isn't so great. Was I insecure over a child's word I trust? — Gina

Gina, buying a house is a stressful event under the best of circumstances. Add the stress of his health problems and maybe you're both being super sensitive. If he has never given you a reason to mistrust him accept his explanation and forget this ever happened. If he has been unfaithful to you in the past then perhaps you should rethink your decision to move in with him. —Queenie

♥

Dear Queenie, I have been married for 12 years. We have had periods where our sex life has been terrible. Last year I discovered he was looking at internet porn while avoiding me sexually. I was really freaked out and we worked on our relationship. Our sex life, communication, and relationship seemed to be more real and stable then it had been in years.

He is kind, a good father, a good provider. He has been working out consistently for the last year and is also in great physical shape. We have begun doing more activities together.

Last week I was looking in the history of our internet files and noticed he has been looking at personals. I do not know if he is communicating or seeing any of them but they are all 18-22 and live within 10 miles of our house. It is not like he is looking at anonymous porn that I was so hurt by before now it looks like he is looking for a date.

When I confronted him he became very angry and denied everything. His honesty is what worries me most. He denied just recently looking at porn videos that I found on our Windows media player. I am tired of the lies. We have a long history together and a young child. Should I finally give up and try and find someone else? Or am I blowing this way out of proportion? -- Valerie

Valerie, you need to talk with a counselor and you and he need counseling together. Whether or not he is actually seeing these women he certainly is leaving enough clues so that most anyone would interpret his actions the same way that you do.

Trust is important in a marriage and he isn't doing too much to earn your trust. Don't give up without trying to see if there is something that can be done to repair your marriage. Counseling is a good start.— Queenie

♥

Dear Queenie, my husband recently got busted. I found out he was having a relationship with a neighbor. He said he did not sleep with her but I do not believe him. We separated for a month and I became ill so he moved back in. It's difficult for us to get back what we had or should I say it's hard for me.

I have to see her almost all the time and there have been a couple of arguments almost fights with her. If we're walking down the same street together she will purposely walk up close to me as if to start a fight.

I just don't know what to do. I feel like I'm in a bad dream; I'm trying to pretend this never happenened but it's killing me inside slowly. I really think they slept together. — Rae

Rae, if you don't trust your husband there's not a lot of hope for your marriage succeeding at this point. Some marriages can be repaired if both people really truly love each other. How much do you love him? How much does he love you? You can't pretend nothing happened because it will destroy you. Counseling is a good start, either with him or without him. — Queenie

♥

Dear Queenie, after 14 years, my husband walked out on me and the kids for another woman. They both were using drugs and when he decided to get clean they parted ways. My husband would blame me for him using drugs saying that I stressed him out so much. I never used drugs in my life. He said the reason why he cheated is because I don't love him enough.

I don't know why but I took him back thinking that he had changed for the better since he was clean and going to church. The kids would tell me he's only back because he had no other place to go.

He is retired now so all he does is stay at home and watch tv or go to church; he does nothing to help me at home or financially or emotionally. I came home from work one day and heard him talking on the phone to his friend about how no good I was and how sweet the woman he was cheating on me with was. I told him to leave but he refused.

I don't know how much more I can take of this man. I thought it would be good for the kids to have him back since my daughters were so close to him, but even they want him to leave because they say that he's changed and he's mean now. I don't know what to do, he walks around the house as if he doesn't have a care in the world. Please give me some advice on what to do. — Yvonne

Yvonne, you know what you should do. Your kids don't want him there, he wouldn't be there if he had someplace else to go, and he's doing nothing to pay his way. If he is treating your daughters badly, that should be even more incentive to get him out of the house. Go see a lawyer and find out what your options are. Then make some decisions. — Queenie

♥

Dear Queenie, I caught my husband running his hand up another woman's leg, all the way up. I confronted him and he told me nothing like this has ever happened and he was drunk. Also he told me he never slept with her but I don't believe him.

Would you consider this cheating and what should I do? I feel sick and I can't look at him without shaking from anger. — Carrie

Carrie, it's amazing how many things people do when they're "drunk" as though that's the perfect alibi for being totally stupid. If he was drunk, how can he be sure nothing else happened? I, personally, wouldn't consider the hand up her leg to be cheating but maybe there are more details you know that you're not sharing. Be sure you're ready to handle the truth if you go searching for it. — Queenie

♥

Dear Queenie, I just found out that my husband cheated! We have been together for nine years and married for three and a half of them. We have a young daughter. Last night I found out he had a two month affair with a co-worker. My first instinct was to throttle both him and her. After the truth came out I told him what I wanted. Please tell me if I am nuts.

We separated last year. He started smoking pot and hanging around his buddies who have no responsibilities, no kids, no wives or girl friends. He also is battling depression. We went to marriage counseling and he to drug counseling. It took us a while to get back anything near what we had. It still wasn't the same. I was having a very hard time being sexual with him and it's been that way since our daughter was born.

Though things were going smoothly for a while I knew something wasn't right. Until this last month we were so happy. Everything was great. Sex was right on, there was no bickering about the little things.

So here it is, I told him that I want to stay together for right now, the last time we separated it was hell on myself and my daughter. I told him that there are no promises and that I want him to go back to counseling by himself and marriage counseling with me. Of course he agreed to it. I think he would have agreed to just about anything at that time. He says that he loves me and that I am the one for him. Also about how sorry he is.

Do I sound crazy? This hurts so much! I told him that I can't guarantee anything to him right now, that I need time and I want to see him making a big effort. He doesn't want a divorce. He said at one point in the affair he was planning on leaving me. Though he says that it wasn't for her. Do I believe him or am I just as much of a fool as he is? — Lola

Lola, of course it hurts! And I think you're being quite reasonable considering the circumstances. Counseling for him and for the two of you is an excellent idea. There's no way that it'll be easy to get past this betrayal but if there is true love within this relationship you'll put it in the past and leave it there. Don't expect that you'll be able to do this instantly or without a lot of tears and anger.

It sounds as though you could also benefit from individual counseling for yourself as well as the marriage counseling with him.—Queenie

♥

Dear Queenie, my husband recently went to a bar, took off his wedding ring, flirted with a girl then took her phone number when she gave it to him. He says he was drunk and only flirting. He took her number because he didn't want to be rude. What do I do? — Tina

Tina, being drunk is no excuse. And he obviously has no problem with being rude to you even if he doesn't want to be rude to someone he flirted with in a bar. He has his priorities all wrong. You have a marital problem. Counseling for the both of you might be an option to prevent this marriage from becoming broken beyond repair. What do you think?—Queenie

♥

Dear Queenie, can you please help me with this problem? I have been married for almost 28 years. It has been a comfortable marriage but for about the last dozen years I have felt pretty unhappy, mostly stemming from non-communication between us. Somewhat because of this I have sought other sexual companions, always being careful and most recently I found my ex-fiance, who is recently divorced, over the Internet and we have been corresponding.

After years of keeping it from her, I told my wife of my indiscretions and my ex who she knew of from my past. She overlooked the sexual encounters I've had but could only forgive me for this other woman if I promised not to communicate with her any longer. Also, my wife and I have begun counseling to fix our communication problems.

My problem is I agreed to this but have not kept my promise and have talked with my ex many other times. I want to give myself every opportunity to make my marriage work but I cannot stop thinking about my ex. I feel that I am still in love with her.

Can you see my confusion? I want to give myself all I can to keep this marriage going but I can't help wondering will I be happy single with the good possibility of getting back with my ex-girlfriend/fiance.

I cannot say anything to my wife about this because that would kill any chance we may have. My ex is even supporting me with my try to save my marriage but has also said that whatever I do I will never be alone, she will always be there for me. Will you kind of give me some advice on where I should go from here? — John

John, lucky for you, your wife has an extremely high capacity for forgiveness. Unlucky for you, you don't have a high capacity for faithfulness. You are an adulterer and have been for approximately half of your marriage. A lot of men would have been out on the street for what you've been doing, but you're luckier than most because your wife wants to give you another chance. Unfortunately, you're not strong enough to resist the temptation of an ex-girlfriend who has now reappeared and is ready to resume a relationship with you even if it means ending your marriage.

No one else can make the decision for you. You have to weigh the pros and cons of each of these women and decide whether you stay or whether you go. Your ex has already told you her door is wide open should you decide to leave your wife. Your wife has already shown she's willing to forgive if you have enough strength to leave the other women alone.

Tough choice. Screw up with your wife and you're out the door to your girlfriend. If that happens, you better hope the differences that split you up before can be worked through this time or you'll have plenty of time to regret leaving your marriage for nothing. —Queenie

♥

Dear Queenie, my husband told me he has a problem with looking at women. I really do not understand what that means. I never knew that I had to worry. What does that mean? He cheated on me probably twice, but he is a very good liar.

We now have a house that we just bought and our son is almost two. Everything is fine but I always remember what he said, "I have a problem looking at women." Please help me understand what that means!!
— Peggy

Peggy, I don't know what that means. Looking isn't a problem, touching is. If all he's doing is looking, don't make his comments into something worse than they are, and concentrate on the "everything is fine" aspect of your marriage and family.

If you treat him as if he were a cheater when he isn't, he loses nothing by turning into one. Treat him as if he is the best husband and father in the world and hopefully he'll be able to live up to your expectations. If he doesn't, you can make other decisions at that point. —Queenie

♥

131

Dear Queenie, I am a young single mother. I recently broke up with my boyfriend because I found out he never broke up with his previous girlfriend. He even made up stories about her, saying she cheated on him. I don't see how he could do this to anyone, especially when he says he attends church regularly. Is it even possible that he loved me?

He still calls me looking for a chance to be with me, however, I cannot stop thinking about what he did. I know I shouldn't carry these feelings in my heart, but its hard to forget him when he keeps calling. How can I tell him to leave me alone politely, and make it work?

Before I discovered the deception, I actually thought one day we might get married. We had a lot of the same interests, he had a good sense of humor, and was a hard worker. We always had fun whenever we went out. I was so stupid. I feel like I might never click with someone on those levels the way we did. How can I get over this feeling? — Brenda

Brenda, "young" is the key word here. You are young, you will experience many things in the years to come. One thing you've already experienced is a boyfriend who cheats and lies. One thing you don't want to experience, if you can avoid it, is a husband who does the same.

The world is full of good men. You don't have to settle for this man who may go to church but who doesn't understand the lessons he supposedly learns there. You don't have to be polite when you tell him to leave you alone; tell him in a way he will understand you're serious about not wanting further contact. —Queenie

♥

Dear Queenie, I am a 46 year old married man. I love my wife. Since we were married 28 years ago we have never really had a romantic relationship. I think she loves me as much as I do her. I have never been unfaithful to her and as far as I know she has always been faithful to me.

When we have sex (which is not too often) we never have any foreplay and never did since we have been together. I am on the brink of infidelity but I still love her. I have talked to her about it but she doesn't want to talk about it.

What should I do? I love her and hate to cheat on her. I need the sex and intimacy. I have been asked by another lady to sleep with her and haven't yet but am almost ready to. My conscience is bothering me bad. Sometimes I wonder if I am being punished for something I haven't done yet. — Ben

Ben, when people want to cheat they'll come up with the dumbest reasons to justify what they do. I have to admit, 28 years of bad sex would drive most anyone to look for sex elsewhere. It's amazing you held in for so long! However, you might want to consider some couples counseling before you break your marriage vows. Once you get your sex outside your marriage, your wife will have ample reason to get everything else in a divorce settlement. – Queenie

♥

Dear Queenie, I have been dating my boyfriend for four years. I am very much in love with him. He had a very unfaithful ex-wife, and it hurt him deeply. For the past two years, he has also been having a long distance relationship with an old girlfriend. He says they are just friends, no sex.

He sees her in hotels three to four times a year for a long weekend plus spends a two week vacation with her. This breaks my heart so bad but I always take him back. He just returned from his last vacation with her but this time he actually brought her where I live and took her to two parties (he wasn't invited to) in front of all my best friends. This hurt was the deepest of all but to make the pain go away, I took him back again.

If it were you, would you call the other woman and tell her the truth about him? Do you think as long as I keep taking him back he will ever change? Should I break up with him and start dating other people? Please remember I love him deeply. I don't know if it's better to live with the hurt with him, or without him. -- Carole

Carole, do you think his being hurt by an unfaithful ex-wife gives him the right to act the same with you? Apparently he does, because he's doing the best he can to show you how little he really cares for you.

This isn't the way you treat someone you love. You already hurt, so you won't hurt much more if you dump him and kicking him to the curb might just give you back your self respect. —Queenie

♥

Dear Queenie, how does a wife deal with the fact that her husband has been involved in a nonsexual, emotional affair? We've been married for 12 years and out of the blue he was ready to end our marriage because he was in love with another woman. Now he has ended the affair after finding out she wasn't who she pretended to be. He wants to pretend it never happened and go on with our lives. I don't know how to do that. Help!! -- Julie

Julie, you can either make him pay for this betrayal and maybe eventually you will feel better and it certainly might teach him a lesson, or you can do everything in your power to forgive him and work toward strengthening your marriage so that he has no need to get emotionally involved with someone other than you.

Paybacks destroy everyone involved. You might feel that he deserves to learn a lesson but what has been done cannot be undone no matter how much he may "pay." Many couples have recovered from infidelity and turned unhappy marriages into strong, happy relationships. Now is the time for you to talk it out and get closer emotionally. Betrayal is extremely painful but so is divorce.

If you can't handle the pain without help then consider counseling. I believe in second chances. No one is perfect. Third chances? Probably not. -- Queenie

♥

Dear Queenie, I am a 35-year old female with a 43-year old husband who recently told me he was having an affair with a young co-worker. He assures me that the relationship is over and that he is willing to work on our relationship.

We have been in couples therapy for a month. The therapy has focused on all my mistakes and has not addressed the issue of a possible midlife crisis even though my husband fits the description. I love my husband dearly and I will accept any suggestions! -- Tammy

Tammy, why is it important that his situation have a name affixed to it? The two of you have a marriage that is in trouble. It's not just his fault, nor is it just your fault.

You are in couples therapy. That is a very good sign that the both of you care enough for each other to try to make this marriage work. Hang in there. -- Queenie

♥

Dear Queenie, for three years I have worked together with a girl that I felt from day one was my "other half." The problem is that I am married, happily.

We worked together for all that time and nothing inappropiate ever happened. The chemistry however was always there, we just never crossed the line. Then I was transferred to another job. We admitted our love to each other and kissed two or three times, knowing that "us" just was impossible. We parted, both crying. She is 27, very religious and a virgin, I am 35 married with children.

Afterwards we started e-mailing and calling every now and then. We met secretly one night 3 months after I left. We slept in the same bed, but did not make love, just hugged and kissed silently for the most part, both feeling utterly in love and utterly guilty. Afterwards we continued talking by phone.

She changed jobs, and I suspect she just could not stand to go to the same office were we had been working together. She is being counseled by her "father" who obviously told her not to talk to me anymore.

Last month we spoke and for the first time confessed our love for each other, saying we should disappear from each other's lives. Then I sent her a card, saying I miss you. I called her a week later, and she broke down in tears and said please do not call me ever again.

We love each other, unfortunately we crossed the line and now maybe cannot even be friends anymore. Should I really never call her again? What will happen next? I know I have to dedicate all my effort and love toward my family, but I feel heartbroken, I'm very sad, I cannot concentrate, I worry about her. Can we ever be just friends? -- David

David, leave her alone. Let her get on with her life. Try to get your marriage back on track. There is nothing but trouble for the both of you if you continue this relationship. No, you can't be any type of friends. -- Queenie

♥

Dear Queenie, I found an email that my husband sent to a female friend. Gave her the times that I work. Told her to e-mail him then because I would not understand. I have never any doubts about his faithfulness. Should I be concerned about this letter that he thought he had deleted and how do I bring up my concerns to him? -- Nel

Nel, I have a suspicious mind so I would probably be concerned about such an email sent to a female friend. A question to him might be appropriate, something such as "I found this and wondered what you meant." It could be innocent. Follow your instincts depending upon his reply. -- Queenie

♥

Dear Queenie, I have been married for 16 years and caught my husband looking at another woman. Not just once or twice, but alot. It really bothered me so I have been talking to him about it. He thinks it is normal for a man to look at other women and think about them sexually and think about touching them and what they would look like with their clothes off.

He says that he has never had an affair. But to me lusting after women is coming very close. To me it feels like he has had an affair and I

135

don't want to have sex with him because I will be thinking about him visualizing all these other women. I think he is a pig. Am I out of line? Is this normal? I don't know who to talk to about this. I am miserable. -- Ella

Ella, most men (and women) like to look at other people. When that "looking" turns to an affair, then there's a problem. I, personally, think your husband is normal although telling you details of what he fantasizes about is out of line and hurtful. Perhaps he needs a little spicier sex life and *you* can change that. A counselor might be a good choice if you're having a serious problem with this. -- Queenie

♥

Dear Queenie, my husband of 13 years moved out to live with his girlfriend. He says he doesn't love me anymore and that he wants out. But yet he comes over every day to check on things and he worries about my car.

My question is do you have any suggestions on getting him back or showing him how much I love him. Right now whatever I do is wrong and whatever she does is right. I don't know if I am fooling myself or not but I think there is a chance for us. -- Sylvia

Sylvia, when the new wears off that relationship he might return to you. That could happen next week, next month, next year, or ten years from now. How long are you willing to wait? Or would you rather get on with your life, and if he comes back, maybe you'll want him and maybe you'll have found someone else you love even more.

If it were me, I'd tell him things are fine at home and he doesn't need to keep checking up on me. Then I'd get some legal advice and start working on protecting myself. -- Queenie

♥

Dear Queenie, I've been with this man for almost 3 years and we have a child together. When I first met him, he was staying with another woman whom he didn't really care about, because if he did he wouldn't have let me come to her house and pick him up, she knew all about me.

After I had my baby a year in the relationship, she stopped seeing him so that drew him closer to me. But now he doesn't spend a lot of time with me like he used to. Women call his cell phone all day and he stays out of town a lot. I ask him if there someone he is seeing and he tells me that he doesn't have time to mess with women but when he comes back, his cell phone keeps ringing. I ask him if he's having a sexual relationship with any of the women calling him and he says no, can't he have a social life?

He says I'm always accusing him of cheating on me but I can't see any other reason, because he leaves every morning and comes back at three the next morning after being out all night. I ask myself do I think he is cheating on me or is he just taking care of business like he always says.

Should I stop assuming because I really don't have proof besides women calling the cell phone or should I accept that he is cheating and I should just move on with my life? — Simone

Simone, from what you say it doesn't appear he knows how to be committed to one woman. He seems to be doing to you what he did to his girlfriend when he met you. It sounds to me that you're wasting your time. — Queenie

♥

Dear Queenie, I recently discovered that my husband has been unfaithful. This was a woman he met on a chat bulletin board, and chatted to for about 5 months before deciding to meet "for coffee." She is also married. After meeting several times, he told her "I love you" because she's so understanding, patient, kind, etc.

According to my husband, the most they did was some heavy kissing. I do believe this to be true. Then, one day she quit answering his e-mail and he was brokenhearted. I found out about this by discovering logs of some of their conversations. I was devastated, and to make a long story short, we are trying to improve the intimacy in our relationship.

We were in a sort of boring relationship and I know that I wasn't meeting his emotional needs, because he was so needy for intimacy on the internet that it led to this "affair."

My question is this: how can I get over the fact that he didn't end this affair, she did, and the fact that my husband is in love with another woman? I can't believe it was love. I think it was "great literature." I am bothered that he thinks it was love. How can I deal with this? -- Darla

Darla, how would you want him to deal with it if you had been the one who made this mistake? Would you want him to constantly remind you of this? Would you want him to never trust you again? Would you want him to leave you? Would you want him to forgive and try to forget?

From a male friend comes this response: "She needs to come to terms with reality; i.e., what's more important to her, an on-going marriage or to be lost in single space. My own experience suggests that first and foremost try and make the marriage work. That's quite likely what her husband's cyber partner is doing.

She's on the right track to begin with by working on their communication, though she refers to it as intimacy. Encourage them to ceremonially 'burn' the file of love notes with the thought of putting that into the past and out of sight. Finally, plan a big adventure together for some months in the future and concentrate on the planning. Foremost, talk to each other."

I think what he says is valid. For men, sex with another woman is cheating. If they didn't have sex there isn't a betrayal. Women, on the other hand, are hurt to their core when their husbands commit the much more intimate act of sharing thoughts, dreams, and desires, with another woman. Most women would prefer their husband be sexually intimate in a brief affair rather than emotionally intimate in a long-term, non-physical tryst.

He hurt you. You can let this destroy your marriage and it easily could. Or you can move on, the both of you growing and expanding your lives through good communication and sharing of common interests. Everyone makes mistakes. If this is his mistake first of this kind, work on your part of the marriage so that he doesn't feel the need to get emotional support from someone else.

You are lucky that this woman is so distant. If she were a colleague and they were in daily close contact, you would have more to concern yourself about, particularly if he still has thoughts of love. -- Queenie

♥

Dear Queenie, my husband and I have been married for 8 years. Last Sunday after almost a year of suspecting, I found out about an affair he had been having. He says he is sorry and after cutting out the sexual part of their relationship, they continued to talk on the phone and see each other for lunch. After I found out, he called her and told her not to call him anymore. It took a couple of days, but she finally stopped.

We have an appointment for counseling and we still love each other. I am really worried because I ask him if he ever told her he loved her and he said no but he cared for her and still does.

My heart is broken and I am truly devastated by this. We have two healthy, beautiful young children and they really love their dad as much as he loves them. What are the odds for us? Please help! -- Sheila

Sheila, he has betrayed your trust, hurting you as deeply as a man can hurt a woman. It is now up to you to make every effort to forgive and forget so that this does not poison your love for him and destroy your marriage. Counseling is an excellent start.

What brought your husband and this woman together in the first place? Do they work together or have some type of common bond? Since he still has feelings for her, the more he can avoid contact the better the chance of those feelings subsiding.

Your husband made a very bad mistake. It has been done, and it cannot be undone no matter how much you or he might wish it to have never happened. Don't let the past destroy your chances for a happy future together. Learn from this mistake, let it help your marriage grow stronger. -- Queenie

♥

Dear Queenie, why do I have such a broken heart longing for someone that is not my wife? I know it is wrong. I feel such rejection. I have begged her to be my friend, but it is such a chore, then when I hope to see her and it does not work out I feel so rejected because I feel like I have to beg her to be my friend. Should I get away from her and take the year or two to heal? -- Don

Don, she obviously knows the difference between right and wrong. You apparently do not. While you still have a wife, you might redirect your "broken heart" in her direction and hope that she loves you enough to forgive you. -- Queenie

♥

Dear Queenie, I have been married for 15 years to the same man. We have 2 teenaged children. The problem is that my husband is military. At every location we have been stationed there has been some problem with other women. Once I walked in on a friend kissing my husband in a more than friendly way. One night my husband followed around a female leaving me on my own while she offered sexual favors. Most recently, he was sent overseas and was there for 5 monthes before we arrived.

During that time, I was very concerned because he was so uncertain about moving the family to another country. The day after I arrived, I met a female that he claimed he only played raquetball with, but she made it very clear that they had done many things together. Sometimes as a couple and sometimes in a group. Supposedly, they were just friends.

I began hearing rumors that he had an affair with another woman. My husband claims that he did not have an affair with her. I know that after this many years of marriage, I should probably give him the benefit of the doubt. The problem with that is he lies. He will lie to me without batting an eye. When I catch him in a lie, he says "I'm sorry, I won't lie again" or "I'm sorry, the truth wasn't worth fighting over".

My husband claims that this is my problem. I have admitted to him that I have some insecurities. I am at a loss. What do I do? Where do I go from here. I believe that I still love my husband, but I am afraid of being hurt again. Is there any advice that you can offer? Is there any way to get my husband to not flirt with other women. He thinks that I overreact when I get upset, because other women are touching him in an intimate way. Please help. -- Maxine

Maxine, you cannot change your husband. He's a cheat and a liar and he doesn't care how much his actions hurt you.

He is correct that this is your problem. He isn't unhappy with the situation, you are, therefore, it is up to you to either accept him and his lifestyle or get out of the marriage.

You will continue to be hurt as long as the situation remains as it is. You must decide if life with him is better than life without him. This has nothing to do with economics because you will do fine on your own. This has to do with how he makes you feel.

Life is too short to spend it like this. Make a decision. -- Queenie

♥

Dear Queenie, my girl and me have been together for almost three years. We've been living together in a beautiful home for about five months now. In addition, we have a beautiful son together. We recently were engaged and have been planning a wedding. However, lately, I've been having second doubts about getting married.

I mean, I love and care for her with all my heart. I do. But I just don't know if I'm ready for all this yet. I'm only 24years old and she's only 22. That's young and I'm still feeling that little itch in me to be a "playboy." But although we're both very young there's a lot of love and trust in this relationship; especially on her part. I know she loves, cares, and trusts me more than anyone. And see that's where the real problem kicks in because just recently I betrayed her trust in me.

A couple of weeks ago, I went away on a business trip and she stayed home and took care of our son. After my meetings were over my friends convinced me to go clubbing with them and we drank, danced, and talked, mostly to women. I left the club earlier than my friends, went back to my hotel room, called my girl and then went to sleep. Early in the morning my friends came back to the hotel, along with a couple of the women from the club. I didn't plan on anything happening, but it did.

The next morning, the girl said that I should tell my girl what had happened that night, even if it means breaking up a "happy home." She

gave me a hug and a kiss on the cheek and that was it. What happened "that night" was an honest to God mistake but I know if tell her what happened "that night," I'll end up losing her and our family. I lose all her love and trust in me and I don't want that. If this does happen, then how do I regain her trust in me? How do I make this relationship continue?

It's hard to tell a woman something like this when she's constantly telling you how much she loves and cares for you, and that you are her everything. I watch her ecstatically plan the wedding and tell all her girlfriends how good of a man and father I am to her and the kids. How she can't wait to get married and the infinite reasons on why she loves me so much. I just really don't know what to do at this point. I don't. -- Steve

Steve, in some other time and some other life I would perhaps say how stupid you were, but you've done that and you'll continue to beat up on yourself so I won't get in the middle.

You didn't have an affair, you didn't "cheat" in the traditional sense, you were compromised by a woman who then expected you to further compound the damage by going home and telling the woman you love how some predatory female, with a few good moves, erased years of trust and faithfulness. Just as some men get their kicks from turning a "no" to a "yes," so do some women. You were had.

Should you tell her? I don't think so. As a matter of fact, if one of your friends says something about it, deny that anything happened! (You were wearing protection, right?)

Yes, you are young and yes, those needs to be a "playboy" are very real and can damage your relationship in the future. But it's time to take a look at the complete picture. You have a woman you love, and a son. Maybe it's time to decide what's more important for the long term. It's your decision, not hers and certainly not mine. -- Queenie

♥

Dear Queenie, I was with a guy for a few months in an off and on kind of way but there was really no commitment and I became pregnant and I decided to keep it thinking that we will end up together some how because I love him a lot but I don't think he feels the same way about me.

During my pregnacy he started going with his ex-girlfriend again and this really hurt me and made me jealous but the one thing I don't understand is he still calls me at night to have sex and I do being stupid because I just want to be with him. I've already tried to talk to him about it and it didn't work so what should I do? -- Crystal

141

Crystal, do you understand that sex isn't the same as love? Do you understand that a guy will be glad to call if he can get sex without commitment? I don't know if you're mature enough to stop having sex with him. I hope you are using protection so that you don't have another child by him. As far as love? I don't see it.

What should you do? If it were me, I'd drop him fast and forever and try to make the best life possible for my child. What will you do? I suppose that depends on how desperate you are to make this loser fall in love with you. -- Queenie

♥

Tit for Tat

Tit for Tat

"My husband cheated on me and now I find a friend on the internet that makes me feel really good about myself. He can make me laugh and smile but it's hard for me to do these things around my husband."

He cheats on her, she's devastated, then she cheats on him. How does his betrayal lessen hers? If he's a cheat, what is she? What justifies her actions when she can't forgive his?

There are people whose moral code would never be compromised regardless of what type of pain their spouse put them through. There are others who feel that they are justified in giving "tit for tat" once they have been betrayed.

I don't see a difference between the spouse who cheats first and the spouse who cheats in retaliation. They're both guilty of adultery.

♥

Dear Queenie, about a year and a half ago I found out my husband had been lying to me our whole marriage. I was devastated. I tried to work through it, I was working hard on my relationship with God and he was doing wonders in me. I am still married but not wanting to be.

Then, a guy I'd known for several years, married with kids, he and I fell head over heels for each other. We met on a business trip, I adored him, he adored me but he knew he would have to do something at home. He has suspected his wife of cheating on him but because he could not leave his kids, he decided to stay and work on his marriage.

I don't think it's appropriate for us to be friends, but it seems important to him to be friends. He was calling me several times a day but now it's once a week or so. When I try to break it off with him he tells me how important I am and how hot I was.

The last time we talked on the phone I asked if there was any hope and he told me to move on. When I questioned him he got really mad and said he was busy so I told him to forget it and hung up on him. I feel bad for hanging up, I feel bad for not being more understanding of his situation. But then I am angry because I feel used and led on by all the time we spent which has ended in nothing. I so want him in my life, but its hard as friends. Should I apologize, should I be friends even though it hurts?

I need someone who is close to God to help me understand the "right" thing to do. I know what we did was wrong, but I feel like my life is at a loss without him. Will he ever come back? Does he love me deep down? Does he miss me? Should I apologize or just leave it be? — Brittany

Brittany, do you remember how much your husband hurt you? Why do you feel that it's your right to be the Other Woman in this man's life? He's a player. You're being played. You're also a married woman. The "right" thing to do is to stop being a fool.—Queenie

♥

Dear Queenie, I have had two affairs, one due to unfinished feelings and the other due to a five year persiod with no emotional input from husband in my marriage. In my behalf, I want to say that during the last three years I tried diligently to divorce my husband befor giving up and going elsewhere for what I needed, love.

After the last affair, my husband said he would change and even started on a scrip to aid in his emotional instabilities. He did change and became the man of my dreams. I was the happiest I could ever believe possible. That is, until my husband said that he wanted to leave and that he was having an affair. His affair nearly mirrored what he knew of mine and for a long time I didn't believe him, now I have heard the other woman's voice and know her name and have even read email messages from her. I believe.

The advice I need now is, he said it was over and that he wanted to stay with me, but then went back to her for about a week, then told me it was over again. I don't know if I can believe him because I keep finding things about her all over the house, her email address and her name and address. If it were really over why is this information still around. I know that I should forgive, I did it first after all, I just don't know how to forget. Can you help? — Kelly

Kelly, forgiving and forgetting are easy to say but the actual doing is extremely difficult. The two of you have hurt each other horribly and unless both of you have strong desires to work on your marriage and make it work, you're not going to succeed. I can't help you forget. But try thinking about this: you cheated more than once during your marriage and your husband forgave and did his best to forget.

The memory of what you did may have been too painful for him to move past and he did to you what you did to him perhaps partly in retaliation, and partly because he didn't want his heart broken again by his love for you.

This isn't just about you trying to forget, it's about the two of you forgiving each other and working toward a marriage that is between the two of you — without outsiders in your beds. Counseling might be a good first step.—Queenie

♥

Dear Queenie, me and my husband hasn't gotten along in eight years. We have four wonderful children. He has cheated at least two or three times a year for the last eight years. I have filed for a divorce so I can move on. We have been separated for a month.

Within the last two months our friend who is a guy has been there for me when my husband was doing me wrong. Then we let him come live with us for a while. Me and this friend have been very close. He tells me all of his problems and I do the same. He can also feel when I am hurt or depressed. We've got a lot of things in common and he makes me feel like a woman should even though my husband treats me bad. We both feel that we love each other. What should I do? — Kimberly

Kimberly, you are a married woman. Until you are legally divorced you are a married woman. You are not ready to get involved with this man no matter how comfortable he makes you feel or how supportive he is. When you are legally divorced then you can do whatever you feel is right. For now, you are a married woman who is the mother of four wonderful children. What kind of example do you want to set for them? (Did I mention that you're a married woman?)— Queenie

♥

Dear Queenie, I have been married for 6 years to a delightful, spunky, pretty, capable woman who is about ready to deliver our first child.

Great, eh? Well, she had an affair two years ago with my boss at work; simultaneously, I was having the occasional rendezvous with strangers. I have met and "played with" about 40 people, and finally met one person whom I fell in love with and have been seeing at several times a week for nearly a year. We both agree that we make each other feel ways we've never felt before, we have a lot in common, and we are fairly well addicted to each other.

I love both women and I want to be a good father. Aside from whether I "should" or not, can you see any way I can continue this trio without causing major pain and grief to either woman? My wife knows about my lover, but thinks it is over--it was for a while. -- Tim

Tim, no matter what you do, you're going to hurt someone. The question is, whom do you wish to hurt less? Or, whom do you wish to hurt more?

As I see it, you and your wife both screwed up big time. She's over her extraneous lover and trusting you enough to do the mommy thing. You, on the other hand, have "done the deed" with enough people to qualify for lifetime AIDS testing and have come out of it with a lover who is willing to keep this affair going. Who is getting set up for big time hurt right now?

Frankly, you're going to have to make the call on this (you knew that anyway, of course) but my feelings are certainly toward preparing to be a father, keeping your wife happy, and giving her the support she needs at this time. That means dumping the girlfriend and learning how to be the best husband and father the world has ever known. How's that for a challenge?

Affairs can be thrilling because you jeopardize everything you love for that which you aren't supposed to have. Are you ready to pay the price? Illicit love has a way of finally timing out — not without great emotional pain to at least one of the players. It could be you — losing your wife, your child and your lover. You might even lose you life with your indiscriminate sexual history.

Your wife deserves a husband who is there full time in all areas. So does your child. Are you man enough for the job? -- Queenie

♥

Dear Queenie, my husband cheated on me and now I find a friend on the internet that makes me feel really good about myself. He can make me laugh and smile but it's hard for me to do these things around my husband. Which way should I turn? I'm confused, please help. — Sue

Sue, why do you think that his cheating justifies your cheating? Either you love your husband or you don't. Either you want your marriage to work or you don't. If you want it to work, stop looking for love elsewhere and get some counseling, with or without your husband. If you don't want it to work, get a divorce and then look for love anywhere you can find it. — Queenie

♥

Dear Queenie, I have been married for ten years and I have two children. My husband recently went on a trip and had sexual relations with another woman.

I was very angry and I found myself not too long afterword, having secret sexual realtions of my own with one of my husband's friends. My husband doesn't know about this and he hasn't said anything about it when I try to speak to him. What should I do? -- Norma

Norma, in my personal opinion, there is a great deal of difference between a casual sexual encounter and a deliberate affair.

Neither is right, but one is more forgiveable than the other (again, this is my personal opinion).

Too bad you felt it was necessary to punish him by cheating with his friend. This is a no-win situation and I don't have any advice for you other than trying to repair your marriage, if possible, and hoping that he will forgive you (more than you were able to forgive him) for breaking your marriage vows. -- Queenie

♥

Dear Queenie, I am middle-aged and have been married for 20 years, we have a daughter who is in college. I was in the military and away from home a lot, which may have been why my wife had an affair years ago. That ended with some bitterness remaining.

I have left the military and for the past 5 years have worked away from home all week. Some time ago, I became friendly with a married lady, who seemed unhappy in her relationship. We became friends and then lovers -- and I have never had such an honest and fulfilling relationship with a woman in my whole life -- we seem made for each other.

My wife is bored with everything, drinks and smokes too much and generally just doesn't try. I am fond of her, but feel no love.

What am I to do? My friend feels unable to commit, because I cannot make the break either. It is too easy to carry on as we do -- seeing each other during the week, and finding the odd weekend away together. I feel such love for her that I am at my wit's end. I am a "one-person" man at heart - and feel such guilt. -- Rob

Rob, now do you understand why your wife might have had her affair? How is she any different than the woman with whom you are now involved?

If you're at your wit's end, divorce your wife. If your lover feels as you do, she will divorce her husband and then the two of you can be together. Don't expect a full-time legal relationship to have the same high ecstacy as the one you currently have with her. Sneaking to cheat has a way of heightening the experience and blinding one to the realities of day-to-day relationships. -- Queenie

♥

Queenie, my wife of 20 years confessed to having affairs with two men over a 7 year period of time with multiple intimate encounters. The last affair, according to her, ended 10 years ago and she has been true to me ever since. My youngest son may be a product of the first affair which lasted 5 years. She is not 100% sure that he's mine but does feel that he is very likely mine.

When she finally confessed all this several months ago I was crushed and in the course of looking for some emotional support I met another woman whom I've fallen in love with and who also loves me. This woman is unhappily married with two young children -- our relationship has become intimate and now she would like to divorce her husband to marry me. She has had two other extramarital affairs so I am not the first time that she strayed.

I feel extremely guilty about the relationship and the possible destruction of her marriage. I am also very uncomfortable with getting involved with another woman who doesn't value fidelity.

To further complicate things, I, for some reason, still love my wife and feel that she will never cheat on me again -- although I am told once a cheater always a cheater. What advice might you have for someone in my situation? — Butch

Butch, how do you suppose "once a cheater always a cheater" applies to her but not to you? Do you believe it's always the other person that takes the blame? It has been ten years since your wife strayed, so what's your excuse? A little late revenge? You want to show her how much she hurt you by doing the same to her?

Now that you've lowered your morality to your wife's level of ten years ago, I'd say the playing field is even. So, what do you think? Can two cheaters make a marriage work? I don't see much hope in your situation unless the two of you get some counseling.

My greater concern is for your son. You're not sure if he's yours and no doubt you now treat him differently than you do your other children. Too bad, since he's the unfortunate victim of this vicious little movie and the subsequent victim of your anger toward your wife. I'm not sure that you're mature enough to repair your marriage or be a good husband to any woman. Are you? —Queenie

♥

Dear Queenie, my husband of walked out on me and my 4 children 5 months ago. I asked him to try to make it work but he said it was over and to get on with my own life. At the beginning of our separation he led me to believe that if I paid off our debts and cleared our credit that he'd return. We also were still being intimate. I really thought he would come back.

The day after our last sexual encounter he went on what was supposed to be a short trip and when he didn't call or come back I got worried. He met a woman with two kids and moved in with her! I was heartbroken and my kids were upset. I finally went to counseling and came to the realization that I had been unhappy for a long time. He likes to party and I don't feel that it is appropriate behavior for a father. He told me to get on with my life and meet someone else so I'd forget about him.

Two months ago I met that man. I had a hard time with my feelings about not officially being divorced yet, but we have everything in common. He has custody of his two children and is a great father. We love to spend hours talking and only see each other once a week, but we talk on the phone almost daily. He lives about an hour's drive from me.

The problem is that now that my husband is no longer in his relationship and got the news that I have a boyfriend, he wants me back. I don't understand how he expects me to believe him when all I have heard is that he had no feelings for me anymore. I think it has to do with the new man in my life.

Anyway, now my kids are giving me a hard time because I won't get back together with their dad. I have fallen in love with this other man and he feels the same. I don't think it's a rebound thingas he is hinting about marriage in a year or two. What should I do? -- Nanci

Nanci, your husband is a rat. Sorry, you probably still love him but I call them like I see them. The man needs to be out of your life so you can meet a decent guy -- although it sounds like you already have -- and have a real life for yourself and your kids.

The kids don't understand and it isn't appropriate to force them make a choice between you or their father. This is a situation you'll have to work out over the next few years. You cannot let them make decisions about who you spend your life with, though. It won't be too long before they're grown and with families of their own and if you've made the wrong decision based on what they want, you'll be alone or in a loveless marriage.

You sound like you have a good grip on the situation and I hope it only gets better! -- Queenie

♥

Triangles

Triangles

*"He is dating and has a girlfriend but yet he still tells me he
thinks we might have a future together. He had said he just
needed time alone but if that were true why does he now have
a girlfriend?"*

Relationship triangles will usually cause problems for at least
one of the members of the triangle: the wife who discovers her
husband's lover, the husband who discovers his wife's lover, the
other person who wants more than his or her married lover is willing
to give.

Unlike polyamory relationships in which a couple agrees to
the intimate inclusion of a third person into their otherwise
monogamous relationship, most triangles are formed when one
partner becomes intimately involved outside the relationship
unbeknownst to their spouse or partner. The triangle takes on
dynamics of its own when the betrayed partner discovers the
interloper and begins a competition in the hope his or her partner
will break off the affair.

Sharing is difficult to do when it means sharing a husband
or wife with a lover. Like a poorly written soap opera, wives and
girlfriends pull and tug in an attempt to get "their man" to choose
them and let the other go. Men aren't the only ones to be at the
center of these struggles as emotionally needy or sexually frustrated
women look for love outside the home and find it with lovers that
are sometimes male, and sometimes female.

Monogamy may be a difficult concept to grasp when
hormones rage and emotional needs are unmet. Being honest with
a partner and working toward a solution instead of going outside
the relationship sounds much too simplistic, doesn't it?

♥

*Dear Queenie, I'm a single parent with two boys and I'm in love
with my best friend who is also single. Both of us are divorced, and she has
a young daughter. She's in love with me but she can't let go of her ex, even
though she says she doesn't love him, for fear of sharing her daughter.*

*What should I do? We've tried going back to being just friends but
it never works and we end up sneaking around (no sex) to just be together.
I don't know what to do. -- Don*

Don, she is using the child as an excuse. She may be too
scared to commit again or she may not be ready to commit again,

but I suspect she is still in love with her ex. Whatever the reason, you're the third part of a triangle and you need to resolve yourself to the fact that this relationship is going to cause you pain.

When you love someone you put yourself into their care. You have faith and trust that the two of you together can solve all the problems either of you may have. You don't have to sneak around.

This relationship is flawed. You need to find yourself a lady who won't put you second to an ex. You deserve much more than you're currently receiving. Good luck. -- Queenie

♥

Dear Queenie, I am a 35 year old female who was married for 12 years and have been divorced for a year with no desire for reconciliation.

I decided that I wanted to establish myself alone before starting anything serious. I have dated a few guys, never serious on either part. That is how I wanted it.

Here is how my problem started. A casual friend was always having problems with her live-in boyfriend and talking very badly about him. He was abusive and horrible. They went out occasionally so I knew who he was but I avoided contact with him because of what she said.

My roommate and this friend's boyfriend grew up together so he began coming over to my house. After the first few times he began flirting with me. I would tell him "not interested" and go to my room and read. But, the more he came over the better I got to know him and I liked him. He was a really nice guy. He never complained or said bad things about his girlfriend. He was always concerned about his kids.

His girlfriend would call for himand ask "is the idiot there?" or "where's the scumbag?" and I began to see a different side to their situation. He continued to flirt with me and I continued to say no. I really didn't want a part of that mess.

Then it happened. He said all the right things and I answered all the right things and we both agreed that it was not to be anything but a fling. That one night has now has turned into full blown love. He fell in love with me as hard as I have him. He left her and moved in with me under the guise of staying with my roommate. We didn't plan on telling her until much later just so things wouldn't get even more complicated.

We have both found our soulmates in each other. He has turned out to be everything I have been looking for. Then she started telling him he can't see the kids as long as he is here. He has no rights to make any decisions concerning them as long as he isn't contributing to the house (he pays child support). I tried to tell him that it will all pass and when she wants a sitter she'll be calling. But he is younger than me and hasn't had the experience that I have had. He went back with her and I agreed with the move because I felt that he wasn't really "done" with her yet.

We still see each other as friends almost every day. Occasionally we have crossed that line and made love. I know that their relationship is done and that if I just wait it will take its course. In the meantime my heart is breaking. I can't believe that with all we have he would still want to be abused by this girl. At the same time I understand it.

The other part of me says end it, friendship and all. But I'm finding that I simply can't do the latter. I don't know how to act or how long to wait or even whether I should wait. I feel like I am cheating if I flirt with anyone. I can't stop thinking about him. He can't stop thinking about me.

If I thought he would be happy with her then that would be one thing. I don't want him to waste all the time I did especially since we could be so happy. Am I making any sense? Please help. -- Kiki

Kiki, first, let's just say no one is ever too old to be confused about love, but experience does help to prevent some repetition in the mistakes we make. Sometimes.

In my opinion, he is in a perfect situation with you waiting for him, providing everything he needs, when he needs it, and getting the rest of what he needs from her. Make no mistake, he needs her or he wouldn't have gone back. He went back voluntarily; the world is full of parents who live apart from their kids.

This is a love triangle. Love triangles vary from relationship to relationship. He has the two of you, you have him occasionally, and she has him as a live-in. Who has the better deal here? Draw it out and see what you think.

Triangles can't survive when one of the players drops out. If you dropped out, what would that leave him? Her. Would that be enough for him? Is it worth it to you to find out? Is it worth the rest of your life, your self-esteem, the soul mate you believe he is for you? Or, if she isn't enough and you're not playing the game, would he simply find someone else to replace you?

You put your life on hold. You did that in your marriage when you discovered you weren't happy. At some point you're going to realize that he isn't going to make a move without a strong enough motivation. When you show him you're ready to get on with your life, with him or without him, you just might give him the motivation. -- Queenie

♥

Dear Queenie, I am in a situation where I have been dating a man for approximately 5 months. He is a great guy, but there's just not a "connection" there, although I care a great deal about him and he says he cares about me.

I recently separated from my only true love, the father of my children. He did me wrong in the past and I gave 5 years of my life to him, hoping he would change. I finally decided to end the relationship because I could not get over the past and I did not feel it was fair to either one of us.

At the time he said he did not want to go to counseling. He now says he didn't know what he had until he lost it and that he will do anything to get his family back. He says he realizes how serious the problem is and that we definitely need counseling. But, my family doesn't like him, nor do most of my friends because they feel he will only hurt me again.

I believe he is being honest and that he is sincere about wanting to work things out. I think about him constantly, but I can't just run out on my current relationship. I don't like to hurt people. Should I stay in the relationship I'm currently in and hope that the connection happens someday or try to work things out with the man I truly love. -- Cora

Cora, you aren't in love with the man you're currently seeing so you aren't doing him a favor by prolonging the relationship. "Connections" are either there or they aren't. It appears there isn't one with this man.

Since you're still in love with the man you call your "only true love," and since he wants to come back for another chance, and since you have kids together, and since he is ready to try counseling, what are you waiting for?

Yes, it's going to hurt the guy you're with but he's going to be hurt sooner or later anyway. The fact is, right now, everyone involved is hurting. The quicker you make a decision and start mending your life, the quicker some of you are going to stop hurting. -- Queenie

❤

Dear Queenie, I am 31 years old and have been divorced for five years. It hasn't been an easy five years. I've dated plenty of jerks and haven't had much success in the single scene. Then I thought I had finally found "Mr. Right." I loved this guy more than I loved myself. He was 32 and divorced. He is gorgeous and made me have butterflies in my stomach. Every time I was with him I would just melt. After a few months of dating, he was already talking marriage. He said he wanted to wait at least a year so we could both be sure.

As time went on, things took a turn for the worse. I commented on his drinking habits and he told me that if I couldn't live with him the way he was then we didn't need to be together. I did everything possible to make it work. You see, this guy is very hard-hearted and although he told me that I was the best thing that had ever happened to him and that I treated him better than anyone had ever treated him, for some reason he just decided that we weren't meant to be together.

It's been seven months since I've seen him. The last time I spoke to him he told me that when it came down to a choice between his happiness and someone else's that his happiness came first. As much as I would love to know how he's doing or if he's already with someone else, I have stayed away.

In the meantime, my ex-husband has come back into the picture. Now, this is a wonderful guy who thinks I'm great. He is kind, considerate and thoughtful. He wishes that we could have worked things out when we were married. There is just one major problem for me. There's no butterflies, no fireworks. I'm still in love with my ex-boyfriend and I just can't seem to get him out of my head. I'm tired of hurting and I want to be free of this pain. Any suggestions? -- Randi

Randi, this man is an alcoholic, hard-hearted, self-centered jerk who does not care to establish a meaningful relationship with you. This man can't make it any plainer than he did when he told you that the only person's happiness he cares about is his. We should all love ourselves then we should expand that love to include others. The man is bad news and if you enjoy pain he will be able to provide you with plenty, assuming you can get him to resume the relationship with you.

There are of people who don't think they deserve to be happy. It isn't something they readily recognize, but something may have happened far in their past so that they were made to feel they aren't good enough. They believe they don't deserve happiness. Playing on that script, they seek out the people who will insure that their lives are lived in pain. It's what makes otherwise sensible women fall in love with abusive men and otherwise sensible men fall in love with abusive women. That internal script is a lie because we are all good enough and we all deserve to be happy.

Look again at the description you give of your ex-husband. What a dream! It sounds as though he has butterflies and fireworks enough for the both of you. What you describe is a man upon whom you can build a lifetime. A man who will be there when you need him, through the good and the bad. A man who won't deliberately harm you, who will provide the emotional support you will need as you progress through life's surprises. A man who would be your best friend. He may not seem to be your perfect mate, but there are plenty of women who would be happy to make him theirs. Better take a long look before you throw him away.

Butterflies fly away. Fireworks are brief flashes in the dark. Seek the man who treasures you above all others and treasure him the same. -- Queenie

♥

Dear Queenie, I was set up with a friend of a friend and fell for him instantly, It turns out he has a beautiful daughter and an ex-girlfriend living with him who was to move out at the end of the month, but things have been postponed.

I'm unsure whether it is worth pursuing this or not, as I really care for him and I know that he feels the same way but we can't spend the time we wish together and when we do we have to sneak about in order not to upset the ex-girlfriend due to the fact that she might flee with their daughter to another town and cause a large problem with custody etc.

As my best friend is the friend that has set us up, she offers little assistance because we both know that this guy is right for me. I just wish I knew how to proceed with this. I would appreciate any assistance you could offer! -- May

May, from my point of view I see a guy who is cheating on his live-in girlfriend, the mother of his child, and a guy who doesn't mind sneaking around if you don't. Don't you think this is a little degrading?

If it was my decision, I'd leave him alone until he was free and clear. Otherwise you may be "stuck in the middle" for a long, long time. -- Queenie

♥

Dear Queenie, when I was a senior in high school I dated a girl for about 8 months which were really the best of my life. I moved away and we broke up. However, we kept in touch over all the years, although I never saw her over all that time.

Two years ago, she got married to a person who cheated on her before and after they married. When I found out, I sent her a card saying that I was happy for her but not totally happy, as I always had the idea that somehow we would get back together. She wrote back echoing my feelings. But I was there and she was here, so I more or less tried to forget about her.

Recently, I moved back down to the area and I got a call from her that she was getting separated -- he cheated on her, and it is over. So I saw her for the first time a couple months ago and we had a great time, and have been writing letters, speaking on the phone and have seen each other around ten times or so. We have talked around a possible relationship, but never really talked directly about one.

I really feel like this is the right person for me, but I am scared to death to tell her as I know it is probably not the best time for her. Should I wait it out, or tell her everything? My brain tells me to let her come to me, but I am a hopeless romantic and I am finding it hard to wait. -- Allen

Allen, a woman who is separated is still married. As such, if you and she get together, she is no better than her husband when it comes to cheating. It doesn't matter who started first, if they're not legally divorced, they're still married.

I would suggest you wait until she is legally divorced and then slowly get reacquainted and see if time has brought your relationship to one that will survive better than the first time you were together. -- Queenie

❤

Dear Queenie, I'm in love with a man that doesn't want me. I haven't heard from him in nearly a year even though I have tried to contact him. If the feeling was returned I don't know what I would do because he has four kids by four women and I don't know if I could handle that.

Beyond that I am dating a former friend of his but they weren't on good terms when I met the other guy. He's decided to marry his girlfriend in a few months but he keeps stringing me along. I need help. I don't know what I'm doing anymore. -- Naomi

Goodness, girlfriend! Where's your pride? You need to learn to love yourself before you go trying to find someone to love you!

You need to dump all of these guys out of your memory and do some "I'm okay" classes. You deserve much better than you're getting from these losers. -- Queenie

❤

Dear Queenie, I am a 23-year old male from Europe and I need some advice. I am in love with a 37-year old woman from America I met on the Internet who is going through a divorce.

We have known each other for 3 months and she says that she loves me and has never felt so much for a person as she does for me. Another guy

that she was seeing who she also met on the Interent has come back after 3 months and said that he still loves her.

We haven't talked for about 3 weeks now because she said she needs some time to get her life together. She isn't talking to the other guy either. I guess my question is will we ever get together? She knows how I feel about her. It's just hard. being so far away though I told her I would move to be with her. We write to each other once a week. -- Carl

Carl, how can you be in love with someone you have never seen? You can be in love with the idea of love, and you can very much like the image of who you think the person is based on your correspondence, but to really be in love, you must have face-to-face, day-to-day contact.

There are many hazards of "falling in love" on the Internet, one of which being the person may not be who/what you think they are. In this case, this is an older married woman (going through a divorce is not the same as not being married), you "met" 3 months ago, who apparently had just "broken up with" another guy she met on the Internet who is now back in her life. There's a lot wrong with this relationship from its very start.

I suggest that you concentrate on someone closer to your own age, who isn't going through a divorce, who isn't also involved with others at the same time. This woman sounds like heartbreak. -- Queenie

♥

Dear Queenie, I have been seeing this man for 2 years and I know that he is the man I would like to have a future with. I love him very much. At this time he has family obligations (children) he must attend to and he is such a good man that I am not worried about him playing around and being deceitful. I just cannot see my life without him in it.

My four children call him daddy and he is everything I ever wanted in a man. The problem is he does not have a lot of time because of the obligations and his work.

Do you think I am holding myself up? The idea of trying to find someone else does not appeal to me. And if I do talk to someone else they are not good enough. This man was there when my child was very sick and you can not tell my son that this is not his daddy! Please help. -- Maria

Maria, if this man is married then you are holding yourself up. If he is not married and has no other female interests and cares as much for you as you do for him, then only you know if it is worth the wait until he has fewer obligations and can spend more time with you and your children.

The amount of time spent with someone is not as important as the quality of the time spent together. There is no quality time spent waiting for a married man to take care of "obligations." -- Queenie

♥

Dear Queenie, my boyfriend and I have been dating for two years. My boyfriend had a one-night stand that brought about a baby. He claims that he never knew of this pregancy until the girl told him that she now realizes this baby needs to know his father. He visited with an attorney who advised him what to expect in a situation like this.

After meeting with her, he was told that this has nothing to do with him, she just wanted a baby. Now he is seeking paternity testing, however, he has decided to be 50/50 with the situation until testing is done.

First, she allowed him to visit and the visits are always just once a week. Second, she is requesting support and he has agreed to give support for now. Since he has shown interest in this baby, she has begun demanding that he (as a possible father) spend several days a week with him. They are constantly arguing about visitation rights (which she would like for him to commit to days and times).

At the beginning she knew nothing of his relationship with me. Once she agreed to let the baby visit at his place he felt that he should tell her of our relationship, so that she would not feel that he is doing something behind her back. I think because of the mention of a relationship, she has made arrangements for the visiting at his place, but always seems to cancel (sometime not even giving reasons).

Because I am concerned with him visting at her place, he has agreed to visit once a week, until this matter is proven whether or not he is the father. A date has been set for this paternity testing.

Questions: 1. What can I do that might help me forgive, but not forget? 2. Should I take some time out from him to grieve and to see if I want this relationship? 3. How can we handle this mother (who I think cares for my boyfriend) and baby if it turns out that he is the father? -- Angelica

Angelica, you can't turn back the clock. You can't forget what happened because there is a child that prove to be his. The child will be a constant reminder to you of his mistake. The child will also bind him to her because of visitation, support and any other "fatherly" things that he might choose to do with or for the child.

Your anger about the situation will not get less unless you are able to resolve yourself to the fact that this baby exists, that your boyfriend will do his paternal duty, and that the child's mother is also now a part of your life. Unfortunately, this is a lifetime commitment.

Only you can decide if you want to spend your life with a man who made a mistake with the wrong woman and ended up being a father. I say the "wrong woman" because if he'd cheated with someone who didn't want to have a baby, you would never have known. Or, if he had used protection, the baby wouldn't have been conceived.

You probably do need time away from him to think about your options and decide if your life is better without him or if it is better with him even with the complications this child and his mother will bring.

If you love this man, don't let your anger destroy that love. If you can't get past the anger then you're better off without him. As far as her having an interest in him, that won't get far if he isn't interested in her.

If he was a divorced man with a child, would you still love him? Would you be able to accept an ex-wife and a child? -- Queenie

♥

Dear Queenie, I have an ex-boyfriend that can't seem to get himself out of my life. I keep telling him that I'm not in love with him and he doesn't want to believe me. I don't want to kick him completely out of my life because he has a bond with my 5-year old son. I have found someone else I care for dearly. What should I do? -- Nell

Nell, if he is not the boy's father, perhaps you need to make that bond disappear. What will happen when you do meet someone who becomes the permanent man in your life and this ex-boyfriend is still around because your son and he are bonded?

What if this ex decides to use your son as the wedge to get between you and anyone you date? Is there a family member who could be the male influence in your son's life at this time?

Your "no" may be sounding like "maybe" to your ex-boyfriend since you're not kicking him completely out of your life. As long as he's around that new man you care for may feel that he's wasting his time with you. -- Queenie

♥

Dear Queenie, I just found out that my boyfriend of three years has been having an "affair" with another woman. He says that he feels that it's okay and he has done nothing wrong except get caught.

He tells me that there is nothing wrong with keeping his "options" open because he is just now sowing his wild oats and was unable to before now since he got married at a young age. He is 43 and I am 34.

I am hurting! But I am inclined to believe that he's sincere about wanting to keep both relationships going to see which one of us is more important to him. I am confused and depressed that I could even entertain the thought of just waiting,and even more concerned that I don't want to lose this guy.

Am I being stupid? I think so but I don't want to believe it. And I don't feel strong enough to just walk away from it all. What should I do? Is this really the way men feel and the way relationships are made? -- Loretta

Loretta, he's right, there is nothing wrong with this arrangement. Nothing wrong, that is, as long as all of the persons involved are aware of the rules of the game. Apparently he changed the rules somewhere along the way and didn't tell you and I wonder if he has told her. In my opinion, in order to get yourself back to feeling as good as you can about this situation, you should amend the rules so they are workable for you.

Establish some firm ground rules if you want to continue in a relationship with him. Specifically, if you're living together one of you should find another residence. Physical intimacy should be well protected (safe sex) or stopped entirely. As long as he dates, you also should date. In other words, if he has options then you also must have equal options.

What happens if he chooses her instead of you? Since he's so unsure, and needs to sow the oats he feels he missed out on when he was younger, both of you might lose out to a third or fourth "option."

He has told you he doesn't treasure you above all others. Don't limit yourself to a man who might eventually decide he loves you. Get control of your life again. Date. Be busy when he calls. Let him know that you care deeply for him but that you are keeping your options open in case someone better comes along. -- Queenie

❤

Dear Queenie, I'm a 30 year old divorced man. She was new in the office. The first week, we didn't get to talk, but I felt I was being observed. When we first did talk it was because she had a computer problem and

asked my help. I invited her to lunch and she said no, I kept asking and when she finally accepted it caught me by surprise.

At lunch we talked a little about ourselves and I asked whether she had a boyfriend and she said yes but he was out of state and she implied that she wasn't very happy with the distance. On the way back, she lets me know she's living with her parents, but she feels that's uncomfortable since she was living by herself all those years while she's studying. Then she asked about my house. I told her I own a house, and I live on my own.

Next day at work, I ask her out to lunch, she refuses. As I know some important people in the company know her family, I assure her nobody will get a clue from me and ask if I can call her at home. She refuses to give me her parents' number, because of her boyfriend, and so on.

Since then she won't talk to me except when she needs some help on equipment or other business stuff. I catch her watching me and she's always wearing short skirts and high heels. It seems as though she is always looking for me when she comes into the room but she won't smile or acknowledge me.

I talked to a coworker best friend about this and he thinks maybe I pushed too hard and that I should just wait for her to notice that I'm a good guy. I don't really care for this approach because I think it's a little too shy.

When I discussed this with a cousin of mine he said he thinks she wanted something else since she made the comment about her boyfriend. That when she asked me if I lived alone, she was probably insinuating to go there and that I scared her when I wanted to call her at home.

I think of her several times during the day, and I ask myself what's my mistake? Is the boyfriend for real? If he is, what are my chances? If it's ok with her I would take them. Would you help me, please? -- Stan

Stan, if the two of you start dating, everyone in the office is going to know. You've already talked to enough people about the situation. You can't be discreet, even this early in the game, and I shudder to think what you'd talk about if you started dating and things went sour between the two of you.

She has a boyfriend. So what if she wears short dresses? So do millions of women. It's today's dress style. So what if she looks at you. She knows how you feel, perhaps she's making certain of where you are in a room so she can avoid the same area. Whatever the reason, do you really expect her to completely ignore you? Do you really think she's expecting to get some action at your place as your cousin suggests?

Cool down, back off, leave her alone. You jeopardize her job, your job and heaven only knows what else. -- Queenie

♥

Dear Queenie, how do you move on when you love someone you can't be with? I love a man that wants to spend as much time with his child as possible and his ex-wife will allow it as long as he's not with me. So he chose his child over me.

I love him more than anything and want him back.. We were talking marriage and now we aren't talking at all. I will love him for the rest of my life! I know my heart belongs to him and I can't forget him. What am I supposed to do, I don't want to spend my life alone. I want to spend it with him.-- Nikki

Nikki, he had a choice to make. He chose his child over you. You don't have any options. You can't have him back. He has the right to make that choice, and he has a responsibility to his child.

Let go. It will hurt. You will feel depressed and in pain for as long as you want to be. It's your choice, too. -- Queenie

♥

Dear Queenie, I fell deeply in love with an older man two years ago. I'm 35 and he's 49. He was just out of a 30 year marriage. After 18 months of a long distance romance, during which he begged me to move with my children and marry him, he changed his mind. When I finally said yes he freaked and said he wasn't sure he wanted to raise another family.

We've been broken up for 4 months now and we still talk almost every day. He is dating and has a girlfriend but yet he still tells me he thinks we might have a future together. He said he just needed time alone but if that were true why does he now have a girlfriend? I'm tired of waiting for him to make up his mind about me. He was truly my soul mate but why doesn't he just let me go if he doesn't want me? He is the one maintaining contact. — Janice

Janice, if you want a soul mate who has a girlfriend then this is the guy for you. If you would rather be in love with someone who didn't treat you as though you were yesterday's leftovers you'll stop talking with him every day and tell him goodbye. He's learning to be a middle-age player, which is fine for him at this point in his life but it's not fine for you. You don't deserve that kind of treatment.— Queenie

♥

Dear Queenie, my wife of 7 years felt that we have "grown apart" and wanted to move out for a while to get some "time and space" (you

know the line). A month later, she felt she had enough "time" and decided she wanted a divorce.

Needless to say I was very distraught for a little while afterwards. But then, like magic, a person who I had a relationship years ago called me, leaving messages on my answering machine, things like "I miss you so much" and "I still love you". I don't know if it was coincidence or what, but it happened.

I wrote about this before. You told me to back off on getting involved with L and wait until some of the dust settles after this very trying time. Well, my problem is that, as I've said in my many previous emails, I always had feelings for L, even after I got married. Now, my feelings for my wife are almost totally dead - if she wanted to come back to me, I wouldn't want to try again. No, what I think I want is L!

The other night, L called me and we talked for 8 hours! We talked about everything, the last 11 years, jobs, friends, lovers etc. Near the end of our conversation she told me how, in spite of the fact that I left her rather abruptly and put her through years of pain and hurt, that she never stopped loving me and always wanted me to come back.

She said she had a few chances to build relationships with other men but she never did because she would always compare them to me and deep inside she felt if she started something, it would be like putting the last nail in the coffin. In short, she wants me.

I finally asked her: Can we start again? She didn't say yes or no, but she did say that it is something that she has wanted to do for years. My gist on it is that she is afraid of coming right out and saying it but she makes it obvious that she wants to get together again. But she is (understandably) being very cautious. She is afraid of getting hurt again. She is fearful that the minute my wife comes back, I will leave her.

Some of her friends told her not to get involved with me again, but the majority of them have told her that she makes it very obvious that she is deeply in love with me and, if she really wants to, she should see me again.

It tugs at my heart to know that she could still love me so much! And I am so angry at myself for losing such a wonderful lover, such a close companion. I know that I won't go back to my wife if she wants to try again, but how can I convince L?

Talking to her the other night, all night, was so good, it made me feel so good again. My therapist is even slowly becoming convinced that this is no mere "rebound" thing - he is starting to feel like I genuinely love L and always have. I feel guilty for feeling this way even while being married but who can change how they feel?

How can I convince L that I really love (and always have loved) her, and that I won't get back with my wife?

L and I still haven't actually seen each other yet (we've only talked on the phone). I want to meet with her, though. What should I suggest? This is not like a "date" - this is about two former lovers seeing each other after 11 years! Should I suggest dinner, a walk on the beach? Having been married for 7 years I forget how this whole "courting" thing goes. -- Neil

Neil, it has been just a little more than a month since your wife said she wanted a divorce. You aren't even remotely close to getting issues within your life resolved to a point that you should be declaring your love for someone else, even if they were part of your prior life.

Those long hours you and she spent talking on the phone were nice but they don't mean that whenever the two of you meet face to face that you will be compatible. That phone talk was nice because you could close your eyes and listen to her voice and fantasize about her, and she could do the same about you. Reality is different and if you haven't found that out with your current marriage, you will find it out if you get involved too fast, too soon with L.

Somehow, though, I think you're going to do what you want to do no matter how logical it is that you get through this divorce and take some time to really discover yourself before you try to add another person into your life. Good luck whatever choices you make. -- Queenie

♥

Dear Queenie, I am a 30 year old divorced man who needs advice as I reenter the dating scene. I am currently in a platonic relationship with a girl who has a boyfriend back in her hometown. She says her relationship with her boyfriend has pretty much stagnated to the point that he either marries her or she will end it.

From what I understand, her boyfriend is a spoiled rich kid and I see her as being just the only accessory to his comfort package that his parents will not provide.

During the eight years they have dated, they have broken up three times but all three times she reunited with him. This time though she is expecting him to come here; that is if he wants to continue with their relationship.

The problem is that I've discovered that we think alike, like to do the same things, and just have so much in common that I frequently have to stop myself from falling for her. She is marriage minded and obviously would wish her boyfriend was the same, but I know that's not the case.

Because she has a very poor image of herself, I'm afraid that when she travels back home to see him that he will propose to her and that she will accept for all the wrong reasons. I know because I too loved and married for the wrong reasons.

I have tried to tell her my experiences but she is being optimistic and hanging in there for him. Is there something I can say or do (or conversely, not say or do) to convey to her that she should give me a try as a lover? Is there a way I can get her to fall in love with me and have her feel justified in breaking up with him? At the very least, what can I try to keep her from saying "yes" to marrying him? -- Sammy

Sammy, it is unfortunate that many marriages occur for the wrong reasons. You cannot say or do anything that will change her mind. You can only get hurt in a situation like this. If you are able to remain a friend without getting emotionally involved, fine. Otherwise, leave this situation now.

If she were perched on a ledge twenty stories up, I would tell you to do everything in your power to get her down. This is a different situation. It may cause her pain in the future, but it will be because she has made the decision that she considers right for herself. You and she have known each other for two months. They have a shared history of eight years. Whether or not they should be together, that history is going to keep them together perhaps even into marriage.

You cannot appeal to intellect when emotions control the situation. This couple has been together for a long time, essentially since their mid-teen years. They probably have never seriously dated anyone else. They are accustomed to each other. They are a habit. Habits, whether good or bad for us, are difficult and sometimes impossible to break.

She must want to move on with her life. She must want this in order for it to happen. You cannot relate your experiences and expect her to use them as her guide. This technique wouldn't have worked with you and it won't work with her. We all have to make our own mistakes and hopefully grow in wisdom from them.

You cannot make someone fall in love with you. The only person you can control is yourself. And in this instance you need to find out why you have an urgent need to get involved with someone who is involved with someone else. Are you trying to protect yourself from commitment?

You said you are reentering the dating scene which would indicate you are newly divorced. You don't really need to get involved in a serious relationship at this point. You need to discover yourself, get comfortable with yourself, find out what makes you the happiest, and then let your life expand to include a partner who fits with the "new you." In other words, you are not ready to make a permanent commitment to this lady just as she would not be ready for quite some time to make a commitment to you should she get disentangled from her current relationship.

My suggestion? Run! -- Queenie

♥

The Other Woman

The Other Woman

*"I had never been to his home and what I found shocked me!
His wife was there, she didn't know about me and of course I
didn't know about her."*

Who is the other woman?

Is she a predator who only wants a man when he is already committed to someone else? Does she delight in the challenge of "stealing" him from his wife and family? Does she stalk her prey and wait until a moment of weakness to pounce?

Is she the betrayed wife who needs to prove that she's attractive and desirable and the best way to prove it to herself is to do to another wife what was done to her?

Is she a naive and lonely woman who falls for the practiced lies of a man who has no qualms about betraying his marriage vows?

Is she a bored housewife stealing a few hours of fantasy and excitement because she doesn't want to give up the security her marriage provides?

Is the other woman the victim or is she the prey?

The other woman is all of these and more.

♥

*Queenie, he's married. We're in love. You got a problem with that?
-- Sweetness*

Sweetness, if you're happy I'm happy. But, since you asked, I couldn't help but notice that you sent your message quite late Saturday night.

What is a really sharp person like yourself doing home alone, in front of the computer, searching out singles sites and advice columns, on a Saturday (date) night?

Is it because he was home with his wife and family? Or perhaps on a nice family trip somewhere? Or maybe he has another girlfriend. Of course you're used to this by now, spending prime time by yourself. Bet the holidays have been a real blast! Does he give you lots of nice presents, too?

You don't give a lot of details but your attitude says a bunch. May I suggest, when you get tired of just getting a piece of the pie, that you dump this loser and go in search of a whole pie of your own? You probably deserve better. -- Queenie

♥

Dear Queenie, I am a recently divorced 25 year old who has been divorced for a year and I would like to know why I seek out more married men as companions rather than single men. -- Lola

Lola, I really couldn't answer that question for you. It's a dumb thing to do, but then you know that. Perhaps therapy would get closer to the answer. -- Queenie

♥

Dear Queenie, I met my boyfriend in a bar. We went to a hotel for the night where he confessed he lied to me about his age and marital status. He is 43, married with 3 kids. I am 27 and single. He later called and we talked for many evenings. He told me the first night I met him he would leave his wife which I said I didn't believe.

He did leave his wife on the day he said he would and we spent 6 fantastic, fun-filled weeks living together. Then he went back to his wife, then back to me, then back to his wife and so on. He is with his wife for one night before he calls and says he can't handle being with her and that he loves me, but he can't leave his kids.

Will this routine ever change and will it change to the way I want it to? Or am I being a moron? — Andrea

Andrea, you see the pattern for the rest of your life with this man. He won't change. He has lied to you because he knows you'll believe him. It's your choice: stay or go. If I were you, I'd choose "go". —Queenie

♥

Dear Queenie, I have been having an affair with a married man for a year now and we have come to the terms that we have a strong desire to be with one another, sexually and emotionally.

He moved his family away to another state because of his job four months ago, but he still commutes back and forth. We are stuck in a hard place, because he loves me very much, but he says that it isn't fair to separate from his wife because there is nothing she has done wrong.

He doesn't want me to date anyone else, I don't want to anyway. But it is hard to be separated from him for half of the month. I truly believe that he is my soulmate, because we connect on so many different levels. I made a promise to him that I will wait for him as long as it takes.

What do you think about my situation? — Dakota

Dakota, every guy who cheats has a line that works best for him when he wants to sink the hook in deep. Now that you've heard his and fallen for it, are you smart enough to spit out the hook or are you going to waste your life waiting for this loser? Maybe his wife "hasn't done anything wrong" but what kind of excuse is that for him to cheat on her and to keep you from finding someone of your own who can provide you a life that's not full of lies? —Queenie

♥

Dear Queenie, this problem may be a little different but it really has me bugged. It is about my very best friend. This is a person who I have trusted with my life and my heart. I confide in him about everything. I found out he has been lying to me for over a year.

He has been cheating on his wife. I have even met this woman and he told me nothing was going on between them. He did tell me she propositioned him and he turned her down. He said he would never do anything with her. I suspected but I truly believed he would never lie to me.

I feel like my best friend betrayed me. I feel for his wife too but I will keep his confidence. He has always been able to confide in me but this time he felt like he couldn't. He said he was afraid my opinion of him would change. I am having a hard time getting past this. It hurts that he could trust that woman with something he couldn't trust me with. I still want his friendship but I don't feel like I can ever trust him again.

How can I get past this? He knows I am hurt and he feels bad about that. He says it is over between him and her and I want to believe that but I have my doubts. Do you have any suggestions how I can get past all of this? And whether or not I should forgive him and really try to trust him again? — Chloe

Chloe, the way I read this is you're hurt because he "emotionally cheated" on you with someone else by having an affair and not telling you when he shares everything else with you but probably not his wife.

You don't know that you can trust him? You really need to get a life, or at least get a man in your life who doesn't belong to someone else. First of all, this man is married. Maybe not faithfully, but he does have a wife. That's who he should be confiding in, not you.

Second, the man is a cheat, plain and simple. He cheats on his wife with you by sharing emotional intimacy that belongs to her and then he cheats on the both of you with this other woman.

Stop acting hurt, you have no right. If you continue this "best friend" charade, you will get what you have earned. —Queenie

♥

Dear Queenie, I am a 51 year old woman involved in a long distance relationship. We live across the country from each other and we first met at a conference last fall while he was in a relationship. He had been previously married twice, is friendly with his first wife, the mother of his children. The second marriage was a disaster from the beginning.

Shortly after we met, I flew out to visit him. He had not broken up with his long time relationship yet. He said he loved her and if he had not been married to his second wife, he would have married her, but was afraid of failing again.

He tells his children that he loves her but does not know what he wants. He tells his children we are just "friends". He sent his ex-girlfriend an expensive Christmas gift, and is upset because she has not acknowledged the gift. I have been to visit him twice and he has been to see me twice.

Do you think there is any hope for this relationship? — Peg

Peg, nope. — Queenie

♥

Hello Queenie, I have been "friends" with a man for 25 years. During all that time I have always wanted more, but he didn't. Over the years we each had relationships and he has been with the mother of his son for 15 years. Hes also had a girlfriend on the side for 8 years. I know, "loser". I have made a lot of mistakes in my relationships and just now, at 43, learning the whys and am changing the way I think about myself and what I deserve.

I am now not satisfied with the crumbs that unavailable men offer. So, with this particular man, we periodically had sex, call each other as friends, and have an off and on relationship. During the last 2 years we have become emotionally closer, but that is still not enough for me. He of course tells me that he cares for me.

Now, I am pulling away because I am sick of chasing the carrot and I think he gets an ego boost because he knows I've always wanted him. Now, he claims he doesn't "get it" why I put off seeing him, or why the rules of the game have changed even though I've explained it to him.

Do I need to cut him off completely? Or do you think I can still talk to him (no sex!) and still respect myself? I have noticed that as I feel better about myself, he becomes less important. — Betty

Betty, of course he's going to complain when you change the rules of the game. All these years it's been his way and now you're trying to make it a little more equal and he just doesn't want to play the game that way.

You already pegged him. He is a loser. Tell him you're not nuts, you're just getting older and wiser and you've decided to stop wasting your time waiting for him to become someone he's incapable of becoming. Then mean it and move on. — Queenie

♥

Dear Queenie, I have been dating a married man for almost a year now who I first met on-line. He originally told me he was divorced and when I first met him in person he told me the real story. His wife did not want to be married to him anymore - that was a year ago- he lives in a separate part of the house and they have a teenaged son. Just recently they decided to tell their son that they are separating and going to do their own thing but that they will still be living in the same house.

His wife knows that he is seeing me and that we have a loving relationship. She wants him to stay in the house for the son's sake. The son does not know about me yet. We talked about him moving out but he thinks it will upset his son and wants to wait. My problem is that I feel insecure about this arrangement and don't know how long I should or can wait. — Bitsy

Bitsy, when you "date" someone who's married you can expect to feel insecure particularly when they use every tired excuse for not ending their marriage. I can't help you. You can help yourself by telling him goodbye. — Queenie

♥

Dear Queenie, I have a good friend, well it started out that way, but now it has turned into a sexual relationship. The problem is this man is married. He filed for a divorce, but the wife won't sign the papers. He also has a girlfriend, which is to say they are only friends now but dated for 4 years. She came to visit him last month, and he did inform me that she was coming, and they spent time together alone.

I didn't ask him what happened between them, he never told me either, only that they are friends now. I love this man and need to no what should I do to insure that they are only friends now, what do you think? — Dottie

Dottie, I think you need to get away from this man. He's married, he cheats on his wife with you, and he cheats on you with his *other* girlfriend. And why shouldn't he? He has a perfect set-up because everyone lets him get away with it. — Queenie

♥

Dear Queenie, I have been in a relationship for two years with a man who is married. I am deeply in love with him and he feels the same way

about me. I feel like he is my soulmate and I know he is the person I want to spend my life with. He has three children and is worried about getting a divorce because of the impact on their life. I don't know what to do. I don't want to be with anyone else but him. Please help me!! — Carrie

Carrie, he sold you the old "you're the only one for me but I just can't get a divorce because it would hurt my children" routine! And you fell for it? You are in a relationship with an adulterer. If he'll do it to the mother of his children, he'll do it to you. Think about it. If you're smart you'll tell him so long. —Queenie

♥

Dear Queenie, I have been with Mike for almost a year. The problem is of course his children's mother and I do not get along. I know Mike loves me. She won't let the children come to my house with him. He is so confused because she says either it is me or the kids, which I feel is insane.

So do I just walk away from him? I know that is not what he wants but I feel if I love him enough then I should step out of the way. What do you think? — Crystal

Crystal, are you dating Mike or are the two of you in a committed relationship such as marriage? Did he leave her for you or did you come into his life after his divorce? Or is he even divorced at this time?

If he isn't divorced, then you need to run, not walk, away, fast. If he is divorced and there is a custody arrangement in place then he and she should abide by that arrangement. It sounds, however, as though you have some doubts as to your place in his life at this point.

Maybe you should walk away so you can decide if you want him (and her) in your life on a permanent basis. They are parents and they will always have a bond because of the children, whether you like it or not. —Queenie

♥

Dear Queenie, I have been dating this man for over one year now. When we first met he was adamant against an exclusive relationship so I vowed not to get too close but we did. I recently found out he was married.

I knew that he had a daughter and his child knows me and hangs out with us a lot. So the mother has known about us for about 9 months. I found out because the mother doesn't like me and picked a fight with him because she didn't want me around her child. All along I thought she was a jealous ex-girlfriend but what she really was, was an angry wife.

He hasn't hid our relationship from her and they have never lived together. He married her because of convenience. I believe that is why she waited so long to get mad about our relationship. He let her know when we first started dating that I am his lover. Now after finding this out I feel really weird and confused.

He says that we are friends. I disagree because friends confide in one another and trust one another. If he really thought of me as a friend why didn't he feel close enough to me to confide in me that he was married but that they were separated or whatever it is that they are.

Even though he has admitted that we mean much more to each other than we ever thought we would he cringes and gets really uncomfortable when I use the word boyfriend to describe him. He would much rather I use friend. I don't think of him as a friend yet and I don't know if I should continue the relationship. Please help!!! — Cindi

Cindi, you know that sign that people make when they hold up the thumb and forefinger at a 90 degree angle? It means "loser" and that's what this guy is. He is married, he is a parent, and he is an adulterer. Of course you should let him go. He has a wife regardless of why he married her.

You deserve much better than this. Treat yourself to someone who will be proud to acknowledge that they're your boyfriend. Stop being a willing third party to this ugly little game he's playing. — Queenie

❤

Dear Queenie, years ago I fell in love with a guy, we went together for 2 years, then I hurt him really bad and we broke up. I never stopped loving him, and we stayed in touch but he married someone else after I got married, but neither one of us have gotten over each other.

We have been seeing each other again and we know we are soul mates, but can't change things because we would both lose too much if there was divorce. We spend a lot of time together and we are happy again and I have grown up. Do you think this is wrong? — Ginger

Ginger, it's adultery. Call yourself soul mates or whatever else you want to but he's a married man who is cheating on his wife with a woman who is cheating on her husband. If you two were really soul mates what you would "lose" in divorce wouldn't make a difference — you'd live on love alone if you just had to be together. You may get to test just how strong your love really is if either of your spouses discover what's going on. –Queenie

♥

Dear Queenie, my boyfriend of 3 years just broke up with me last weekend. He went back to the mother of his child. I am having a really hard time dealing with this and all I want is him to come back to me and give me a second chance.

I also have 3 children of my own and he has helped me raise them. I have tried running to other men and that just makes me feel worse. I don't know if there is anyway that I can do to get him back. But how do I get over these feelings. It is hard for me to eat, sleep, and work. Can you please help? -- Dee

Dee, if he loves you, he'll be with you. If not, he won't. You can't beg, plead, cry or demand that he return. You can only get your life together for yourself and your children and live each day one at a time. —Queenie

♥

Dear Queenie, I am 22 yrs old and well I feel like I am 42. I was in an abusive marriage to an alcoholic and finally got the courage to leave, and moved out with my infant son.

Then meet this guy on one of those personals phone chats. We spoke for a couple of weeks on the phone before we finally meet and it was wonderful, I really thought that I had found the person I was looking for this whole time. I completely fell in love with him. We started to see a lot of each other. He meet my family and friends, he was a big part in my life. We almost had a child but I lost it.

Everything was fine for about a year except he would never take me to meet his family or friends, saying he was just a personal person. Then one day he called and broke up with me, over the phone!

I was upset and cried for days and then decided to go see him. I had never been to his home and what I found shocked me! His wife was there, she didn't know about me and of course I didn't know about her. And I didn't know she had just had a baby with him. He was so angry that I was there and that everything was out in the open.

I left after telling her I was sorry and that I was mad at myself for falling in love with him. I still love him but how could I ever trust him again? I want to call him just to hear his voice. I am so alone and mad at him for putting me through so much pain. How do I stop loving him? -- Deanna

Deanna, he didn't put you through this pain, you believed a man who fed you pretty lies when he recognized someone who needed to hear pretty lies in order to feel better. You were down. He saw that. He used you. He took advantage of the fact you had been in an abusive marriage, the fact that you were hurting, the fact that you needed some comforting. He played you. If that wasn't bad enough, the two of you had unprotected sex and you became pregnant. Of course, at the same time he was having unprotected sex with his wife.

Why would you continue to love someone who was such a cheat? It doesn't matter how much sweet talk he gave you, they were lies, big lies! Feel sorry for his poor wife, the one who just had his baby, the one who is trapped into a situation with an adulterous husband. Is this really the kind of man you want for yourself? I'm having a difficult time imagining anyone who would be less deserving of your love.

As far as trusting again, maybe this will teach you never to trust a man who keeps his life secret from you. No one is that much of a personal person, and if they have so many emotional scars that they can't introduce you to their family or friends after a reasonable amount of time, you just need to have enough sense to turn your back and walk away. Fast!

Have some pride, girl! You deserve much better than this but you certainly aren't going to get it if you keep mooning over this cheat of a husband.

Perhaps he broke up with you because he found himself a new girlfriend, someone who wasn't making demands on him, someone he could play for a while before she got serious and wanted some kind of commitment out of him.

Guys like this don't stop with one time. They are players for life and they destroy a lot of nice girls because they know just the right words to make them feel so very special when all they're looking for is a little outside entertainment. You're far better off without him — Queenie

♥

Dear Queenie, I'm in love with my boss who is also my mentor. I've been working for him for almost 5 years. We started committing a relationship only at the beginning of this year. He's married with a kid. He loves his son a lot and so do I.

When we just started out, the both of us were very happy. Of course, on and off, we've been asking ourselves did we do the right thing. This question have been bothering us for many times and we've tried many times to end this but always in vain. We both know that we love each other very

much but because of responsibility and religion, he just can't divorce his wife. This is what I think and I bet this is what he's thinking too.

I love him very much but I'm deeply hurt because I can't be with him forever and I'm always waiting for his love, attention and care. I've tried very hard to stop thinking about him, try to talk less to him, try to give him a cold shoulder in order to forget about him. But the more I try to do so, the more hurt I am.

What am I going to do especially when I'm seeing him every day? I'm confused. Does he love me? -- Myra

Myra, falling in love with a married man can only cause pain as you have found out. I don't see how this situation can improve for you until you're no longer working for this man. He took advantage of the situation.

It is not easy to fall out of love. It's even more difficult when you work for the person you love. You feel helpless because you're not in control of the situation. You see him all the time but you cannot acknowledge your relationship. It's a mess.

Take control of your life. Don't let this man's unprofessional behavior cause you any more pain. Think of his wife and put yourself in her place. No matter what he may tell you, at some time he wooed her the same as he has wooed you. -- Queenie

♥

Dear Queenie, I was in a relationship with a married man for 16 years with a lot of false promises, and deprived my son from having a father and someone for me to enjoy at holidays and just being out in the open with. He took good care of me, but something hit me one day and I said it is over between us.

The love faded away a long time ago from lies, it gives me a mean feeling at times, but I feel it is never too late to try and put your life on an even scale. Can I ever forget him now because he did help me with my son through school and financialy it was more than generous.

Now his youngest son is in college and he wants to get married, but he is still married, living at home! So you can see why I called this to a halt. What is he trying next? -- Ria

Ria, he isn't available until he's single. You wasted 16 years dating this married man, why waste more time waiting for him to terminate his marriage so he can marry you? It sounds like more stall tactics on his part. Time for you to find a man who can be yours alone. -- Queenie

♥

Dear Queenie, neither of us are kids and we've both had our own broken hearts in the past and can tell when things are clicking and when there's trouble on the horizon, but this has got me baffled.

We dated for almost four years. We seemed very compatible from the beginning. Then, he tells me that he's not divorced, but has been separated, has no financial obligations to his wife, has no children with her and, but for the legal papers, is essentially divorced from her and has no plans to go back. I was somewhat upset by this since I had made the mistake of dating a married man before and didn't want to play that tune again.

We saw each other every weekend, somtimes twice a weekend. Since we live an hour's drive from each other we didn't see much of each other during the week. We spent all the holidays together.

I asked him if he would work on getting a divorce. I figured that if he was at all serious about our relationship, that he should at least be free of prior commitments. I also didn't want to be "wasting" my time dating a married man if he was never going to be truly available. He agreed to getting the divorce, but was confused as to why I put so much emphasis on it.

We went on a trip together and had a great time, stopped in his home town and I met his parents and brother. Things were wonderful, the sex was terrific and I was very happy. I thought he was too.

After we had been back for a few weeks he says his career is not developing into something that he thought it should be. He said the house was too much to keep clean, it costs too much in mortgage payments, and that he was really thinking of moving back to his home town.

I finally asked if I was anywhere in his moving picture and he said that our relationship did not mean enough to keep him from moving and that we should stop having sex because it implied more substance to our relationship than it deserved.

I was crushed and still can't figure out what happened. He has not even put his house up for sale yet, nor left his job, so it was obviously an excuse. But why would he change so fast from having such a good time with me one month to dropping me the next? -- Maye

Maye, he changed because you wanted him to make the relationship an honest one. He gave you the "I'm married in name only" story and you believed him. Then you told him to make a decision and he did but it was not the one you wanted him to make, it was the one that shows you exactly what he feels about you and the value of this relationship. Please, forget him and next time make sure the guy is legally divorced, not just pretending. -- Queenie

♥

Dear Queenie, I've always been a magnet to married men and for the last 13 years have been involved with one long distance very passionate man until his heart attack, and that ended. I am finding it hard getting over this. I am 53 year old divorced woman with grown children. -- Samantha

Samantha, does this mean that you are agreeable to affairs with married men? Do you try to get involved with married men because you don't want full time commitment or because you want a man who has already been "housebroken" by a wife? Or are you so desperate for love that you will settle for whatever you can get? Settling for what a married man can give is a losing situation as you're finding out.

When relationships end, there is pain. You're going through it now. You'll get over it in time. Unfortunately, the longer the relationship, the longer the cycle of pain.

I would like to think that you'll learn to say "no" to married men and "yes" to men who aren't already committed elsewhere. You'll stand a better chance of not having this happen again. -- Queenie

♥

Dear Queenie, I was in a relationship with my boyfriend for 3 years. Then I found out he was cheating on me. I was depressed and cried all the time and thought I couldn't live without him. I told him I wanted nothing to do with him. But he kept coming back, begging for another chance.

At first, I said no, but then I began to speak with him again. But I still noticed that he was very distant with me. I found out that he got the girl pregnant and he was still hanging on to her because of the baby. So I told him it would be best for us just to go on with our own lives. He said he wanted no relationship with her but would take responsiblity for the baby.

He kept begging me to take him back and again, I began to talk to him. I guess at that time, I was in denial, I couldn't believe he could ever love anyone else but me. I just left it alone and would talk to him every now and then on the phone.

At first when the baby was born, I didn't hear from him, nothing, not even to ask how I was taking it. He said he just needed some time because all of this was too much for him to handle but he said he loved me and wanted to be with me.

We began to see each other again but every day that went by, I knew in my heart that things would never be the same for us. I guess from all of the lies and him pulling himself away from me, I began to fall out of love with him and now I am beginning to see I don't really need him.

I asked him if he still sees her. He said he doesn't treat her like a girlfriend but he will go to the store with her sometimes. I was very angry because to me, that is cheating on me still. I got upset with him and said I wanted nothing to do with him anymore, I was giving up and I am moving on. He begged me to stay and said that I was being selfish and only thinking of myself.

Do you think I am overreacting? I don't want to be known as a girlfriend who was obsessive. Please give your advice on this. I don't want to be with him any more. But I just need a few words to help me understand him or this whole situation. -- Tamara

Tamara, he sounds like he's more trouble than he's worth to you. This baby is a lifelong commitment. What you're experiencing now is only the beginning. If you can't handle his involvement with the baby's mother and his child now, you won't be able to handle it in the years that will follow.

It's your choice. Either learn to live with her and the child as a part of his life, or move on and get a boyfriend who doesn't have so much baggage in his life. -- Queenie

♥

Dear Queenie, I am in love with a married man who is unhappily married. I think the only reason he stays is because of his son. We have flirted over the phone for the last couple of months. We got together one day while we were drinking. I haven't seen him or talked to him after that night because of our different work schedules, its only been a couple of days. Is it just a one night stand or could there be more? -- Molly

Molly, the key here is "married." It sounds like you had a one night stand. Don't you know that all married men who cheat are "unhappily married"? It's the oldest line in the book after "I'll respect you in the morning." -- Queenie

♥

Dear Queenie, I've been involved with this man for about 3 1/2 months now. He said he loved me and I in turn told him I loved him. I really only get a chance to see him on the weekends. He rarely calls during the week, because a lot of time he's out of town and claims he doesn't want to run up phone bills.

When I first met him he was in a bad relationship with another woman and was in the process of breaking up with her. Once he broke up with her, he started seeing me and we became intimately involved. I found

myself falling in love with this man who seemed very sincere, sweet, honest and open. Seemed very kind and understanding.

Well within the past few weeks, we haven't seen very much of each other, just periodically as he says, it's because of his job. So, last week I paged him because I hadn't seen him in about two weeks, had talked to him on the phone probably two or three times.

Instead of him paging me it was another woman. She wanted to know why I paged him and how I knew him. I told her the complete story - I had nothing to hide. She told me she was his girlfriend and had been dating him for about two years and that they lived together and wanted to try and make things work. I told her if that was the case I would not interfere. The next day I receive a phone call from him and he said everything she told me was just lies and that he wanted to be with me.

He came over and apologized and said he didn't want her. We had a nice time together and he said he would see me the next night. Now the problem is, when he left, I have not heard anything from him since.

I paged him on several occasions, but he has not returned my phone calls. I do not know how to take this. I do care for this man a lot and think about him constantly. What should I do? -- Polly

Polly, it sounds as though he has either made his decision and you are not a part of the picture or he is at least trying to make a go of it with her again.

You probably would prefer to hear something else, but, if it were me, I would forget him until he is completely and totally split up with and over this current girlfriend. In other words, stop paging him or trying to make contact.

If he really loved you, he'd be with you, not her. Words of love are cheap to come by; actions are what count. No matter what he may tell you, he's still with her. -- Quenie

♥

Dear Queenie, I am in my 50s, divorced twice. I have one grown son from the first marriage. My situation in a nutshell is this: I have been seeing a married man for almost 15 years with no future in sight. I know this is a convenience for him and also has been for me.

I am now ready to relax and settle down, and I met someone at my high school reunion who seemed to be very nice and we started talking to each other by way of long distance. He said he was coming visit me, then, after a month or two, he slowed down in calling and when I pinned him down about it because I was ready to move back to my home town to be with him, he told me he met someone else.

Now, a few months, later, he calls and wants to renew our relationship. I agreed to start from scratch which is where we were, and I am going to visit my home town soon, but this is where I am not sure since he has shown me signs that he is possessive and jealous. I do not want to go there and learn more about his possessiveness or jealousy. I will stop right now and hope you will answer and point me in the direction of where I should go. -- Camille

Camille, I think you already know the answer — follow your instincts. A man who is possessive and jealous this early will not get better over time. This is the beginning of the relationship when you're seeing the best of him.

When you go for your visit, why can't you see him on a casual, no strings attached, basis? Not every date has to turn into a future husband. Learn to date for the fun of it and choose men who are not encumbered with wives or long-term girlfriends. -- Queenie

♥

Dear Queenie, I have recently gotten out of a four year relationship. I am twenty-one years old and the relationship started out when I was seventeen and he was twenty-seven. He was married at the time. His wife found out and they separated and six months later I was living with him. I have recently moved back home because I began to doubt that he was ready for marriage with me.

Our problems weren't out of the ordinary, but I was young and had never been in love. He was a womanizing jerk that would build up my self-esteem only to break it back down. He was very controlling on some issues and at other times, he was very loving and gave me a lot of attention.

My father hated him and we didn't speak for a long time. Now I've moved back home, everything is fine. Here's the worst part: My ex started dating someone else three weeks after we split and she moved in with him last month. I live in a very small town, and I can't get away from him or her. I hear and see everything. It's pretty obvious that he's gone on with his life, and I'm stuck being afraid to open up my heart to someone else.

I feel that the only reason he got into a relationship so soon with someone else is because he can't stand to be alone. I feel like he has replaced me and she is living my life. I'm sure he treats her like a queen just like he did me at first, but it doesn't last for long. I'm so afraid to let myself go with another person. What do you think? -- Liza

Liza, this man was the most important person in your life for four years. It doesn't matter that he didn't deserve that honor, he held the post anyway. It takes time to get past the hurt and the bitterness. Some days the need for him will be stronger than others but at some point he will not hold such an important role in your life. You saved yourself a lot worse heartache by dumping him now than by living more of your life with him. You know that already.

Most probably history will repeat itself with his current girlfriend but guys like him can always find some women who believe "all he needs is the right woman" to straighten him out. There's no way the next woman would ever believe that "her" love isn't just what he needs.

No one plans on getting hurt in a relationship. Denying yourself a chance at a new relationship to spare yourself pain from its failure is to deny yourself the possibility of the ecstacy of success. -- Queenie

♥

Dear Queenie, I really appreciate the advice you gave to me about my boy friend who never had any time to spend with my kids and myself. You were right. He is married! And I have moved on with a rather nice man.

The problem is the married one keeps calling so he can stay in my mind! And I do still care! I am trying really hard to give the new guy a chance, but he is just not the same as the old one. What should I do? -- Mercedes

Mercedes, what is there to ask? Put yourself in his wife's place. Doesn't his cheating make you mad? Now keep that feeling and tell the guy to take a hike! Caring about him only hurts you and your current relationship. -- Queenie

♥

Dear Queenie, I was with my boyfriend for almost 3 years. Our relationship was going stronger and stronger and we are both very happy. I can say that ours is simply perfect and I really cannot ask for more except that he's married (actually he's separated).

Sometimes I can't understand why things happen to me. I mean for 3 years I'm keeping this relationship hidden from my family although all of my friends know but not my parents and I know if they found out they will surely forsake us as well as his parents would be very much disapproved by our relationship.

It seems that the world is against us but now it won't bother me any more. I'm in a very committed relationship with him and plan to marry in a couple of years once his marriage is annulled. It's like getting through

hell before you get your marriage annulled. In fact his ex-wife is not willing to cooperate.

I just want to ask if we make arrangements with his ex-wife stating that if he ever gets married she will not go after him in court as well as after his property although their child would have the right to his property. Can we get his ex-wife to sign it in front of a lawyer and then if she should go after him when we got married, can we accuse her for breach of contract? Would a contract protect us from his ex-wife runing our marriage?

Please advice me, I need your response badly. If we will wait for the ex-wife to file the annulment I know it will take forever and my bf can't file the annulment himself because he's the one who abandoned his family so you see how can we get married without fearing that his ex-wife will ruin the tranquility in our relationship. -- Lora

Lora, if you are looking for someone's blessing on this relationship, you've come to the wrong woman. And if you're seeking legal advice, you need to ask a lawyer.

You are worried about his wife ruining your marriage — so far, you're ruining hers. Referring to her as his ex-wife doesn't change the fact that she is his legal wife and you are what can only be called "the other woman" in this threesome.

As far as annulling this marriage, isn't it a little difficult to say something never happened when there is a child involved? Does that mean the child no longer exists? Or perhaps it was grown on a tree in the backyard?

You are worried about the church, the courts, your family and your friends. Why? You aren't worried about the fact this man is committing adultery and has been for the past 3 years. At one time he supposedly loved his wife, isn't that why they married and had a child. If you marry him, the same thing may happen to you. Take notes now so you'll know what to expect when he starts cheating on you.

There will be a time, years from now, that you may wish this man had never been a part of your life. You could save yourself some heartache by telling him "goodbye" now and walking away from a married man who is putting you in bad graces with your family, your church, and your community. You say it doesn't matter. It does. -- Queenie

♥

Dear Queenie, I was in a long term relationship with a married man for a year and a half. He made all sorts of promises including the one to

leave and divorce his wife. Finally I had enough, even though I truly do love him, so I ended the relationship.

I met a new guy at work and began going out with him. It has been 8 weeks that I've been dating this guy and for some reason I'm still thinking about the first guy. The first guy and I are still friends, we talk and get together twice a week and hang out. Since I've dumped him he has filed for divorce and is now telling me that he will do whatever I want that will help the relationship, if I get back together with him.

He knows he has to prove to me that he's going to stick to keeping his promises, but I truly do like the second guy, but I can't get the first one out of my mind.

I did go straight from one relationship to the other. Could it be that I should just take my time and only be friends with both of them, until I can get my feeling straightened out?

Help me please. I don't want to hurt either of these guys, the second one is just way too nice and sweet and doesn't deserve this. The first one has told me that no matter what he'll always be waiting for me, till forever if that's what it takes for me to decide which one of the two I really want to be with. -- Connie

Connie, you have the answers yourself. You said: "Could it be that I should just take my time and only be friends with both of them, until I can get my feeling straightened out?"

Right now the first guy is still married and I would suggest that you leave him completely alone, let him get his divorce legally over with and then give him space to make it on his own for a while so that he gains some maturity. Of course you think you love him, but so did/does his wife. He made forever vows to her once. Do you want to end up in her spot in a few years? It could happen.

This isn't going to be easy, and people are going to continue to get hurt as long as the relationship stays as it is. -- Queenie

❤

Dear Queenie, I have been having an affair for the past four years. When it began, my lover told me he was going to get the divorce, but due to 20 years of marriage, he needed some time to make the break.

Things began to progress, he started breaking the ties and preparing his family for his potential exit. Right after that he had a heart attack. He has since had another one and several other major health concerns.

I have remained with him through all of this, but he stated it would be a lot harder to get away from his marriage now and he was worried that I could not accept all of his health problems.

I am younger than him and in very good health. I have tried to assure him that I would be there no matter what, especially since I've been there this long. He still says he's afraid to make the break but he wants me to remain with him and not see other people.

I only see him about 3 times a week and talk to him a few minutes every day. He does not support me in any way other than buying me nice gifts. I have broken off with him several times only to return after a short time due to his pleading and my own wanting him. I love him more than I have ever loved anyone.

I know he is the one I want to be with for the rest of my life. I am not young, nor do I consider myself foolish. I have dated several men. I have been single for several years and my lover is the only man I want even though I do date others.

I have dated some very neat guys. Some have cared deeply for me and talked marriage. I am not lonely nor am I desperate for someone to be with. I know it is wrong to have this affair and probably he won't leave her yet I still want only him. What can I do? -- Candace

Candace, will you please read and re-read your letter? Read it until you understand that he is not going to divorce her. Read it until you see that you are wasting your life for a few nice gifts. You are being foolish.

He has it all: a wife and family, and a girlfriend who will stand by him no matter what shape he's in. Shall I spell it out far too bluntly? You are much cheaper, safer and more reliable than paying for sex on the street.

Words have no value, actions do. It does not matter what he says, it is what he does that shows how he truly feels about you and his family.

If you want to spend the rest of his life waiting for him to divorce his wife, you're going to pass up a lot of opportunities for happiness. It is your choice. I would like to think you're smart enough to see how you're being used and then walk away. -- Queenie

♥

Dear Queenie, when I was 17, I dated a 24 year old man who was separated. He was only the second guy I was with and after a pregnancy scare and six months together he moved out of state for a job transfer. Even then we were still close and talked every weekend. We spent the weekend together to celebrate my 18th birthday.

The next time we talked he said I was too immature and young to handle a long distance relationship and I needed to get out and experience

life before I settled down. Now it's been 6 months since we talked and I still think about him and miss him. What should I do? I'll be in his town next month and am transfering to college there next year. Should I call him? Or continue to feel alone and miss him? -- Missy

Missy, are you chasing him by visiting his town and transferring to college in the area next year? If so, I certainly think it's a bad idea. This man is still married (separated is not the same as divorced) and getting involved with a married man is bad news no matter how mature you think you might be.

He doesn't want to have anything more to do with you. Why waste your time with a guy who doesn't care, and who is married besides? There are a lot of nice guys you've probably ignored to be with this loser.

Nope, I wouldn't call him. Not unless you want to get involved in a sex-only relationship, be even more lonely than you are now, and miss out on meeting some nice guys. You're just beginning a very exciting life. Why give it all up for this loser? -- Queenie

❤

Dear Queenie, I'm in love with a man who has been separated from his wife for over two years. We've been living together for over a year. He continues to stay married to help her with insurance purposes. I want something more permanent than just promises of a future together. By the way, they have children together.

What can I say to him without putting him off and still make him understand my point of view? I don't want to push him but I don't want to be kept waiting either. -- Dolly

Dolly, you're living with a married man. Big mistake. His wife has his legal name and his health benefits. Good for her, bad for you. Say goodbye. If he divorces her and marries you, you have what you want. If he doesn't, you have your answer, even if it isn't the one that makes you happy.

Those children will continue to be his responsibility even if he divorces her and marries you. Child support will cut into your living expenses and sometimes strain your finances. Custody and visitation arrangements will keep him tied to them and to her regardless of how you feel about it. Can you deal with this? -- Queenie

❤

The Other Man

The Other Man

"I'm in love with a married woman. I know she loves me too.
But her situation doesn't seem like it will change anytime
soon."

There are advantages to being the other man. He has the excitement of an affair, sex without commitment, and no responsibilities of marriage. He may also be married or involved in a second relationship.

For some men, it's the perfect relationship.

Like women who end up as the third player in an affair, some men get emotionally involved and want more than what a casual affair provides. They want marriage and kids and they want it with the woman they're having an affair with. Instead of accepting the limitations of their relationship they push for it all and they're heartbroken when the affair ends.

The other man may be naive and inexperienced in love or he may be an experienced player, moving from woman to woman as relationships turn serious.

Some "other men" never come out of the shadows. Some, like Michael Bergin, write books to capitalize on their affair. If you don't know who Bergin is, he's the man who says he was the other man in the marriage of John F. Kennedy, Jr., and Carolyn Bessette Kennedy. His book, *The Other Man*, was published after the Kennedys died in a plane crash.

♥

Dear Queenie, I have a question about a situation in my dating life that I am confused about. I am now a graduating senior from college. I met a young lady in my senior year of high school that I fell in love with and planned on marrying. However, fate would have it a different way.

She had an encounter with her ex-boyfriend and later told me that she was pregnant with his child. I stood by her side all the way through being disowned by her parents to telling her ex-boyfriend. She went back to him and I returned, brokenhearted, to college.

She called me over a year later, apologetic for leaving and told me she had her baby and was pregnant with another. She called me several times more then disappeared again. I had the usual bad luck with women over the next couple of years.

Then, three weeks ago, she calls and tells me she's unhappily married and wants to know if she left her husband would there be a chance of us having a future together. I told her I thought there was but I couldn't be with her if she was married because this is not my way because I don't break up homes.

Should I persue this? Is it morally correct to see her? Should I still love her? Tell me your thoughts on my next move. -- Charley

Charley, my thoughts are that if you are really seriously considering getting involved with this married woman, the mother of two children, the same one who cheated on you when you were dating her, then you're too far gone to listen to anything I might suggest.

No, it's not "morally correct to see her." She's married. Should you still love her? Only if you like being used. Your next move? Out of town, if that's the only way you can get away from her. -- Queenie

♥

Dear Queenie, please help me! A year ago a friend of mine moved in with me after she separated from her husband. We've been friends for a few years, she's a little older than me and she has a couple young children.

She stayed with me for three months and during that time I fell in love with her and told her how I felt but she really didn't seem affected by it. She said when she starts dating again, I'll be the first one she goes out with. She's been away from her husband for a year now. Her husband moved out of her house and she moved back in. I don't think they're getting back together but now I hardly see her and we are fighting all the time.

I try not talking to her and staying away from her, but it doesn't work. I still feel like I love her. We used to spend alot of time together I could see her whenever I wanted. Now she just makes excuses when we are supposed to spend time together. Instead of me, she spends all of her time with a female friend. They go everywhere together, the friends sleeps over, and I'm always second to her. I'm beginning to think that she may be gay. And, if she is, what am I supposed to do?

I used to be a nice person, always happy and cheery. Now I'm depressed. I love her so much, I don't know what to do. I've even asked her if she was gay and she said no. I just feel like she's the only thing that will make me happy. I don't have any friends and now I don't feel like getting any. I just like to be alone. I love her so much. What can I do? -- Stan

Stan, it's too bad that you're looking for all kinds of excuses why it might be her fault that she's not head over heels in love with you but you won't face the fact that she is still married (that's what it is until her divorce is actually, legally finalized), and as such she cannot begin another relationship.

Even if her marriage were final, it takes a minimum of a year, and many times much longer, for a divorced person to get their emotions back in line so that they can make a decent and happy love commitment with another person.

Back off. Stop questioning her choice of friends. Stop pushing for commitment. She cannot give you what you want because she isn't ready or available. Maybe she will never be available in the way you want her to be because she may not have the same feelings for you and she may never have those feelings.

Because you seem to be in need of a person to commit to now, I suggest that you look for a woman who is single and available and forget about women who are married, separated, or newly divorced. -- Queenie

❤

Dear Queenie, I have known this girl for four years and fell deep in love with her. I have recently retired from my job but she still works and has been transferred to another town. When I went to visit her recently we became close and she says that she loves me. She wanted me to stay with her but I needed to come home for my son and to look for another job.

Just as soon as I left she started dating another guy. She is always having trouble with relationships due to her moodiness. So now every time she gets hurt she has to let me know. I am extremely jealous but try to hold back because I want to see her happy.

She says she loves me and I make her happy and she could see having a family with me. I have asked her on numerous occasions to marry me just to be turned down. She said she'd rather just live together. I don't believe in that but came around to her point because I really want to be with her. Now she comes up with excuses for not doing that.

I have always been there for her and have been through this "being put on the back burner" many times but she always comes back to me. She is currently going through a divorce and I can understand being gunshy about marriage but what I don't understand is if she loves me and she says I make her happy why go and try find what's already availble to her. I love her very much and am lost as what to do. -- Evan

Evan, the first question that comes to my mind is, how long has she been married? You casually mention the divorce but somewhere in this four year relationship either she has been married the entire time or she married someone within that time and is now leaving him. Do you understand what it means to be "used"?

You have done everything possible to get her to love you as you love her. Her response is to date others, while married, and run to you for sympathy when the relationships go bad. Is this how you treat someone you love?

You've offered marriage, she turns it down. She offers living together, which you don't believe in, but to please her, you compromise your own moral code and say yes, after which she decides no.

I cannot help you. You must help yourself. If you want a better life, get away from her as quickly as you can. There are many fine, respectable, honest and deserving women in this world. She doesn't appear to be one of them. -- Queenie

♥

Dear Queenie, I'm in love with a married woman. I know she loves me too. But her situation doesn't seem like it will change anytime soon. I've told her that I'll always be there for her, and that all I want is her friendship. Am I doing the right thing? Can I just be friends, or will this only hurt me because I still love her? -- Daniel

Daniel, this is a losing situation and as the person outside the marriage looking in, you'll lose the most. You can't be "just friends" with this woman. Let it go. -- Queenie

♥

Dear Queenie, I am involved with a married woman who is also my best friend, I am a woman. I love her very much and want to wait for her until she leaves her husband. Do you think that I am crazy to wait? I love her very much and I do not want to give up the relationship. -- Pearl

Pearl, your situation is no different than a man in love with a married woman. You'll do what you want to do, but you're in for a lot of heartbreak on your present course. -- Queenie

♥

Dear Queenie, I'm recently divorced after 23 years of marriage, most of which were not happy. We stuck together committed to raise our children through school. I now have a lady friend who I first saw three years ago, before my divorce. She was in a crowd of people, I saw her from behind and for some reason stared at her. Almost immediately she turned around and her eyes met mine just like she knew I was there.

I had never felt the way I did when she smiled at me. I saw her a number of times after that and since my divorce have become quite good

friends with her. I have really strong feelings and desires towards her. How do I know if these feelings are true or a result of the divorce?

This lady had a very unhappy childhood, and is currenly involved in an abusive marriage. She says she wants out and plans on doing something soon but she is afraid for her and her children's health. I want to be there for her and I've let her know this.

Because of her past she is reluctant to trust any one especially men. How can I get her to understand that I am sincere? Should I continue the relationship considering the circumstances? -- Calvin

Calvin, "soon" can be a lifetime. She's either married or she isn't. If she isn't then nothing should stand in your way toward developing this relationship further. If she is, then walk away.

Put yourself in her husband's shoes. If she had been your wife during these last three years, and her husband had been you, would you be happy to have him providing emotional support to your wife or would you be angry and consider his involvement unwelcome?

If the abuse is physical, and she needs protection, there are legal steps she can take as she removes herself from this marriage. Your involvement at this point could possibly jeopardize a child custody agreement and maybe more.

I'm not saying you shouldn't be a friend if she critically needs one, but you might be a little too emotionally involved to be "just" a friend. -- Queenie

♥

Dear Queenie, I have been in a close loving relationship with this woman for the past year. Every day has been great. She is married and has been going to get a divorce the whole time. Recently they started the divorce procedure and now she has distanced herself from me.

She says that, unlike she felt a few weeks ago, she now feels outside herself, confused, numb, and out of touch with herself. We hardly talk. When I try to find out does she still love me, does she still think about us, etc., all she says is that I am being selfish and not thinking about what she is going through, that this has become a very tramatic time for her.

All I want is to help and to know that we are still together and that everything will work out. Please if you can let me know how I should react or if there is any advice you can give, I could really use it now. -- Benjamin

Benjamin, this woman is married. She was married a year ago and she is married now. To tell you that you should have waited until she was divorced is a little late in this emotional game but I would like to hope you've learned a valuable lesson: don't date married women, no matter how bad they say the marriage is. No matter how much they say their husband mistreats them. No matter how much they say you're wonderful, marvelous, and the best thing that ever happened to them.

Legal separations are not the same as being divorced. Unhappily married is not the same as being divorced. Thinking about getting a divorce is not the same as being divorced.

It's possible she is changing her mind about the relationship between the two of you. She may have enjoyed your company while she had the safety and comfort of her marriage, but she may not wish to get more deeply involved now that she may actually be getting a divorce. Time will tell.

In the meantime, stop calling, stop sending cards, flowers, gifts, or having any contact whatsoever. Let her become divorced and legally available. Let her contact you if and when she is ready. Don't wait for her to contact you, though. Get out and date. And leave the married ones alone. -- Queenie

♥

Dear Queenie, I'm really not so sure where to begin, but I guess I could start by saying I'm madly in love with someone I work with, and the crazy thing about it is that she's someone I never thought I'd fall for. She's in her 30s, has been separated from her husband for a good couple of years, and has a couple of kids.

We've gone out a couple of times, but always with the kids. Please don't get me wrong because I love her kids; my problem is that each time I spend time with her, I find myself more in love with her, and the craziest part about is that we haven't kissed or anything, we're supposedly just friends.

I finally told her exactly how I feel, that I'm crazy about her and her response to me was, she's not ready for any kind of commitment just yet because she just came out of a real bad marriage. Her husband used to beat up on her. And of course she's also seeing other guys that she claims to be just friends.

I really understand her situation; I understand that this is her time to find her self, and that I shouldn't be in her way, but somehow my heart is so weak to admit that all I could be to her is just friends.

Should I just quit while I'm behind? Or keep just being friends, even though it hurts knowing she's also spending time with other guys? -- Donald

Donald, she isn't ready for commitment. Actually, if she is only "separated" she is still married. If she is recently divorced, she has a lot of "healing" to do. Most experts say divorced persons shouldn't even consider thinking about serious relationships until at least one year has passed since their legal divorce is final and, depending upon the length of the marriage, it may be much longer. That is so that they can get themselves together emotionally.

If you must have commitment now, you'll probably have to seek it from someone else. And, there's always the possibility she may never be ready for anything more than friendship with you. Only time will tell. I hope you don't put your life on hold any longer waiting to see how her life turns out. -- Queenie

♥

Dear Queenie, I met this woman, married and a few years older than me sometime ago. We were good friends for months, talked occassionaly, became best friends, shared each other's secrets, helped sort out each other's problems, literally laughed and cried together, and from there, became so close, that we started talking to each other daily, for hours. She called me her best friend, but for me, it was much more than that.

The next time I met her, I kissed her and she responded, but she regretted it later. We still haven't made love, but I've asked her to marry me and she's refused. I was willing to give up everything for her, but she doesn't feel the same. She says she still loves her husband, but I doubt that.

I've decided to finish all contact with her, I feel I'm going to go crazy from wanting her. I've tried this before, but she always convinces me otherwise. With me, it's all or nothing. If she can't commit to me, why can't she let me go? Am I being selfish in demanding too much, or is she being selfish in keeping me hanging on.

The only way I can get on with my life is by trying to forget her, which seems like an impossibility. I thought about ending my life too, but I wouldn't ever go thru with it. I decided never to marry, ever, but she convinced me otherwise. Tell me, am I too dependent on her? -- Merv

Merv, she's married. The two of you can get in a lot of trouble if this continues. Ending your life is too permanent for this temporary problem.

You will get over her, it just takes time and making your mind up that it is best to leave her alone. You must for your own sake. -- Queenie

♥

Road to Divorce

Road to Divorce

"How do you tell your mate that you no longer love him
because you just realize that the two of you are not compatible
after ten years of marriage and you feel that you do not want
to try anymore?"

No one gets married expecting to get a divorce. Divorces, even the "friendliest" ones, are painful to everyone including family and friends. Unfortunately, some marriages are just too bad to continue and divorce is the only solution.

What is the measure of a marriage that can be saved instead of a marriage that needs to be ended? Some men and women have the capacity to accept and forgive behaviors that others cannot and won't tolerate.

Every marriage has highs and lows. It takes maturity to navigate between those highs and lows and to not take the other person's mistakes personally.

Love can conquer quite a lot in a marriage but for some behaviors even love isn't enough. Domestic violence of any type should not be tolerated. Abuse in any form should be unacceptable nor should behaviors that put the other partner at risk, such as sexual addictions.

It's difficult to make the decision to divorce, even harder to make a new life once a bad marriage has ended. Many spouses have "what if" and "if only I would have" thoughts that will plague them and hold them in the past long after their divorce is final.

Even so, some marriages just aren't meant to last a lifetime.

❤

Dear Queenie, my husband of almost 20 years moved out a year ago. Told me he doesn't love me any more and we were through. I know it's because of friends of his that are using him. I went by his place today to drop off the kids and he's living horribly. I hadn't seen his place before and my heart broke for him.

I really want him to come back but I know he's afraid that his friends won't be his friends any more if he does. What should I do? I hate to see him being used and I hate that he lives the way he does. But most important I love him very much. — Gayle

Gayle, your husband is an adult. That means his friends can't make him *do* anything, they just become the excuse for doing hurtful things. He is doing what he wants to do and right now he wants to be with his friends and out of his marriage. All the love in the world won't make him turn into the husband you want him to be.

If he'd rather lose you than lose his friends it sounds as though you come in a very distant third in his life. If it were me I'd have to start working on getting myself back on track and developing a life without him. You deserve better than this.— Queenie

♥

Dear Queenie, me and my wife have split up and now we're trying to get back but she wants to be friends and take it slow. I'm afraid that we will just be friends and that's all. I want to know if we can be good friends and still be husband and wife and how can I show her that I want both? — Peter

Peter, what you're really asking is how do you fast forward through all the friendship stuff and get right down to having sex again. While sex may be your top priority, developing a strong friendship is hers. If you are serious about wanting to repair your marriage you'll put your sex drive on hold and work on the friendship for now. — Queenie

♥

Dear Queenie, I am 51 years old, my husband is 43 and he has decided that he wants a divorce to see what the other side is like. He says he has only been with 3 women in his lifetime and feels that he is missing out. I love him very much and thought we would be together forever.

This started when we decided to have separate checking accounts. I make a lot more money than he does and he felt I was controlling the account. He liked the independence and said for a long time he felt he wanted out but didn't think he could make it on his own. Now he has become a lot more independent and wants to be single again.

This is the second marriage for both of us and it has been a little rocky but I really thought we were committed to each other. Now, he's never at home at night, he drinks, plays pool, and works another job to keep from coming home. And he keeps reminding me to split everything and to file for divorce. What should I do? — Debbie

Debbie, it sounds as though your husband may be working his way through a midlife crisis. You might find some answers at the Midlife Club: www.midlifeclub.com.

Only 3 women, huh? So he wants to start sampling the current crop? It's a little difficult for a married man to check out those "greener pastures" although those hours he's spending away from home might just be leading up to more than playing pool and hanging with the guys.

One thing I've noticed is that a lot of men aren't very anxious to be independent and away from home until they have a little nest waiting elsewhere. Could it be that he has a "nest" somewhere?

This isn't something that is easily fixed and the only help I can give to you is to tell you that what's happening is more common than you might think. Visit the Midlife Club link above and you'll understand. Otherwise, take care of yourself because he's most definitely taking care of himself without regard to your welfare. — Queenie

♥

Dear Queenie, I have just seperated from my wife of 15 years; we actually are a one-night stand that ended in marriage a couple years later. I am not in-love with her but I care for her. We have only been separated for a week and she wants me to court her again and have sleep over visits.

As concerned as I am for her, I am not prepared to go back to her. I need advice how to handle the situation without making her bitter and resentful towards me. I want to move on with my life, but also I do not want to destroy hers. Please help me. — Tony

Tony, divorce will always hurt the person who is being left. If you absolutely see no future in the marriage then the price for ending the marriage may be her bitterness and resentment. If you are leaving her for another woman, her feelings may be justified.

You can do your part by being generous with the divorce settlement and not pushing the matter of your first night together as this makes it seem that your marriage started on less than respectable terms. All relationships start somewhere and yours just happen to begin with a one-night stand; it took two years to culminate in marriage.

Leave as a gentleman and treat her like a lady. Respect the fact that she loves you and wants to spend her life with you even if your feelings have changed over the years. —Queenie

♥

Dear Queenie, I need some advice that could help save my marriage and relationship with my wife. My wife and I had a talk about a week ago about some things that have been bothering her and why she feels unhappy. She told me that she is not getting enough help around the house and that I have forgotten to notice things about her.

She feels like she doesn't want to be married any more and that she wants to be more independent. She tells me that I cause problems whenever she wants to go to dance clubs with her friends, that just because I don't want to go with her she shouldn't have to stay at home, too. The reason I feel uncomfortable with her going to the clubs is that there are a lot of guys that go to the clubs to find a woman to take home and get laid.

After my wife told me how she feels and that she wants to do things that she wants to, not that she doesn't want to do things with me but to have some time to herself, I now understand what she has been dealing with in the past and I am ready to work things out.

She told me that she wants to spend some time away from me and the house so that she can think about what she wants to do. She tells me that when I say "I love you" to her she can not say it back. A part of me feels like she is not going to give me a chance to change and that she doesn't want to be a part of my life anymore.

I have always been faithful to my wife, it's just that I didn't want her to go out and do things without me. Some friends of ours have real problems in their marriage because he has cheated several times but still his wife stays with him. I would think that if one of the partners cheated on the other it is worse than what's been going on between us. Can you help me out with some helpful advice? -- Bill

Bill, I don't know what you've done in the past so that your wife is trying to decide if life without you is better than life with you. I really don't want to know.

It doesn't matter if your friends have a marriage in which he cheats and she forgives. Comparing your marriage to theirs is not valid.

If you truly love your wife, and if you really want to change, start now and examine the relationship. Make a list of all the things you do which she says make her unhappy. Then, if you can, stop doing them! Of course it's not easy but neither is it easy to give up on a marriage if you have the capability of keeping it together.

Have you neglected her, taken her for granted? Do you believe that it's her place to keep the home in perfect order without your help? Does she have any girlfriends to talk with, any hobbies or outside interests? Does she have a job outside the home? Does she have a chance to "grow" within herself? Does she have an opportunity to take time for herself?

She obviously enjoys dancing. When she asks you to go with her and her friends to the dance clubs, go. And dance with her. Rekindle the flame that used to burn between the two of you.

Is she sexy? Tell her so. Is she pretty? Tell her so. Do you love her? Tell her so regardless of whether she can tell you the same in return. Romance her.

If she must leave, let her go. Let her rediscover herself. Take the time to rediscover yourself as well. This is not a license to date others. This is time for introspection and evaluation of your relationship with each other, where it is and where it should be. If she loves you, she will return.

Incidentally, those men in clubs cannot pick up women without the women being in total agreement. Not all women go to clubs to be picked up. Sometimes they're there just to be somewhere. Sometimes they're there to better appreciate the man already in their life. And sometimes they're there to hear the words they desperately wish they would hear from their husbands. -- Queenie

♥

Dear Queenie, how do you tell your mate that you no longer love him because you just realize that the two of you are not compatible after ten years of marriage and you feel that you do not want to try anymore? -- Deb

Deb, it took ten years for you to discover this? Or have you had ten years of aggravation that has just gotten to the point that you can't take any more?

Before you do something you might regret, take a few deep breaths, relax, and think of life without him. Actually, think of life with another woman holding him. Then make a list of all his good points and all his bad ones. Think back to how it was in the beginning, and why you wanted to marry him in the first place.

If you're just bored but he's a good guy and there might be some hope for the future for the two of you, don't kill this marriage. Try to repair it with counseling.

If you've discovered someone else thrills you more, be sure you aren't trying to turn a fantasy into reality with someone who may have more faults than your husband and who might not be ready to make the ultimate commitment when you're free to do so.

If your marriage has fatal flaws such as abuse, alcohol, cheating, etc., then maybe it shouldn't be saved.

A simple "I think we should talk" is a good beginning to this important conversation. -- Queenie

♥

Dear Queenie, is there such a thing as a "friendly" divorce? -- May

211

May, perhaps some divorces start out as "friendly," but it's difficult to keep personal feelings out of such an emotional issue. -- Queenie

❤

Queenie, my wife has done me wrong and I want to know how I keep us from getting a divorce? I don't want one but she does how can I make her love me again? — Art

Art, you cannot keep your wife from getting a divorce if her mind is made up. You also cannot "make" her love you. If she won't discuss it, if she won't go to counseling with you, if it's over, then accept it.—Queenie

❤

Marriage Repair

Marriage Repair

"This relationship means an awful lot to me not being how it used to be is hurtful. I still think deep down inside that it can be nurtured back because I know him better that he knows himself."

Some marriages start failing before the marriage ceremony but with so much hoopla already committed to, the marriage takes place and then the couple begins an agonizingly long journey toward divorce.

Other marriages begin in the heat of lust but don't have enough foundation to build upon when the sexual heat cools.

Yet other marriages are successful at the beginning because each partner's needs mesh with the other's. When those needs change, such as an alcoholic who quits drinking, the new needs may be too much in conflict for the marriage to survive.

Too many repairable marriages end in divorce simply because one partner doesn't feel like working on the relationship any longer. Regardless of how difficult dating and pre-marital relationships may be, marriage will be even harder work over the long term because of the added responsibilities of family, finances, and other obligations that the vast majority of dating couples don't have to deal with.

Despite the love one person in a marriage may have for the other, it takes two people to work together to repair a troubled marriage.

♥

Dear Queenie, I am married to a wonderful guy and he means the world to me but I just do not feel that special kind of feeling any more. I know I love him more than life itself but the feeling is gone and I do not know how to get it back.

What do you recomend that I do to help this situation? I am up for any suggestions. -- Sandy

Sandy, how would you feel if he came home one night and told you that he was in love with someone else? Envision it then do everything in your power to rediscover all those special things that made you fall in love with him in the first place.

Marriage is the most important "job" you can have. It has its good days and its bad days, its ups and downs. The real fireworks won't always be there, you exchange them for the comfort of someone who you trust and depend upon, your companion and soul mate.

Go take a look at him right now. What if he said it was over? How would you feel? Visit some of the romance sites on the Web and find tips to add the romance back into to a relationship. Treat him to some special romantic rendezvous. Make him your lover again. The payoff for you will be worth it! -- Queenie

♥

Dear Queenie, my wife of 2 years has filed divorce papers, and, if everything goes on schedule it will become final in three months. I love my wife in spite of all her shortcomings. In our culture marriages cannot be thrown away that easily. I have been married before twice and she was married once before and her husband is deceased.

Her son from this first marriage doesn't live with me because she would rather her mother take care of him because of the way things are between us. I think he needs to be living with us so that we can become a family.

I think this marriage is failing because we don't communicate well with each other although I think I do a better job of expressing myself to her than she does to me.

She says my anger is bad and that we are very different. I say that I only get angry when she talks of leaving or says that it was a mistake to marry me or when she is leaving the house to go stay at her mother's house as she has done several times before this.

I am very tactile and expressive in love, she isn't. I feel that she does not love me because if she did she would show it somehow. -- Thom

Thom, marriage is a compromise. That means that both people adjust their differences so that there is less conflict with their marital partner.

From what you write, you wish her to change to meet your needs, because they are more important than hers. If this is a part of your culture then so be it. If this is your strong personality making demands on her milder personality, then I can see why she would struggle to be free. What you have written about your anger being bad says much in a few words. Also the fact that you love her "in spit of all her shortcomings." Isn't that nice of you?

Communication is each person alternately talking and listening. Listening and understanding. Can you do this? Or must your wife always defer to your wishes? Or is that how your culture expects women to behave? -- Queenie

♥

Dear Queenie, what do you do when the love your mate had for you is gone and trust is gone, but you still love your mate and don't want to get a seperation or a divorce but you want to try to work things out and your mate at the time is not willing due to school and the kids, and your mate treats you like you're seperated? -- Janice

Janice, have you tried counseling for the two of you or just yourself? This marriage is in big time trouble. Depending upon the situation, you may need legal advice also, which I cannot provide. Visit divorcesupport.about.com and maybe you'll find some resources that can give you some direction to either save your marriage or end it equitably. Good luck. -- Queenie

♥

Dear Queenie, I feel taken advantage of all the time by my husband. I work, cook dinner, clean the house, handle the finances, etc. Anything that needs doing I'm always the one for the job! I don't know how I ended up this way. But it's been this way from the very begining of our relationship, so I can't blame him. I knew what I was getting into before I married him.

So my question, these things cause me to feel miserable and dissatisfied most of the time and knowing I still love him are these things important enough to leave my husband? Sometimes I think so. Am I the one being selfish?

I did leave him for a month and he begged me to come back and said all the things I needed to hear from him. I thought he finally understood me. But then in a couple weeks things were back to normal and other things even got worse. I feel out of control of my own life. Do you have any suggestions? -- Danielle

Danielle, you need to regain control of your life. It's as easy as deciding that you are happy with your life as it is and you're going to work through your feelings with or without your husband's input.

Being miserable and dissatisfied is no way to live a life. Unfortunately, you knew what you were stepping into but you went ahead and stepped anyway.

There's nothing wrong with taking charge, nor with being the one to whom everyone looks when something needs to be done. You just have to know your limits and let everyone else know them, too. When you've had enough, say so.

Stand up for yourself, take time for yourself, learn to say "no" when you need a break. Things will not fall apart because you can't do everything to perfection all of the time. If it means dinner isn't on time or it's out of a can, if that's not good enough, your husband can cook or order in. If it means there's dust in the corners, hand him the broom if he complains.

If you can change the situation from doing these things because you have to do them, to doing them because you want to do them, you will have a much more optimistic attitude about your life and your marriage.

It's not selfish to need some time for yourself. However, don't throw a perfectly good marriage away as you desperately try to make that time for yourself. -- Queenie

♥

Dear Queenie, he is asking me to move on with my life. His decision is that I can stay at the house while we sleep in separate rooms. We talk a lot but there is something different about it, he listens to me more earnestly. One reason for this is that his business is encountering a lot of problems. He says he just can't give me the comfort that I need because he can't even give it to himself at a time like this.

I tend to bring up the involvement he had with another woman six months ago too frequently when he specifically told me to put behind us. So now he says a relationship is not what he wants with me or anyone. I am willing to change because I did not realise what damage it could have done.

This relationship means an awful lot to me not being how it used to be is hurtful. I still think deep down inside that it can be nurtured back because I know him better that he knows himself. Could he just be saying this because of the extreme pressure of life? He says sometimes he doesn't know where he is heading. Or should I just be strong for both of us at this moment? Things are never always terrible it has to get better some way or the other. No one will ever understand how much I care about him or no one will ever care as much as I do.

I don't want to be like his exs who ran off but it is hard when that someone shuts you off and says things to you that are not positive. -- Norma

Norma, this is a relationship with problems, and they don't necessarily sound as though they are all caused by you. He told you to put his involvement with another woman behind you? That's fine, but you had unresolved feelings of betrayal. Despite his need for you to forget, it doesn't happen overnight and it very rarely happens as quickly as a cheater wishes it would.

If his business stresses are causing him to be confused about life in general, there may be nothing you can do at this point except take care of yourself.

Can you stay in the same house with him as a "platonic friend"? I think this could be extremely painful. What happens if he decides he wants to date someone else? Could you handle him dating and perhaps bringing a date home?

Life will get better but only after you take control and make some positive decisions about your personal happiness. That might mean moving out and moving on. -- Queenie

♥

Dear Queenie, how can I make it easier to be without my husband when he is driving long distance? He is going to school to be a truck driver and we have only been married for 2 months. We have one child and another on the way and I am not sure how to make the situation easier on myself and my 5 year old son. — Ginny

Ginny, you'll be handling a lot of the parenting by yourself and that won't be easy but it should be easier knowing that your husband is working hard to support the family.

Plan some private time for you and your husband when he's home so that he really looks forward to being home, and don't complain about the fact he isn't around so much. Lots of women are married to long distance truck drivers and their marriages survive because they make the most of the time they are together. — Queenie

♥

Dear Queenie, I've recently gotten married and already we are already having problems. My husband has a fixation on scantily clad women like you would see in "nudie" magazines, videos, and on television. It doesn't help that I'm 7 months pregnant.

I've had discussions with him over and over how this bothers me and it's even gotten to the point that when we go out in public together and he thinks I'm not paying attention he'll ogle a female right in front of me. It drives me insane. I think that he's still in "single" mode. He doesn't go to these females and say anything, he just stares.

I almost left him because of this problem. I feel that since he married me, I should be enough but he can't stop his wandering eyes. I know that he won't cheat on me but he does this and then denies it.

He tells me that his friends do it and they're married and that their wives don't care and I tell him that we aren't his friends. He seems to still not want to listen and blames it on me being pregnant.

I love him so much and now that I've voiced my problem with him, he hides and looks at his nudie magazines. I've cried over it and he said that I can throw them away. I've come close but never had the guts to do it, so I took them and hid them, letting him think that I've thrown them away. He hasn't said anything about it yet. But now he runs to the internet and looks at the porn sites. What should I do? — Rosie

Rosie, if he was doing this before you got married, you probably thought you could change him once you were married. It seems to be a female trait to try to make a less-than-perfect boyfriend into a perfect husband. Well, guess what? When you marry someone you marry them faults and all. You have a man who ogles women. If that's the worst he does, you're very, very lucky. I think you're making too big a deal over this. —Queenie

♥

Dear Queenie, I am 39 years old and have been married to my husband for 2 years. We have a great relationship in all respects except one: when I am sick or hurt, he ignores me. I feel like I become invisible to him.

He gets busy with his computer games and I have a hard time getting his attention for help with things like cooking meals, walking the dog, bringing me hot soup, etc. even though I am sick or hurt. I've tried to explain how I feel but he says he just doesn't have a good bedside manner and is busy with other things. He has been this way as long as I've known him.

This is especially ironic since when he had major surgery I nursed him night and day through his recovery. He was very grateful and said he couldn't have pulled through without me. I did everything for him, gladly, and would do it all again.

During that time period I pulled my back doing some heavy work around the house and now I need him to tend to me a little, but he acts like I'm invisible. He doesn't even ask how I am feeling.

Am I asking too much for some extra consideration and help when I'm hurt or sick? What happens if I have to have major surgery, or get extremely ill some day? I feel like I cannot depend on my partner to be there for me. Please advise. — Nicole

Nicole, why did you marry this man? You knew he wasn't the type of caring individual you need. You knew exactly how he was from the beginning of your relationship yet you married him and now are upset because he is the same as he was then. Did you think marriage would make a better man of him? Why can't you be happy for his good qualities and accept his faults?

Some men and some women have a difficult time as caregivers but it doesn't make them bad people. Are you ready to bail out of your marriage in order to find someone who has a better bedside manner? Or, would it be more beneficial to consider hiring a nurse should you ever need the type of care you're thinking may be required in the future? —Queenie

♥

Dear Queenie, I am 27 and have been married for 3 years, but I think about my ex-boyfriend constantly. When my husband and I were engaged I broke it off mainly because of my feelings for my ex and we got back together but then my now husband came back into my life and I made the choice to marry him. I think I did it because everyone likes him because he's such a stable guy and hated my ex because he had a pretty wild past. The thing is, I think my ex was and is my soul mate.

My husband and I were always best friends but since we've been married, he never wants to have sex (he admits he is rarely in the mood) and our marriage is slowly fading. I found my ex on the internet, but I did not communicate with him so far.

What do I do? I have been praying to make our marriage better, but I know there is more to life than this--I have no life in this marriage--I feel more like a roomate. What do I do?— Serena

Serena, you have to do more than pray in order to make a marriage work. Having your mind constantly on your ex means you're very rarely thinking about your husband. That cuts into the intimacy factor of your marriage.

How would you feel if your husband constantly thought about his ex-girlfriend and felt that she was/is his soul mate? Would you feel hurt? Betrayed?

If you actually love your husband then you should forget about your ex and concentrate on putting the fun and sizzle back into your marriage and your marital bed. Otherwise, do him a favor and let him go so he can link up with a woman who will put him first in her life, not second behind a guy she used to date that she's considering making contact with again. —Queenie

♥

Queenie, I am a Catholic and my wife is not. I have asked her to go to classes conducted by my church to learn more about my church and what I believe and she refuses. Does that mean she cares so little about what I believe that I can assume that she just wants to use me as a meal ticket and does not care about me at all? -- Chip

Chip, why must your wife have the same religious beliefs as you do? Why can't you have the same religious beliefs as she does? What's wrong with each of you having your own religious beliefs?

Didn't the two of you talk about religion before you got married? Did you get married expecting to change her to your religion? Why must you change her now? Perhaps you care so little about what she believes that you can't understand that she has a right to her own beliefs. —Queenie

♥

Dear Queenie, my wife of 6 months and I have had disagreements lately about lifestyles. The major problem for me is that she has many male friends, most she knew before we got married, and they are still very much an active part of her life. She calls them or they call her on a regular basis and she even invites them to our home while I am at work. She says this is perfectly innocent since she never has been nor never will be unfaithful.

To her, anything short of getting naked in bed is perfectly acceptable including social drinking after work, hugging, kissing, even sitting on their laps. Two of these are ex-boyfriends she was intimate with.

My position is that this is not acceptable behavior for married people, regardless of the innocence. She criticizes me for being jealous and possessive. I don't think I'm wrong here. It has gotten to the point that I have made myself an appointment with a psychiatrist. Any advice? -- Carl

Carl, I think your wife needs to visit a counselor to learn why she feels a need to act single when she's married. No one should have to put up with a mate that causes so much anguish.

No matter how much she says she would not be unfaithful, she has the door wide open to the opportunity. I see nothing wrong with married people keeping their single friends, but when those single friends cause a problem in the marriage, something needs to change.

Would she like you to invite your former girlfriends over when she's not there? Would she be happy that you hugged and kissed them and let them sit in your lap? Probably not. I'm not suggesting that you do this because I don't think this would solve the problem in your marriage.

The two of you need to talk about what you each expect and need from the other in order to have a solid marriage. If your needs are too far apart, you're going to have to decide the course of action you want to take at that point. Good luck. -- Queenie

♥

Dear Queenie, I'm married with two lovely daughters. Recently, I found out my husband had a short affair with somebody from abroad who was here on a holiday. He admitted the fact and told me he is very sorry and will never do such a thing again.

His life is as per normal, golfing, football, etc. My life is in ruins from the day I found out about the affair which happened just after our second daughter was born. I love my husband as much as the first time we met about six years ago but I cannot understand why this is happening to me and I simply cannot accept it.

I want him back and he is trying to make me forget about the affair. However, after two weeks, I'm still crying in public and especially in the middle of the night. In my mind, I keep imagining how they made love together. I'm also afraid that once I'm over this, he will do it again.

My husband was everything to me. I am dependent on him emotionally. But now I feel betrayed and it hurts so much that sometimes I think of just leaving him and going somewhere else. I cannot do that because my daughters are so young and they are both very attached to both of us. Help me, please! -- Amy

Amy, it is a very terrible thing that he did. But it is done and no matter what he does now, he can't undue that foolish affair. It has happened. He may wish with all his heart that he had never betrayed you, but he cannot go back and erase the happening. History cannot be changed.

You have every right to feel the pain and hurt of this betrayal. It comes at a particularly vulnerable time for you, not so long after the birth of your daughter. Your emotions are raw, it is a deep black place that you have fallen into as a result of this. It is understandable.

Of course it won't help to say that millions of women have been betrayed in just the same way. It won't help to say that many of them have learned to push the memories back so that they can reconstruct their marriages and continue forward. It won't help to say that life goes on and it's up to you to pull yourself together because if you don't, your marriage surely will end.

Do you love this man? Forgive him. Do you want this man? Forget what happened. Do you want a happy marriage? Continue into the future and put the past behind you. Do you want to learn from this? Pull yourself together, be the best wife and mother you possibly can be. Become less dependent on your husband and develop yourself as an individual.

Many of your feelings right now are feelings of helplessness because you don't think you could survive without your husband.

Right now, you might have an extremely difficult time on you own. But you're an intelligent, mature woman who can do anything she puts her mind to, so get going! Forgive. Forget. Don't worry about if this might happen again. None of us knows the future. We only have control of right now. Make the best of it. -- Queenie

♥

Dear Queenie, several years ago I was married to a man that obsessively cheated. I was both mentally and physically abused. I have worked through most of the pain, and I realize this was his problem and not one caused by me.

The only lingering problem is my inability to trust. I married again to an absolute godsend of a husband. He cooks, he cleans, he is kind, he is considerate. but if he is late coming home, I panic. I know I shouldn't, his past has shown nothing but honesty. I get extremely jealous, too. I just need to know how to put this behind me before I lose him. It can't be fun to be accused all the time. -- Maryanne

Maryanne, your first husband cheated and abused you, and your second husband is paying the price. That's about as fair as if your husband accused you of infidelity because his first wife cheated on him.

You're being unfair to him and yourself. Put what happened with your first husband in the past where it belongs. Forget him. Move into the present and think about the future with this wonderful man who loves you. Put the ghost of your ex to rest. Get some counseling if you need it.

PS: Your husband sounds like a dream! Cooks and cleans? On top of being hard-working, kind and considerate? Lucky lady! -- Queenie

♥

Queenie, how can I learn to trust my mate again after he has cheated on me? How do I get over it and stop throwing it in his face? -- Doreen

Doreen, if he's cheated once, he deserves another chance, without being reminded of his mistake. Why destroy a good relationship over one mistake regardless of how wrong it was?

If he has cheated more than once, dump him and move on. That's my opinion, anyway. -- Queenie

♥

Dear Queenie, my husband cheated on me and I forgave him. I will never forget, but I understand why he did it. We were going through a rough time and I have a son who at the time demanded a lot of attention and I was dealing with my child more than my husband and he had an affair.

It was a short affair but to me you only need to do it once. In some ways it brought us closer but I do not trust him. I'm not sure I ever will as he is the one person I would have bet anything that he was not the type to cheat. How wrong we are sometimes. -- Maureen

Maureen, it doesn't really sound has though you have forgiven him. He made a mistake which he may truly be sorry about but if you won't let go of your mistrust, it will create a situation that will bring even more unhappiness into your relationship.

It is impossible to change history. For that very reason, try to forget as well as forgive and love him as though this never happened. Why waste the present and the future because of something that happened in the past. -- Queenie

♥

Looking for Love

Looking for Love

"I am scared to death to tell her as I know it is probably not the best time for her. Should I wait it out, or tell her everything?"

Love doesn't solve anything but tell that to someone who has just had a relationship end. Suddenly they're "nobody," as the song goes, because they don't have somebody to love them. Regardless of the fact that the great majority of us came into the world alone, most people would much prefer to travel through life as part of a couple rather than cope with going home alone.

The rules for the dating game change after divorce. There's baggage that comes with having been married and someone who has never been married may not wish to get involved with a ready made family or spiteful exes or reduced finances due to child support and alimony payments.

When a marriage ends and new relationships begin before the bitterness has been resolved and the old relationship is put into its proper place in history, the stage is set for more unhappy dating experiences. It takes time to forgive the mistakes of the past so that those mistakes won't invade current and future relationships.

There's a desperate need of newly divorced men and women to prove that they are desirable, to have someone hold them at night, to feel secure in the arms of another. That desperation leads too many people into relationships that have limited futures. In the need for a quick fix for the loneliness they feel and the validation they need, they ignore the warning signs of another relationship that will eventually prove bad for them.

As lonely as being without someone to love may be, it's far more lonely to be trapped in a loveless relationship.

♥

Dear Queenie, I have a girlfriend who is going through a divorce. She and I have been friends for about half of our lives. She started seeing me about two months after she left her husband. We talked at length how this was going to affect our relationship, and was it a wise thing to do, and she said that she did not want to deprive herself of feeling good again because she had been feeling so miserable for so long.

She was going to move in with me, we were going to work through things together, and her little boy was going to live with us as well. All of a sudden, she changes her mind and tells me that she doesn't want a relationship anymore.

I had only moved forward with our relationship at the pace I did because she was telling me she wanted to do all the things she wanted to do. She took most of her stuff and said she needs some time, and doesn't know what she wants.

I want to give her time and I don't want to lose her but what can I do? Do I wait around until she decides she doesn't want me? I mean I love her and she doesn't want to blow our relationship either, but how do I proceed? -- Carl

Carl, she doesn't know what she wants to do. Divorce is very difficult under the best of terms, and having someone who's there to lean on is certainly a plus, as you were for her. Sometimes those feelings of dependence and need mask themselves as love.

She really does care for you, but perhaps her dependence and need are not as great as they were when she first left her husband. She is getting her fear of divorce under control.

She is confused about the fact that maybe she doesn't want to get back into a relationship right now, even with someone as good as you are for her. She needs time and space to work through her feelings.

This will not be easy for you. These types of things never are. What you need to do is re-establish your prior friendship with her. Try to be there for her if she needs you but push back your need for intimacy and commitment with her. At the same time, don't put your life on hold while she sorts things out. Get out, meet people, date. Try to make every effort that this does not ruin a great friendship. -- Queenie

♥

Dear Queenie, I am a divorced woman in her late 20s with one child. I would like advice on how to go about meeting a man for a serious relationship. I have been married for a long time. It has been so long since I have played the dating game, I not sure how to go about it. I don't want to meet someone at a bar or at work.

I see men in the sports I participate in that are attractive but I don't seem to send the right signals to show that I am interested but not desperate. I have been having a hard time meeting a man who does not like to play games and is interested in a serious relationship, especially with a woman with a child.

Could you also give to me advice on what to say to someone that I am interested in, to subtly let him know I am interested and not say something that would turn him off. -- Alice

Alice, since you have a child, perhaps your best approach is to go with your child to places that other parents would go. Not every single parent is female and you might find a man with a child who has the potential to be the perfect partner.

Because you and your child are a package, that is probably your best way to market yourself. A man who expresses interest in you would be expressing interest in the whole package. Take your child to the movies and I'll bet you'll see single dads there. If you see someone interesting go up and ask a question about their child. Same thing for walks in the park or at sports events, the market, etc.

The biggest problem I see is that you don't want to play the dating game, you want to go immediately into a serious and committed relationship. That would scare off most potential life partners because it takes time to build a casual meeting into a serious relationship. Your obvious need for a husband for yourself and father for your child may be scaring off some good men. -- Queenie

♥

Dear Queenie, I was married for 11 years until she decided to screw around. I have been divorced for six months now. The problem I am dealing with is my girlfriend. She is 22 and I am 39. I just don't know how to handle this. So far my not wanting anything serious has kept us out of the bedroom. But she is staying in my house in my guest room. And I really think both of us are getting these feelings, but both are afraid to do anything.

My biggest fear is later on. I would not want to go through the rejection I just went through at 50, and I also have a hard time figuring out why such a young pretty lady wants any thing to do with a old fart like me. I know I am not old but consider the age difference. I have never really had a problem finding a date. So I must not be totally ugly either. I am just confused as hell with this. Any advice would be helpful. -- Chris

Chris, it sounds as though you are facing some midlife issues. Midlife can be a very brutal time in a man's life. You still think it's your fault that your wife messed with someone else, don't you? That you probably weren't young enough or good enough or something else, but it had to be your fault?

You're still in the emotional turmoil that comes from divorce, being the dumped one. You need to get back to feeling good about yourself and that might take a long time. Can you keep reminding yourself that you're really okay? Please try.

I have to ask why this new girlfriend is staying in your guest room. How long have you known her? If it's been for a very short period of time, how did she end up living in your guest room? Even if you've known her for a long time, how did she end up in your guest room?

What I'm trying to get at, right now you're in transition from being married to being single. It's important that you get in touch with the inner you. You're also on the brink of the male midlife stuff, and that might be a bumpy ride. You need to be unencumbered for all of this.

With her in your home, you are putting some very severe limits on what you can and can't do in the near future. How can you date someone else when you have this lady living in your home? And, how can you break up with this woman, gracefully and without a big mess, should it be necessary, when she's living in your home?

You haven't been single in the past 11 years. You need to get comfortable with that. This new girlfriend may or may not be a "transition" girlfriend, one who will get you through a part of the process, but not the one who will end up as your new soulmate. She probably seems to be everything you want in a woman, and she may well be. But a few months from now, as your emotions get into better shape, you may find that she isn't the one you want to spend the rest of your life with.

You need to have the freedom to explore your new world, learn about yourself, expand yourself. If you don't take the time to do this now, she might not be the one who does the rejecting when you're 50, it might be you. Good luck, I'm definitely on your side! -- Queenie

❤

Dear Queenie, I need some serious advice. I am 29 years old, divorced with 2 children. I have not had a serious relationship since my divorce 4 years ago.

I met my boyfriend, 23, 4 months ago and I am in love with him. In the beginning he was the one who was falling in love but I was too scared to answer. I feel he took this as a rejection. I told him a few months ago how I feel, that I love him and he does not answer me. He says he loves to be with me, but that he doesn't know what love is.

I only see him on the weekends and that's a big change considering I used to see him a lot during the week. Have I scared him away from me? Will he ever love me again? I think about him all the time. He doesn't even call me much any more. How can he act like he doesn't care but when I try to end it, he says he doesn't want to lose me, that he cares for me very much and that I need to give it time. Help! -- Carole

Carole, you've only been dating him for 4 months which is not a long period of time. You're significantly older than him (not so much physical age as life experiences), and you represent a lot of new responsibilities for him if this turns into a serious relationship. At 23 he may not be ready to take on the responsibility of a ready-made family no matter how much he likes you.

He may be in love but time is what both of you need in order to learn more about each other to decide if love and commitment are part of your future together.

It might ease things if you let him know you're getting on with your life and that if he should feel that he'd like to be a more important part of your life, you'll be glad to talk about it with him. Then cool down, back off, and don't rush into things with him or anyone. That's what I think. -- Queenie

♥

Dear Queenie, I believe I am a reasonably attractive person with a variety of interests and a multitude of experiences to share. I have a lot of women friends, am involved in charitable/social organizations and am even the head of a single's group. My question is still an age old one. "How do you meet interesting women in this day and age who are not afraid to commit?"

I only say this half in jest because I have been married before, and except for my ex-wife, am still friends with most of my ex-"significant others." However, recently, I broke up with someone I was involved with and she got married within a month after we split. I am not unwilling to become involved and married, but I don't want to make the same mistake.

I am a professional and business man but I am starting to feel that unless I lower expectations, of which I don't think mine are out of line, I will not meet someone else, reasonably attractive, intelligent and willing to become involved in a relationship.

As they (whoever "they" are) seem to say, "all the good ones are taken." I know that isn't true, but do you have any suggestions, or advice. -- Paul

Paul, if you're looking for commitment, as obviously she was, why did the two of you break up? Was she ready but you wanted more time? Had the two of you been dating for several years or only for a few weeks or months? Did she want marriage while you opted for an open relationship?

If it has only been a year or two since your divorce, you may not be ready for another marriage commitment yet. If that is the case, when you date someone who is ready, they (as might be the case with your latest "ex") may give you just so much time and then, regardless of who ends the relationship, find a quick-commitment kind of guy and latch onto him.

Never lower your expectations! That says desperation on your side and what about the woman you choose? What lady would want to find out that she was less than your ideal?

You sound like the kind of man women are looking for so don't give up the search and don't get discouraged. Unless you have extremely out of line requirements, there is a lady who will make you glad you waited and who will show up when you're ready.

If this ideal person does show up, what then? If she has all the right qualifications, and she seems to love you as much as you love her, will you be ready to move to a more committed relationship?

All the good ones aren't taken, but they are not going to stay in a relationship that doesn't go anywhere. That doesn't mean meet her today, marry her tomorrow. It takes time to become comfortable with another person, get past the "perfect manners" and see if family, past baggage, habits, interests, goals, dreams and desires are compatible.

Have you ever noticed that when you least expect something, it happens? Love is very much like that. Go looking for it and it remains elusive. Stop looking, relax, enjoy life, your friends, your interests, and seemingly out of nowhere SHE appears. It'll happen. Trust me. -- Queenie

❤

Dear Queenie, I should be happy but I'm terribly confused! After a long hiatus from romantic encounters, I've met someone I enjoy. But as a single mom who has become accustomed to her own space and time, I'm not as excited about it as I would have been in my youth (I'm 44 and my life is pretty complete with or with out a partner).

I'm flattered and I love going out again, and having a social life. But I don't think this is THE MAN of my life, unfortunately. And I think I'd like to be able to continue looking, but still have some sort of relationship with the current suitor.

We've just begun, the new beau and I, but he feels I'm the one. He's attentive and supportive, all the things we women want in a man. I would like to slow down, and have tried to be honest, but he's just the type who jumps in with both feet, and probably takes a lot of hurtful "hits" for not being more cautious even when warned.

Whenever I see him he has lots of little gifts for me, and he's just aglow with energy and hope. Scares me—I like him, but I don't spend all day looking for little things to do for him. So, I feel guilty as well as conflicted!

Since I've been out of the dating scene for a long time, I'm uncomfortable with a lot of the advice currently out there. It seems things have gotten rather cold and clinical, and people are allowed to do whatever is necessary to get what they need. My friends say as long as I'm not married to the guy, it's none of his business if I date other people. That sounds great, but feels wrong. So what do you think?

Should I just break it off entirely, or is it all right to date him and still keep dating others, when the opportunity arises? Is he moving too fast, and if so how do I say so? I've told him, but he's still going full steam ahead! Must I constantly caution him? Is this the big red flag it seems to be? -- Nora

Nora, I'll tackle your friends' advice first. If something "feels wrong" to you, even though it doesn't feel wrong to them, don't do it. They are not the absolute authorities for what is best for you — you are! Not that I would ever discount what my friends said, absolutely not. Sometimes they have a much clearer understanding of a situation, looking at it without emotional ties, than I might. So, listen to what they have to say, sift through their words of wisdom, and then use what fits well with your philosophies and moral views.

This guy does sound like a dream. What might be happening is you're enjoying the freedom of being your own person and making your own decisions so much that you are putting up barriers to the intimacy of a committed relationship. Nothing wrong with that. Of course, you could end up losing a very good lifemate along the way.

It's a shame, too, since he seems ready for commitment, and he's chosen you. Very flattering. Plus he sticks with it even though you push him away sometimes a bit uncaringly. That shows devotion. Why is it a lot of times we don't hear bells and see the fireworks with the people who appear to be the best suited for us? Of course, the other view is that he really is scared of commitment himself and knows that you won't commit, so he's safe with you. (Interesting angle, huh?)

Yes, he's going too fast, at least he is pushing too fast for commitment from you because you don't feel ready. Someone else might have married him by now.

As far as dating someone else, until you have made a commitment to someone, you aren't required to date only one person. Too many people believe that one or two dates means they're committed. Nope. But please make certain he understands that he doesn't have an exclusive on your time, and then be prepared to accept it when he dates. I, personally, think he'll be much more appealing to you when you see him out with someone else. -- Queenie

♥

Dear Queenie, I have been divorced for a year and have a 4 year old son I am raising on my own. I have not been in a relationship or even on a date since my divorce until a couple months ago when a very close "friend" of mine popped back into my life. He was very up-front about wanting to "see" me regardless of the fact that he "was" a friend of my ex-hubby as well. I was very reluctant about seeing him but after looking at things from his perspective, I decided that this was something I wanted to do.

I have always found my friend attractive, sweet and caring. We started dating and eventually we had sex. I have to admit, I have never been with a man that was this sexually compatible with me. It was almost like a sign that we were meant to be together, but now he tends to be rather distant and moody and anti-social.

I have done nothing wrong and he has even told me that. When I try to talk to him about it, he clams up. What can I do to get him to open up to me so we may be able to be together? I think I have fallen in love with him. Please help! — Lana

Lana, you haven't been divorced long enough to be ready for a long term, committed relationship. He's the first guy who made you feel special but that doesn't mean he's the right guy for you at this time. Considering how strongly you feel and how fast this developed he may be what is known as a "transition lover" -- the first big love after a major relationship fails but not usually the right person for the long term.

His very reluctance to go any farther after being intimate says a lot about him and his possible motives. Forget about getting him to open up. He isn't ready and neither are you. Walk away from him. Be cool, forget about intimacy with him, forget about thinking you've fallen in love.

It takes two people to make a love relationship work even under the best of circumstances. You already know that from having had a marriage end in divorce. Take it slow and easy and let yourself heal from your divorce. And you might want to look for "friends" in a pool other than the one in which your ex swims. — Queenie

♥

Dear Queenie, I started a relationship with a man after 1 year of celibacy and post divorce. I thought I could be involved sexually with no emotional involvement. Not so! Now I am hurting because I have fallen in love with this man. To top things off we have moved to opposite ends of the country.

I have told him how I feel and he has shown some indications that it is not all about sex but how do I get over him? How can I bring him fully into my life? -- Ceil

Ceil, which is it that you want? To get over him or to "bring him fully" into your life? Right now he knows how you feel because you've told him. Apparently he doesn't feel the same way so for the time being the option of getting into a more committed relationship with him doesn't appear to be there. Getting over him means you stop thinking about what could be and start thinking about what is. —Queenie

♥

Dear Queenie, I have been seeing my partner for five months now. We are both in our forties and have been married before. She has three children, I have none. We enjoy a good social and physical relationship.

During an intimate moment I asked if I was making her happy. She said "sometimes." I than asked if she loved me, to which she replied "sorry, but I don't." We both want to continue seeing each other but I am afraid that the future might hold nothing for me but hurt and pain. Should I move on? — Marty

Marty, this lady couldn't have been more honest with you about the status of your relationship together. Is that the type of relationship you want or do you want more? Your answer determines whether you stay or go.— Queenie

♥

Dear Queenie, I am involved in a relationship with a man who believes that we should take it slow. I am really enjoying the pace of our relationship right now, as I went through a painful divorce nearly two years ago after a two year marriage. As a result of my divorce, I understand, and appreciate, taking this new relationship easy.

I can say from my heart that he and I both take this relationship seriously. Neither of us considers it casual; we share a mutual commitment to each other. He is not a man of a lot of words, but his actions speak very loudly to me. He is kind, caring, and very attentive to me. In the time that I have known him, he has not let me down!

I really cherish this man, and the consistent, steady pace our relationship is taking. We have been seeing each other for about ten months now. The relationship that he and I have is unlike anything that I've been involved with in my life. My previous relationships went on, full-steam ahead, where I jumped in with both feet before even thinking. That's definitely not the case this time.

There are times, however, when I betray my own happiness by projecting my thoughts too far into the future. My mind moves fast forward to months from now, sometimes a year from now, wondering where this relationship will be at that time. I wonder how long it is going to take for us to move onto the bigger stuff — such as living together, or, bigger yet, getting married.

I know that he is a planner and that he's got his eye on the future. I am very encouraged by the fact that whenever he talks about his plans for future trips, he always includes me in those plans. After the mistake I made in my marriage, I really think that I now have a wonderful gift in front of me, one that is slowly being unwrapped. I don't want to mess things up by wanting to rip the wrapping paper off the package prematurely. I'd appreciate any advice or thoughts you might have for me. — Wendy

Wendy, you already know what to do. You must respect his need to move slowly with this relationship. He's doing all the right things. Don't doom it by pushing it faster than he's ready for it to be pushed. — Queenie

♥

Dear Queenie, I am 33 years old and the man that I am dating is 48. He treats me better than any man I have ever dated before and he is always thinking of my kids. The problem is he worries about our age difference because he thinks that later on I will want someone younger as he gets older. I don't believe that this will happen because I really love him.

I have never felt this way about anyone before. So, what should I do? I feel like he is my soul mate and that we were meant to be together. Do you think that age should be an issue in a relationship? — Sheila

Sheila, the only time the age difference is important in a relationship is when it bothers one or the other of the people in that relationship. It bothers him so it is a big deal. As far as him worrying about the future, he's wasting the present while he worries about something that may never happen. I think the age difference would be more significant if you were 20 and he was 35. — Queenie

♥

Dear Queenie, I've been divorced for many years and haven't really been interested in a serious relationship since. In fact, I have purposely avoided them, choosing instead to have a series of "sex only" flings that I could get out of easily. When I realized that wasn't really what I wanted either, I stopped and have remained dateless and celibate for the past couple years, just to give myself some time for me, my kids and my career.

I have a good friend that I've known for several years now who I met through a mutual friend . We've become pretty close over the years, go camping together, taking my kids on weekend trips, etc. Sometimes he just comes over and we watch TV and talk until late, then he spends the night on the couch.

He's the extremely shy type and, according to his friends, his last girlfriend was probably 8 years ago or more. Until recently, I've always been sure that we were "just buddies." Lately, however, I sense that he may have more on his mind. He used to always treat me like one of the guys. But now, something seems different and he has started commenting on my appearance, has hugged my for no reason, and talks about "us" taking the kids places or planning things for the future.

I'm not sure how I feel about him. There are times when I think that we're so compatible it's stupid not to pursue a relationship and others when I think that after being friends with someone for so long, you kind of pass up that romance window and it just can't work out. Until now, the decision was easy, because I felt like he either wasn't interested in more or that he was just as leary of risking it as I am.

Am I making too much out of this? Or are these sudden compliments and such, a shy guy's way of hinting at more? I can't decide if I'm hoping that it is, or dreading it.

I've dumped so many men in the past, I'm terrified I'll end up hurting him. I've never dated anyone that I actually cared about before and it scares the hell out of me. Any thoughts? — Marilyn

Marilyn, if this man doesn't have a significant other waiting for him at home then I'd have to guess that he has put you into that category. If he hasn't had a girlfriend for eight or more years, it sounds as though he's ready to move your relationship from friend to lover. If this isn't something you'd like to do at the moment you'd better let him know so that he doesn't assume more than you're willing to give or take your rejection to mean you don't want to have anything to do with him.

I've always thought the best relationships were those built on friendship first. Maybe he's the one man who could be the last man you need to date. — Queenie

♥

Dear Queenie, three years ago I met a woman. I was then a widower for one year. Our relationship was very great from the begining. We have very much in common, a similar attitude on life, love and sex. I was really happy.

We still like each other very much but some uneasiness exists in our relation. She looks at almost every man with long promising glances and tries to flirt with many men I know. We have a very stormy sexual life but I feel sometimes really upset and disappointed.

I have tried many times to confront her about this but she denies doing this and says that all this stuff is my insinuations only. I think I am a bit jealous but her behaviour is so blatant that I feel sometimes as if I am being treated as a mat. — Ken

Ken, perhaps you and she are trying to become too serious too fast. I realize it has been three years since the two of you met, but you had only been widowed for one year at that time and maybe you just weren't quite ready for what has developed and perhaps neither was she.

You mention that you are a bit jealous which could be much more jealous than just "a bit" to her and jealousy might be causing her to search for a way to distance herself from you. If this is a good relationship then talk with her and see where she wants it to go — and you decide what you want from it also. — Queenie

♥

Dear Queenie, I have been friends with this gentleman for three years. He held my hand and picked up the pieces when my husband and I separated, and was there for me through subsequent failed relationships. After the last one, he looked at me and said "Haven't you figured it out by now? I'm the one who loves you."

For the first time I went from liking someone to loving them to being in love with them. We developed our relationship slowly and the intimacy was wonderful but recently he has become more detached.

I'm vague on his comings and goings, he doesn't call as often, and he purposely seems to not do normal daily niceties for me that he does for the random public. Each time I've questioned him denies that he wishes to end the relationship and acknowledges that I have reason to be disappointed.

How do I know if his feelings have changed and he wants out, or if he's angry with me and punishing me for something I know nothing about? — Kitty

Kitty, if you think his feelings have changed then they probably have. Maybe you really aren't ready for a committed relationship yet and it also sounds as though he may have thought he was but has since found that what he thought he wanted and what he really wanted were two different things.

The two of you were great friends but taking the relationship to the lovers stage has created a strain. Instead of questioning whether he wants to end the relationship why don't you tell him you don't think the two of you are ready for a totally committed relationship and that it's time each of you had space to breathe.

If you've always had someone to lean on through your divorce and those other relationships, it's time you experience life on your own and learn some truths about yourself before you get into another serious relationship. Just my opinion.—Queenie

♥

Dear Queenie, I have been dating my current boyfriend for about two months now. During this time we have both fallen deeply in love with each other and know that we want to spend the rest of our lives together. He is 35, divorced with two kids. I am 26, never been married, with no kids.

My question is about the kids. They are a very big part of his life and I have heard all about them. We have had many conversations about the kids, and it has come to the point where he wants to introduce me to them. I want to meet them too, just for the fact that I want to be part of all aspects of his life but I am very nervous and looking for some advice on how to act and what to say to them when we meet.

I have a lot of experience with kids, but I wanted to make sure I do everything right when it comes to his kids, because I plan on being a part of his life, for the rest of my life. Can you give me any advice on what to do? — Candi

Candi, don't try to take the place of their mother and don't try too hard to make them like you. Give them time to get to know and trust you and never try to compare yourself with their mother.

Loving a man with children will provide some strong challenges over the years. You will have to accept that he will get calls from his ex about the children at inconvenient times and that he will spend time with her and them when you'd prefer he was at home. And, the financial obligation may mean giving up some of the things you'd like so that the kids get the things they need.

Make sure you can handle the fact you're adding not only these children but his ex-wife into your life for many years to come.

Some second wives aren't able to cope which is why a lot of second marriages fail. Good luck. —Queenie

♥

Dear Queenie, I am currently dating a woman who recently got a divorce. She still has a lot of things from her divorce such as gifts, cards and dried flowers. I know she doesn't want to throw this stuff away, but I am sick of seeing it around. Would I be right to tell her to get rid of it, or put it away? — Dave

Dave, you might be tired of seeing these things but it's her stuff, her divorce, and it should be her choice as to when, or if, she gets rid of it. —Queenie

♥

Dear Queenie, I'm confused with this guy I met. He has been divorced for several years and so have I. We both have kids and we are both very single. We kiss and fool around and he e-mails me and calls me every night, one or the other but he says we are just friends. That is fine but he has told a close friend that he cares a lot about me although he doesn't know that this other friend and I know each other.

Recently he has been traveling and he has written and e-mailed me 3 times while he's been gone. If we are just friends why is writing and calling all the time. I could see once a week and I sure wouldn't call a friend on vacation, I would be enjoying the getaway.

So what do you think is going on? And is he the one that is falling in love? Yes I do care a lot about him and yes he knows. But he says we are just friends. — Rhonda

Rhonda, does your dating book have specific guidelines as to how many times a friend calls a friend and how many times a lover would call? I haven't seen any such guidelines.

Quit trying to analyze this relationship and his actions and slow down. There isn't a need to rush into another relationship — and that's perhaps why he keeps saying you're just friends even though he's very much attracted to you. Slow down and this relationship might turn into something more. —Queenie

♥

Dear Queenie, I am a 23 year-old woman who is dating a 29 year-old man who left his wife one day after their one-year anniversary. We started dating several months later. I know he didn't have enough time to heal from his broken marriage but things really clicked with us and now

I'm having a hard time with him working through the pain of his divorce. I know he loves and cares about me but I have a hard time hearing him talk about loving someone else.

I know he is dealing with a lot of feelings, and I want to be there for him, but I hate that he has shared such a special relationship with someone else. How can I get over my feelings and be there for him without being hurt that he's thinking of her when he's with me?? Thanks for any advice.
— Coral

Coral, you started dating him too soon after his marriage ended. If I read you right, he's now working through the legalities of the divorce itself and may be having some second thoughts about having left his wife.

If you're not willing to help him work through his feelings then do him a favor and back out of this relationship. He's the one who is hurting. You're jealous because he actually loved someone before you met him. He can't turn off his emotions just because you want him to, he has to work through them. Be glad. Otherwise, even if things got serious between the two of you, he'd be able to walk away from you and not look back. –Queenie

♥

Dear Queenie, I have dated a man for two years and we are absolutely best friends. The problem is that I have a real fear of marriage after having a bad one and he wanted to know if I could ever marry again and have another child. He didn't like my answer so he ended our relationship.

Now that he is not in my life I miss him so bad and feel that I really wrecked something that could've been beautiful. I told him that I have had a reality check and that I am willing to marry for the sake of having him in my life if thats what he wants. He feels now that he needs space. How much time should I wait? I feel like I'm dying a slow death. — Nanci

Nanci, when he asked you for a commitment, you weren't ready so the relationship ended. When it ended, it caused the both of you a great deal of pain. You're ready to change your life to get him back into your life, and he needs time to decide if it's the right move based on your prior response.

My question is this: are you ready to do as he wants just because you're lonely or because you truly believe it is the best thing to do? If it isn't the best thing, if you have any doubts at all, accept the pain and let this relationship cool down for a while. You cannot rush into something this important. If you really are ready for the type of commitment he wants, give him time and if this is meant to be, he'll come back. —Queenie

❤

Dear Queenie, I am very much in love with a man who is 54. I am 31 and divorced recently although the marriage ended several years ago. Since I began the new relationship I have been faithful to him and honest. My ex continuously hopes for reconciliation and I continually refuse him. I have made it clear to both men that the old relationship is over for good.

I have to see my ex occasionally because of our daughter and I want to keep a friendly relationship with him for her sake. My boyfriend has up to now understood and encouraged me in this regard. However, he's tired of my ex's constant attempts to get back together. I can't say I blame him. He's had far more patience that I would have. However, now he's given me an ultimatum. He's leaving if I don't cease contact with my ex.

How do I keep the peace? Will he be able to get over this? He's not a jealous person — he's just tired and frustrated. My ex has recently started to work on our daughter so that she gives the boyfriend a hard time. I feel like I'm presiding over a high-school. Please help. — Toni

Toni, it's too bad your daughter has to be the one who will suffer the most in this twisted little game. She loves you both and only wants to have a happy home. Your ex is being unfair but that's probably why he's your ex — that and a lot of other things that broke the marriage. If your ex is about your same age your boyfriend might also be apprehensive that he can't compete with a much younger man in the long term.

I can't tell you how to handle your ex, your boyfriend and your daughter but it sounds as though counseling might help your daughter so that she will better understand why moms and dads aren't always able to live together and so that she'll have some emotional protection from the game playing she's being put through. You cannot cut all contact with your ex because of his role as dad but if you can cut out excessive contact, that's a start.

As far as your boyfriend, he needs to understand that your role as mother comes first and you must do whatever is necessary for the well-being of your daughter which means occasional contact with her father. Your ex and you are tied together for a long time because of your parental responsibilities and if your boyfriend can't handle it, he's going to be the big loser because there are plenty of men who will be able to take the heat of the ex. —Queenie

♥

Dear Queenie, I am 31 years old. I was dating a man 50 years old for a little over 6 months. I fell in love, and wonder if he did the same. We stopped dating earlier this year. He broke it off because he had separated from his wife due to her infidelity and he was not ready to become involved. He did tell me this during the course of our relationship, I just didn't listen.

He is a very good man who just loved his wife and children very much, and does not want to accept that it is over. He could have used me, but he cared too much to do such a thing. He and I work together, and up until now, things have been pretty awkward. He wasn't even able to look at me at first and now he is beginning to talk to me again.

If I want him back, what do I do? He made it clear on several occasions that I treated him better than any other woman, and had he not just went through this with his wife, he would have wanted to marry me. I know his self esteem is in the dumpster, and I do not want to get hurt again. -- Nicky

Nicky, if you want guarantees that you'll never get hurt in another relationship then I'd suggest you get yourself a dog. Otherwise, take your chances on the people you are most in tune with and let the fates have their way.

You already know what's wrong here, he was involved with you too soon. He needs at least a full year after his divorce is final to get himself together, maybe much longer, but since men generally have a tendency to jump into relationships quicker than they should, if you let him go, someone else will grab him and you'll be left to kick yourself for waiting for him to heal. So, if he's shy and old-fashioned, take it very slowly and let him make the moves. He knows what to do; let him set the pace. —Queenie

♥

Dear Queenie, three months ago my ex-girlfriend dumped me, gently, but it hurt and our relationship was very intense. A question of bad timing, I think. She had just come out of a violent relationship and has only recently got divorced.

She had a lot of problems but I loved her and didn't think this would matter. I was wrong, sadly. In fact, at times she has been very nasty to me and I've taken it full on the chin every time. I don't know why I allowed myself to fall in love with her. Normally I would be more careful. I was stupid, I think.

I still love her and we are still friends. I'm hoping that she will get over her past traumas and that we will be able to pick up our relationship

again. I've been hurting so much and this relationship has made me ill at times and I don't know how I've managed to pass my exams. I put all of my effort into this relationship and now I'm faced with the vacuum.

I have a great job to look forward to and it's not as if I have any trouble meeting new girls. The thing is that I'm not really interested in anyone else but perhaps sleeping around would help me to detach myself from this relationship. Do you have any advice? She is 32 and I'm 23. — Paul

Paul, sleeping around isn't going to make you mature. Getting a grip on yourself and realizing that a woman who has been in a violent marriage has a lot of emotional problems to work through before she can handle a normal relationship might. At 32, with her history, she is light years ahead of you emotionally.

Focus on your education and that great job and let time heal her wounds. Maybe in a few years the two of you will be more suited to each other. Maybe not. —Queenie

❤

Dear Queenie, I've been involved with a wonderful man for about eight months. He is so perfect for me. He is extremely handsome, sexy, and kind. He graduated at the top of his class from a prestigious university, is very healthy and health conscience. He doesn't drink or smoke, he's thoughtful, laid back, and sophisticated. In a nut shell, he's the strong, but silent type.

I was a little apprehensive in telling him about my son because I didn't think that I'd continue to see him, but he pursued me until I returned his phone calls and at least heard him out. He was very complimentary about me taking such good care of my son while holding down a full time job and attending college in the evening.

He has made it known on a couple of occasions that he'd like for us to start as friends first. I was all for that and flattered that he felt that I was worth knowing and savoring a friendship. At the same time, I want him in more ways than just a friend and I think it's starting to show.

Lately, I've been having feelings that this relationship is going to crash and burn any minute because things are just a little too perfect. I've been wanting to just let it all go because I'm afraid of the pain that comes with falling in love, especially if you're falling in love by yourself.

I've recently accused him of seeing someone else because when he said he would call, he didn't. He said that he's been busy with work which is believable because he works odd hours. I have never felt so insecure and without confidence in my entire life and I am trying very hard to not show

it because this is really not me. I mean, I have to constantly tell myself that "we are just friends, he is entitled to see whomever he pleases until we define this relationship as more."

I've been considering other dates so that I can at least stop thinking constantly about him. I was thinking that it would help curb my appetite for him until he is ready to fully give himself to me. At the same time, I don't want to risk losing him.

I know I should slow down and "just let whatever happens happen" as he puts it, but I'm a very honest person and it's hard for me to repress such strong feelings. Do you have any little smidgen of advice that will help me to withstand these feelings and give me a little more confidence, patience, and resilience? I want him now! -- Crystal

Crystal, if you know you should slow down so you don't run him off, so you don't ruin this relationship, so you don't get hurt yet again, why don't you?

If you and he don't have a commitment, then it's time you started dating others. Let him see that you are secure and confident in addition to being desireable to more than one person (him). Either he is going to start chasing you or he isn't. If he doesn't then you haven't lost anything, just gained an answer (even though it isn't the one you want).

Keep up as you are and you most certainly may lose him. — Queenie

♥

Dear Queenie, I'm a single mother of a one-year-old, and been going to school for the past year. I'm really good friends with my teacher, and lately been very attracted to him. I've been getting hints from him back to me, but he's extremely hesitant. I just can't shake this one off. He's such a good friend, and he's very good with my daughter.

How do I get him to notice me a little more since I'm just about finished school, and want to move on with him? He always says he doesn't want to go out with anyone with a kid, but he's been the one who's been making the moves on me lately. How do I know when to bite the bullet and do something about this? -- Kate

Kate, I suspect he might be very interested but may wish to stay uninvolved until you're no longer his student. It would seem to be the ethical approach.

After you're no longer in a student-teacher relationship, if he hasn't invited you out, why not invite him over for a nice home cooked meal and see how he relates with your daughter. I suggest this because if he really isn't interested in dating someone with a child, you don't want to get into a "no win" relationship in which you and your daughter come out losers. -- Queenie

♥

Dear Queenie, I am a 41 year old divorced female who has been dating a man 39 for about a year. It was a good relationship and we became very close, were very compatible and I felt that we were the best of friends as well as lovers. My boyfriend lost his job in this area and found another job halfway across the country. Before he left, we spent 4 days in a bed and breakfast at the coast and we had a great time.

While we were there he finally told me that he loved me and when we returned home, he cried that now he had to come home to pack and move away. His new job is a temporary job and we both felt it would be foolish for me to leave my job and home to go with him. He talked about looking for permanent work and he asked me what city I would be interested in moving to. I felt that our relationship was becoming more serious.

A few weeks after he moved things changed. It's been 3 months since he left and now he tells me he loves me but only as a friend. He still calls me and tells me he misses me, he loves me, he wishes I was there with him but he doesn't want us to visit because he feels it will be maintaining the relationship and just postponing the breakup.

He told me not to wait for him and so I told him that I was going out and meeting new people, not dating or sleeping around. He got very upset and said that he knew that was the way things are supposed to be but he couldn't deal with it right now. One time on the phone he cried that he couldn't stand the thought of me being with someone else.

I am terribly confused. If we are just good friends and not lovers then why would he tell me he loves me and cry and get upset about me being with someone else if he feels we have no future together. Is he not in touch with his true feelings, is he lying to himself or me or is he totally confused about our relationship? How should I handle this man? I feel that if there is no future between us and we're not seeing each other then I need to move on with my life and find someone who loves me and wants a future. -- Mame

Mame, you cannot put your life on hold while he gets in touch with his. What happens if he gets in touch but decides you're not the person he wants for a long term commitment?

Continue to take control of the situation and your life. He, of course, would like you to stay completely available should he decide to return. That shouldn't be an option. He'll have more incentive to make a decision about the relationship if he knows that someone else may discover you and want to make you the star of their life drama. -- Queenie

♥

Dear Queen of Hearts, I'm a 53 year old man who has been divorced twice and have three children. I've found a lovely philippina girl 20 years old who says she wants me and that age is not important. Should I go for it? -- Sam

Sam, does she want you or does she want the security you can provide? If you love her and you're sure she loves you, if you think you can handle the age and cultural differences, if you've given this a lot of thought, do what makes you happy. -- Queenie

♥

Dear Queenie, I met a guy 2 years ago, we started out as friends. He has been going thru a nasty divorce, then last year I hadn't heard from him for a couple of months and then he calls to tell me he had cancer surgery and was going through radiation which is why he hadn't called.

We became more than just friends, and he seems to get closer then just pulls away, doesn't call for a while, then he becomes even more passionate and then he just cuts me off. He hasn't made any promises and he was upfront about seeing other women and he tells me all the time he doesn't feel comfortable with himself yet he says he doesn't want to be committed and he really hasn't dated anyone. I mean, what am I?

His behavior goes from erratic to down to earth. I know I should just accept that there's nothing between us and move on and I'm trying to, but what if he calls again? I really care for him and he knows it. Should I just treat him like he's treated me? -- Mavis

Mavis, this man has had two traumatic experiences in less than two years -- divorce as well as cancer. Do you have any idea how even one of those things can screw up a person's perspective on life and relationships?

Yes he's going to be erratic. It goes with the territory. What that means is that anyone close to him either learns to weather the storms or they back off until the storms are over and hope they're still a part of his life.

The man you met two years ago is not the same as the man you know today. Maybe there isn't anything left of the relationship the two of you once shared. His feelings have changed as they would with such trauma.

Should you blow him off, treat him the way he has treated you? It's an immature response and not worthy of you so I wouldn't suggest it. You're hurt and that's a normal thought but try to get past it and if he does contact you try to start fresh and see if there are any common areas left between the two of you that could build into a good relationship. -- Queenie

♥

Dear Queenie, a lady I know is going through divorce. We have been friends for 20 some years and at times more than that. She now tells me that she is not sure what she wants.

I recently saw her out with another guy and this upset me and I'm not quite sure how to handle it. I have to know where I fit in to the big picture. What advice can you give me? -- David

David, let her live her life the way she sees fit. Apparently, since the two of you have been "more than" friends at times, you feel she now belongs to you.

The fact is, she's going through a divorce and she has a major batch of emotions that need to be taken care of before she's going to know what she wants to do with the rest of her life. That means she's not ready (nor willing) to make a commitment to anyone at this time. Actually, until the divorce is final, she isn't legally able to make a commitment.

Most "experts" suggest a divorced person wait a minimum of one year after the divorce is legalized to even begin making any kind of relationship commitments. It takes that long (and usually much longer) to work through all the emotional garbage divorce brings out. -- Queenie

♥

Dear Queenie, I am a mid-30s woman with no kids and have been divorced for 6 yrs. Do you agree that it is difficult to find someone to be in an intimate relationship if you are spending a lot of time with platonic friends of the opposite sex?

Also, do you think it is unrealistic of me to be holding out for a man who enjoys dancing as much as I do and who can also talk about his emotions?

I facilitate a relationship workshop for single adults which makes it even more difficult for me to find someone, because most of the men I meet become intimidated when I tell them about it. I don't tell them about it

right away. Even though it is an important part of my life, would it be better if I didn't mention it until we have become intimate? -- Jewel

Jewel, honesty is a prime qualification of a good relationship so holding back information that you consider important until you've become intimate doesn't seem like a good idea.

The difficult part of finding a relationship partner (of the intimate kind) when you're spending a lot of time with opposite sex platonic friends is that potential partners may see you with someone, think there is more going on between the two of you than mere friendship, and not even try to strike up a conversation.

On the other hand, it can be tremendous fun to pal around with friends of either sex since there are no pressures of commitment, friends allow you to be yourself without being judgmental, and they're less apt to dump you when someone younger or prettier or more successful comes around.

If it was me, I'd hold out for a dancing partner. Life's too short to spend it sitting out your favorite dances. -- Queenie

♥

Dear Queenie, I have a friend I care very deeply about, who is going through his second divorce. We have known each other for over 20 years and we dated several times in school and after his first divorce.

We began seeing each other several months ago but are supposedly just friends. It is very hard for me because I care about him a lot, he is really hurting from this divorce and does not want to go through this hurt again.

How can I make him see that all women are not alike? I know that time should heal all wounds but I'm afraid of losing him a third time but I don't want to hold too tight either. Please give me some advice as how I should handle this situation. -- Myra

Myra, because you care so much for him you feel that you must shoulder some of his pain. Unfortunately, this is a growth time for him and he needs to work through this pretty much on his own.

If you and he fall into a "rebound " relationship, which could happen considering his pain and your feelings for him, when he's worked through a lot of his emotional baggage, the two of you may no longer be a good fit.

Do you want to risk your long term friendship, and the possibility of even more, by getting too close too soon? Besides, until he is legally divorced he's still a married man, which should put him off limits for anything more than a casual friendship. -- Queenie

♥

Dear Queenie, I am a 53 year old male who longs to be in a full time, committed relationship. I have had many, many relationships over the years, but none have ever worked out.

I am currently living with a 35 year old woman who has 3 small children. She is recently divorced, and started dating me before her divorce was even final. We have been together every day since then. We are happy and she says she loves me, and I know I love her and her children.

She is very beautiful and could have any man she wanted. I am, at best, marginal looking. She certainly doesn't want me for my money, as I have very little. I have been told I have a good personality, but wonder how far this will take me in this relationship!

She is currently a full time student, and I am working full time in a dead end job that pays adequately, but not well. What chance do you give this relationship to blossom into a permanent situation? I would like to marry this woman, but am afraid to get my hopes up. What is your opinion of May/December relationships such as this? I often think that my relationships don't work out because I choose the wrong women. -- Henry

Henry, many May/December relationships and December/May relationships work just as well or even better than relationships where the persons involved are close to the same age. So that shouldn't prove a problem.

What I see in what you have written is that you seem to have a terrible inferiority complex. You are negative about your looks and you're in a job that doesn't make you happy. Who has made you feel that you are not as good as anyone else in this world? As long as you have such a low opinion of yourself, and such a negative outlook on your future, you'll not have too much success with the long term.

Most women would take a good personality along with faithful, hard working, honest, truthful, trustworthy, over the gorgeous hunk any day. Hard to believe, I suppose, since men seem to go for looks first and will trade good personalities for good bodies without thinking twice.

Women can appreciate a good looking guy but most women also understand that looks are "skin deep" and there are greater values that don't diminish with age. You're a prize so start thinking of yourself as one! Get some confidence!

Is there a reason you can't improve your job circumstances? What happens when she graduates and gets a more responsible job than you? Not only is your already low opinion of yourself going to sink lower, her job advances matched with your dead end spot just might sabotage your relationship.

Why do you think you choose the wrong women? Do you usually go for looks instead of substance?

You have one life. Make the best of it! -- Queenie

♥

Dear Queenie, I started going out with my girlfriend about three and a half months ago. Since then, I have come closer to her than I have ever felt about anyone in my entire life. Not even my ex-wife made me feel the way she does.

When we met, she told me most of her friends were guys which I don't have a problem with. The problem that I have been having though is that everytime we go to an event where most of her friends are, in particular the guys, the greetings that I'm seeing seem to be a little inappropriate. I'm used to a hug and a kiss being a standard greeting of affection among friends. But there is always one or two that seem to want to hold on to her extra tight and give her extra kisses a little too close to the lips. She doesn't say much to them either.

I have confronted her about this and she doesn't seem to understand the problem that I am having with it, especially since I have never put her in this situation. I know that it may mean nothing to her, but I feel as if I'm not getting the respect I deserve as the love of her life when we are in theses situations.

I would not do allow this type of behavior to go on between me and my female friends especially when she is there because I am sensitive to how she may feel in that situation. Maybe this is the way she was with her friends before she met me and that's fine. Even though to her all of it may mean nothing, I feel like now that she's with me, she should be telling them that it's not appropriate.

I really want to make our relationship work, and I don't want to ruin it by being the jealous type of boyfriend and thinking things that don't exist. I just want to know if I am wrong for feeling the way I do? Should I change the way I feel about the situation, or should she be doing things differently?? Please help. -- Chris

Chris, you are being possessive and you don't trust her. You've been together for three and a half months. You say you deserve the respect of her friends for being "the love of her life." Have you asked her to marry you? Are the two of you planning how many children you're going to have? Are you looking for houses to buy? Have you talked about your goals for the future? Are you in a committed, for life, relationship with each other?

You say "I would not do allow this type of behavior to go on between me and my female friends especially when she is there." Does this mean you would allow such behavior in private with your female friends? Would you prefer she allow such behavior only when you're not around? If so, I think her approach is a more honest one.

I may be missing something here, but I think you're going to ruin a good thing with jealousy. -- Queenie

❤

Dear Queenie, I've been dating a very good, kind, man for a year and a half. We do not live together, we both have children and have both been divorced for approximately 4 years. We love each other.

I have been feeling a need to have him more in my life and to start blending our families more. He is afraid he cannot give me the affection I truly need. He says something inside him just shuts down and he can allow himself to feel only so much.

He said he wants to see a counselor about this because it really bothers him. He knows he loves me, but feels he won't be able to make me happy because he can't give all of himself to me.

I am at a loss. Here is a man I truly love. He loves me and says that he see us together. Now he is asking for "time" to think about it. At first he said we were done because he just didn't think he could fix the problem within himself. Then he said to just give him some time.

I don't want to throw this relationship away, but I don't want to be a chump either. What should I do? -- Olivia

Olivia, men and women view relationships differently for the most part. Men get comfortable in a relationship (as he has in yours) and they don't see a need to take it further if it works just fine as it is. He has what he needs, he feels no need to get married.

Women, for the most part, want the legal commitment of marriage. They feel insecure without it. They cannot understand why their partner doesn't feel the same way.

There's nothing wrong with either view of relationship commitment, until the views conflict, then it becomes necessary that one or the other compromise if the relationship is to continue. Either you accept his way or he accepts yours or you come up with a third option that is acceptable to both of you.

He realizes he may lose you if he doesn't make the commitment you require. He doesn't want to lose you so he is trying to change himself. It won't be easy but he's willing to give it a try. Counseling is a big step.

If you want to speed him up, give him a firm deadline and stick to it. Love is a gamble. How much are you willing to risk? How much is he? -- Queenie

♥

Dear Queenie, I am a 35 year old, single man who is fit, financially secure and in good health. Just over a year ago, work transferred me to a new city where I quickly met and became friends with my co-workers, many of whom were also new to town. Particularly, I have enjoyed the friendship of two married couples.

From the first time I met the wife of one of these couples, I was attracted to her. Being married, however, I resigned myself to a friendship which was simply more meaningful on my end. Far from obsessing over her, I dated off and on continually looking for someone I could be happy with. This being said, I'm afraid that my fondness for this lady was hard to conceal. Even her husband made quiet jokes about it, usually after we had been drinking or if he and I were alone.

Nonetheless, we all continued this friendship and I continued with my search. Several weeks ago, however, her husband left her. She was devastated and I've been trying to be the best friend I can throughout this whole ordeal.

I think this is the best thing that could have happen to her. She's got her head on straight. She has the motivation now to make some career moves that she has always wanted to try and she really seems to be enjoying her new found independence. She still goes through periods of anger and grief for 5 years of marriage that was trashed.

As for our relationship... it still remains friendly. Obviously, I have high hopes for its future being more significant. I know, however, now's not the time to press for that. I keep fighting off urges to confess my feelings for her, all the time wrestling with the fact that she probably already knows.

The divorce is going to happen, that's a guarantee. Should I continue as a friend, and meanwhile date other people, figuring that we'll grow closer together when the time is right and if it were "meant" to be? Should I do as many things as I can with her, all the while encouraging a closer friendship? Should I go for broke and confess my infatuation with her?

What is the time-line for separation/divorce and new relationships? Are there stages that women go through? Wildness, partying, depression? Is it true what they say about rebound-relationships, that they never work out? What should I be looking for to make a move? Thanks for your advice.
-- Norman

Norman, you have a lot more questions than I have answers. However, I do think any move is premature until the divorce is final. The time frame for serious dating or any kind of big decisions is at least one year from the time of legal divorce and it may be much longer depending upon the intensity of the break-up and the length of the marriage.

That may seem like a long time and you're right, it can be. But there are a lot of emotions that have to be sorted out and taken care of when a marriage ends when that divorce decree is final.

This will be a time for her personal growth. She will make mistakes. She will date people who are wrong for her. She may even fall into rebound love. She will be discovering herself. She will need a good friend who can be there when she needs someone in whom to confide. It sounds as though you fit that description. Are you up to the task without letting your infatuation get in the way?

You can confess your feelings after the divorce is final, but she may be afraid to enter into any serious relationships for quite some time. She may prefer to keep relationships light and uncommitted. If she does get involved, the relationships may not last. You might be on much safer ground by being best friends for a while. My thoughts, anyway. -- Queenie

❤

Dear Queenie, I'm a single male parent of two children and I have been divorced for 6 years. There is a co-worker that I am extremely interested in starting a relationship with. We have worked together in the same office for over a year now. She is also a single parent.

I have been out of the dating scene for quite a while. How do I go about telling this woman that I am very interested in starting a romantic relationship with her? I asked her out for dinner and a movie about 6 months ago and she said maybe another time.

We sometimes go out for drinks with other co-workers and at times I feel that she may be interested in getting to know me better. She does things like patting my hand or arm while talking to me, etc. Is this a sign that maybe she is interested in possibly starting a relationship? -- Earl

Earl, some people are more "touchy, feely" than others, so she may be doing this patting without thinking about it. On the other hand, she may be trying to tell you that it's time for you to ask her out again.

Going out on a date and starting a relationship should not be said in the same sentence. Not every first date begins a relationship, nor should it, although that thinking is what gets too many people in a lot of trouble.

Your question makes it seem that your current interest in this lady is to hit the sack with her, and she would probably be much more comfortable if she thought you were interested in getting to know her as a friend before getting her into bed.

You didn't ask, but I have to stick my two cents in anyway: dating a co-worker is asking for trouble. What do you do if the relationship goes sour? Some companies prohibit this activity between co-workers and with sexual harrassment suits and everything else that can happen, it's a good idea (at least in my opinion) to look for love outside of the office. -- Queenie

♥

Dear Queenie, how does an alone and lonely young 64 yr old semi-retired professional meet and or communicate with 55+ ladies? -- Frank

Frank, I'm happy you're looking for ladies in your age range! That's the best way to have something to talk about right from the start. What are your interests and hobbies? What do you like to do? What may seem to be a world without very eligible ladies will reveal itself to be filled with ladies who would enjoy your company if you'll look around and really open your eyes.

When you notice a single lady or two or three ladies out together, and one in particular strikes your fancy, do you hesitate about talking to her? You shouldn't. When you see someone you'd like to meet, walk up and say something like, "Excuse me for interrupting, but I just couldn't help but notice what beautiful eyes you have (or what lovely hair you have... etc). My name is Frank, what's yours?" If she's interested in continuing the conversation, she will. If not, she won't.

Not every contact will turn into something, but if you don't make the effort it's guaranteed nothing will happen. Each attempt will be easier and if you know that sooner or later your efforts will be rewarded by meeting that special person, you won't mind the attempts that don't pan out. -- Queenie

♥

Dear Queenie, I am a respectable gentleman 60 years of age that has been divorced for 6 years after 29 years of marriage and 7 kids. Over the past 6 years, I have found only one relationship that in the end did not work out. Someone give me some advice on how I am missing the boat. I am extremely lonely but just can't find the right one! -- Dan

Dan, looking for love in some ways is like buying a car. If you're looking for a particular make and model, it may take quite a long time, particularly if you're searching for a classic in good repair. If you have your heart set on specific requirements, a certain year, automatic or stick shift, under 100k miles — you'll have to search more than if you just walk into a showroom or onto a car lot and say, "I'll take that one over there." Of course, the one in the showroom may look nice but it might not have everything you require to really be happy.

What type of woman are you searching for? Are you trying to meet women who are significantly younger than yourself? Have you cleared yourself of ill feelings about your divorce or do they carry over into your relationship requirements? Do you have a network of friends, both male and female? Do you belong to clubs? Do you have hobbies? Do you socialize?

When was the last time you saw a lady you would like to meet, looked her in the eye, and smiled? And when she returned your smile, did you then say, "Hi, my name is Dan, and I think we used to work at (your company's name) together." Even if she says no, at least you will have opened the door for more dialogue if she's interested in continuing the conversation.

Don't take it personally if every contact doesn't work out. The more you get out and meet people, the more chance you have of meeting someone special. -- Queenie

♥

Dear Queenie, I need help finding the time to start again. I've been so busy at work and doing everything to keep the house going too (it's currently on the market so I can move to a condo) that I don't seem to find time to go where I could meet new men with similar interests, etc.

It's been overwhelming at times to restructure my life again so that I can have time for meeting new people. What do you suggest? I am ready to start but don't know how to begin! -- Nita

Nita, major life changes can be overwhelming, but part of that extreme activity can be the very thing that keeps us from going crazy with time on our hands.

If you're now at a spot where you think you can make time to start meeting people again, sit down in a comfortable chair, put your feet up, take a note pad and pencil and list everything that you absolutely must do. Add in quality time for yourself. Do you have time to meet and socialize? If not, can you make time?

Do you have a hobby? Are there specific sports in which you have an interest? What about volunteer groups in your area? How about business socials? Turn this into a game and relax and enjoy. It's amazing what happens when you stop being stressed about meeting someone. -- Queenie

♥

Dear Queenie, I have been a widow for a year. My children are grown and out on their own. I still work full time. I am 50 years old, still attractive but I haven't been on a date in over 30 years. How do I start now? I am shy but I like to go out and have a good time. -- Cathy

Cathy, identify the things that most interest you and get involved in them. If you have a hobby, join a club. If you like to dance or would like to learn, find a dance club or take lessons. If you like to travel, join a travel group.

Does your church have a singles group? Does your community have a singles group? How about volunteer work? Or join the local chamber of commerce and attend their social gatherings. Go back to school either as a volunteer or as a student. Open a part-time business.

Your interest in the world around you will translate into enthusiasm for being where you are, no matter where you are! People, both male and female, like to be around others who enjoy themselves. -- Queenie

♥

Queenie, I keep getting into relationships where after awhile my partner finds a reason to have an affair. This started with the one relationship before my marraige, happened in my marriage and continues with post marraige relationships. They are different each time, but with the same conclusion.

Am I attracted to a type of woman that is predisposed to cheating? I hear all the time from them that I am a special, tender, caring, and loving man, that the sex is great and that they have never known a man like me. So if I am so special, why do they want to destroy the relationship? — Scott

Scott, possibly you *are* drawn to the wrong type of woman. Sometimes counseling can uncover the emotional needs that make one type of person more attractive than another. When that type of person is destructive to us, we can then learn how to avoid them. Do you understand what I am suggesting? —Queenie

Dating with Issues

Dating with Issues

*"I am 46-year old divorced female involved with a 30-year old
never married male. We argue a lot, mostly because he says
that I am insensitive to his feelings."*

This is a continuation of "Looking for Love" that could be
sub-titled "Sure We're Wrong for Each Other, But How Can We Make
Our Relationship Work?"

Going on a date doesn't mean a relationship is the natural
next step. Dating is simply the mechanism to separate acceptable
potential mates from the unacceptables.

As the spinster lady who lived next door used to say: "You
have to kiss a lot of toads, but don't let any of them close enough to
give you warts or your prince won't take a second glance."

❤

*Dear Queenie, I'm at an impasse with my girlfriend of over 4 years.
Our relationship began after she was dumped by a man who is in a high
profile job. She's also a high profile person with a very strong ego and she
loved being in the limelight with the movers and shakers. I couldn't provide
that environment for her but, we seemed to flourish, nevertheless.*

*We've had many memorable times over the years but I'm starting
to feel my life is not moving forward toward some form of commitment,
which I want. Actually I'm not sure she hasn't made a commitment.*

*I firmly believe she loves me, but she is unwilling to make any
changes from the lifestyle she has lived for the past 20 years. She raised a
daughter herself, owns her own home, and earns a good living in her work,
which she would leave if I asked her to, yet I am unable to support her
lifestyle on her terms if I were to do so, so I don't ask.*

*I'm low profile but not devoid of an ego and over the years I
swallowed it plenty of times, and would continue to do so if I could see
some concilliation from her. Yet the appearance of her inability to value my
opinions and ideas as valid, or even to humor me from time to time, drives
me crazy, and has caused me to go into some behavior I don't like.*

*I'm starting to feel the only course to take is a fresh one, but I love
this woman and feel I would be giving up if I let it go. She is very strong
willed, but that I view as an asset, and part of why I love her. We are both
contemplating that separation is the only way but I am not sure that there
is no common ground. What do you think? -- Stone*

Stone, good relationships are built on compromises. It would
be nice if that meant each person compromised equally but we don't

live in an ideal world so it means that sometimes, when you truly love someone, you must push your feelings aside and accept your loved one, "warts and all," as the saying goes.

You came into this lady's life when she was in pain from a broken love affair. No doubt your attention and caring were most welcome and deeper feelings have developed, perhaps even love. The possibility is, however, that the two of you are too different in your lifestyle needs that the relationship can't go too much further without one or the other of you giving up some pretty important ground.

Would it be fair that she give up the limelight and high profile lifestyle that she enjoys? Would it be fair that you re-invent yourself to fit into a lifestyle you don't enjoy?

Once the glow of the romance settles into commitment, all the differences will magnify themselves and unless the both of you are willing to work very, very hard, the relationship will turn sour. The feelings you have right now about how she treats you are only the beginning. Your poor behavior can only harm the situation.

When we love someone we must love them for all the things that they are — not love them if they will change to meet the vision we have of them. If you want and need a woman who is lower profile, who can live within your means, who doesn't need the limelight, look for that type of person. Don't find the opposite and then try to exercise your control to have her give up that which she needs and cherishes in order to show how much she truly loves you.

Love is not a contest in which each player shows how much they can sacrifice for the other person. It is a teamwork effort, with balances and counterbalances for the life of the relationship. The give and take is rarely 50-50.

Will you be better off without her so you don't have to worry about her lifestyle, her strong will, the things you can't provide for her on your own? Or would you be better off loving her as she is, accepting the limitations of the relationship, using your low profile approach to life as a counterpoint to her strong ego? It could be a very good match!

How does she feel about the relationship? Does she want it to continue? You say she would leave her work if you asked her, that you firmly believe she loves you, and that you're not sure she hasn't made a commitment.

That sounds as if she's also pretty deep into this relationship. Does she need more, or does she want the relationship to remain where it is?

If both of you have the same strong feelings about the relationship, if this is not just a one-sided effort, then you might want to separate. See how the rest of the world is doing, consider life away from each other. You'll either come back together determined to commit, or the relationship will dissolve. Either way, you'll have your answer. -- Queenie

♥

Dear Queenie, I am a 25 year old woman who has lost herself in a love relationship and can't find the answers. Please help me! You see, when I was 18, I met this guy who I thought would someday be my husband but it didn't quite work out that way. We started out good, he would go out with the guys during the day and call me up later to go out at night.

The problem at that time was that my mother wanted me in by 11:30. So, I asked if we could get together earlier. Okay no problem he said. Everything seemed to be working out until we moved in together after the birth of our child. When I moved in with him, I felt he started taking me for granted. He never wanted to do anything anymore. All he did was work, play ball, and come home to sleep.

When I asked if we could talk, he always said not now I don't have time. Then I would write a letter asking if he would talk when he got home. He replied "yeah okay, we'll talk when I get home". When he got home he never once said okay what do you want to talk about? This has lead us to break up.

It's been 4 years since we've been apart, but I still love him and wish we could work it out. He's just hard to talk to without him getting defensive and yelling. I feel like he doesn't care, but he says he does. It's like he really hates me.

Please, can you tell me how to reach a man who shows no feelings towards nothing. He's a good man, he takes care of his responsibility. I just need to know if he loves me then why can't we try to work it out? I'm willing to forgive the harsh things he has said to me and leave it alone.

At one point we were going to get back together, but he told me if I could not deal with him having other female friends then it would not work. Now, I can accept it if they are friends only. But it's a problem when we are spending time together and he gets a page from one of those girls and he jumps to call them back but when I'm away from him he could not call me back until about 2 to 3 hours after I paged him. Am I being too jealous, do he really cares? Please help. I'm confused! -- Jackie

Jackie, I'm confused about the relationship you have with this man. You say you broke up and that it's been 4 years since you've been apart, but then you talk about the time you spend together now and the jealousy you feel about his female friends. Are the two of you together or not?

You say he's a good man, that he takes care of his responsibility. I assume that means he is supporting his child. If so, he's already experienced the responsibilities of marriage without the ceremony, and maybe he just doesn't see any additional benefit in making the relationship legal. What more would he get out of marrying you? You're already there for him without him tying himself down any further.

It sounds as though there never has been any form of communication between the two of you. He does what he wants, and you either accept it or not. Sometimes it gets mean. You probably nag and that either makes him meaner or he goes where there's not so much nagging. Is that about it?

This isn't the way a relationship should be. Both of you should want to be together and be willing to put the other person first. If he doesn't feel about you the way you feel about him, you won't be able to change him, but you can change yourself.

From what you have written, this relationship seems to be going nowhere. This man can't help but take you for granted! Perhaps when you stop trying so hard to make this man a permanent fixture in your life, he will take notice of you as he does his other lady friends. By that time, you may have found someone else who will treat you the way you deserve to be treated and you won't care about him any more.

He's not the only man in the world, just the only one in your world. Expand your horizons! Don't settle for the crumbs he throws, go for the whole cake! -- Queenie

♥

Hi Queenie, I am a 37-year old divorced, white male. I have been physically disabled for almost 11 years due to a car accident. My wife divorced me after I became injured and I haven't had much luck dating since then. It seems people only see my wheelchair instead of the person that is in it.

I am an average looking guy with an outgoing personality. I am healthy in every respect except for the fact that I use a wheelchair to get around. What can I do to improve my chances of finding a compatible female? I have placed and responded to countless personal ads on the internet with no response. Am I being too honest in telling them in the ad that I am disabled? Help, life is too short to spend alone! -- Ray

Ray, some people may feel that "all's fair" in the game of love, meaning don't tell the truth (or the rest of the story) until you have to. This might work in some instances, but I really think the honest approach is best in the long run. Not everyone is emotionally equipped to take on the extra challenge of a lover with a disability. When you find that special person, though, it will be worth the wait!

Believe it or not, there are a lot of good men, who don't have a physical disadvantage such as yours, who are in the same boat as far as being alone.

Has your accident has made you angry? Has your wife's leaving caused you to be bitter? Perhaps your attitude about the way the world is treating you is influencing your chances with suitable love candidates.

Also, do you look past the pretty face to see the person inside when you meet people for the first time? Would *you* ever consider dating a disadvantaged person?

The Internet is certainly a place to look for a person to "talk" to and there are more and more stories of true love found in cyberspace. But don't put all your efforts in that one direction and don't believe everything you read.

Get involved in clubs, special interest groups, volunteer organizations. Get out, stay busy. Don't look for love, let it find you. There is a special lady out there and I'm betting you'll meet her when you least expect to. -- Queenie

♥

Dear Queenie, I am 46-year old divorced female involved with a 30-year old never married male. We argue a lot, mostly because he says that I am insensitive to his feelings.

I believe that he dwells on things far too long and takes issues to where they should not go. For example, at a meeting, I made a remark that he took issue with which evolved to the fact that I was not taking his feelings into consideration.

Part of this is true as I was trying to listen to what was going on in the meeting while he kept whispering on and on about how I was ignoring him. This issue had nothing to do with him and I was stating an opinion with which he disagreed. I can accept that but why can't he accept my point of view? This is just a very minor problem in relation to others we have encountered.

When I tell him that perhaps our relationship was not meant to be, he says that I do not love him and that I am giving up. Well, perhaps I am giving up because this causes me tremendous anxiety and frustration. I

wish that I could let him down easily as he is prone to certain bouts of depression, especially feelings of worthlessness and self-loathing.

Can you help as soon as possible? This has been going on for two years and I am feeling very anxious about the situation. -- Pearl

Pearl, he sounds like a petulant little boy. I would suspect that you are not as insensitive to his feelings as he is to yours. You have the experience of commitment to a relationship, even though it didn't last, whereas he apparently has never cared deeply enough for someone other than himself to make a full commitment.

His immaturity will continue to cause you pain until you come to grips with the fact that he isn't your responsibility and move out of this relationship. It's not so much a matter of giving up as it is understanding that we each receive one life to live and none of us have to spend it with someone who causes us more pain than pleasure.

Successful older/younger relationships involve partners who are on the same mental/emotional/experience levels. He sounds much too immature to be a good match for you. -- Queenie

♥

Dear Queenie, my problem is a little complicated to explain, but I'll do my best. I am 25 years old and my boyfriend is eleven years older than me. We have been together now for about 2 years. I love him with all my heart and I know he feels the same about me. The problem is my parents.

From the start of our relationship, my parents refused to even acknowledge that he existed. The reasons are because of the age difference, he is divorced, and he has a 7-year old daughter who lives with his ex-wife, he didn't go to college and I'm currently going for my Master's, and we are also different religions. His ex-wife isn't a problem because she has already remarried.

I know it is a lot for my parents to take, but I really think that he is my soul mate. We have been living together now for about a year, and my parents still will not take notice to him. All they do is give me grief about still being with him.

Unfortunately, my parents are not in the best of health, and they like to make me feel guilty by telling me that I have to listen to them and I can't aggravate them because it is all this stress that has caused them the problems that they have with their health. I really can't take it anymore. All they keep asking me to do is move out and to get my own place. I have currently put down a security deposit on an apartment I found with my girlfriend.

My boyfriend is really upset. He says that if I move out our relationship will be over. He said that my parents are helping me to move out so that I will no longer see him anymore. If they find out that I am still with him, they probably won't help me financially to pay for rent while I go to school. He also feels that my parents will be setting me up with so many different people that before long I will find someone new.

I don't know what to do. I know the only thing that will make my parents happy is if I move out. I'm not so sure how happy that will make me, but if anything ever happened to either one of them, I know I would get blamed for aggravating them. My problem is that I always try to do what's right for everyone, and in this case I can't please everybody. What should I do? -- Lacey

Lacey, you're in a terrible spot and you're right, you can't please everybody. So, start by deciding who is most important in your life. I hope your answer is: YOU! You must decide what you truly want out of your life and then do whatever it takes to get it. (Hint: your education is critical to your future regardless of your other decisions.)

Parents know how to hit our "hot" buttons more than anyone else in the world. They have our lifetimes to polish the technique so why shouldn't they be experts? On the other hand, they also know us quite well, sometimes a little better than we know ourselves. And, they have not only the benefit of our lifetime of experience but also theirs. So they see us repeating the mistakes they themselves made and try to prevent us from making the same mistakes.

Overlook their guilt trips, you're not responsible for them. It's not fair of your parents to do this to you, but they love you and certainly want only the best for you. You know that, too, and that's making it difficult when you've found someone that you believe is the perfect person for you.

Your parents' behavior is poor about the situation but they don't want to see their beloved daughter make a giant mistake. Who could blame them? Put yourself in their place, if your daughter fell in love with someone of a different religion, lower education, divorced, and 11 years older, would you be happy?

As long as you are accepting money or support from your parents you have an obligation to them. That means no lying to them about moving away from your boyfriend and then living with him. Be honorable. It's the only way you can be or you wouldn't be having so much trouble with all of this. Stick to your personal convictions.

Your boyfriend is foolish. And you're wrong, there is something in this whole world he won't do for you. He won't work with you in this very important and crucial situation. If he loved you enough, he would accept your need to complete your education. He would also understand that true love waits as long as is required. He would trust in you. He would give you the space you need now in order to continue your personal growth for the future.

He would treasure the weekends. He wouldn't place guilt and stress you even more. Not if he truly loved you.

My hope is that you will move into your new apartment with your girlfriend and continue your education. You have a bright future ahead of you, perhaps with this man, perhaps not. -- Queenie

❤

Dear Queenie, I am in my early 30s, divorced with no kids, and I recently got reacquainted with a 29-year old friend who has never married and has no kids. She's college degreed, has a stable career, very personable and endearing, and is physically attractive. I know this sounds really stupid, but I have a problem with her age.

Like my father who is over 20 years older than my mother, I've always been with girls who were at least 5 years younger than me and no older than 25. My ex-wife was 6 years younger.

My problem with women who are in their late twenties or early thirties is that they need to have kids now while it's "safe" to do so. I feel if we were to seriously date and later marry, we wouldn't have enough time to settle into the marriage before having kids.

If we wait, then she runs the risk of being afflicted with "post-natal syndrome disorder" and might end up like a co-worker's wife who had her last child at age 36, became mentally unstable a year later, and was divorced two years after that. I know this condition is rare, but I've developed this fear of it growing up watching this thing destroy a perfectly good and happy family.

I know it sounds like I've already made up my mind to not date this woman and it seems I'm just asking you to validate my reasons. Instead, being already "once bitten and twice shy," I'm just plain confused. I know she's very much attracted to me. I too am attracted to her, but not as much. I know when I see her in a few days that I will enjoy her company and won't have these concerns. What I'm afraid of is when we decide to date romantically that these concerns will eventually inhibit my willingness to return her affections for me.

Since my divorce, all I know of love is how to live without it and have gotten use to loneliness, because I've learned to live with it. Given my

recent track record beginning with my divorce, I'm a tired, emotional cripple who feels he's on his last leg. What am I supposed to do? -- Len

Len, to truly change your life for the better you should get counseling to understand why you believe that younger women are your only option for happiness. Your co-worker's wife's "post-natal syndrome disorder" is not a valid reason for seeking women within such a narrow age range. What happens when they grow older? Will you divorce again and go after another younger wife?

Your friend needs someone who can appreciate her qualities without being focused on her "excessive" age. You don't fit the criteria.

You will continue to have a life of loneliness until you learn why you're running so hard from intimacy and commitment. Find a counselor. And good luck. -- Queenie

♥

Dear Queenie, my boyfriend and I have lived together for 7 years and have a 5 year-old son. Recently he has become more distant and uncaring towards me and we have been arguing more because of this. He denies that anything is wrong.

Should I just ignore this and continue on or pursue this? The last time he acted this way he left for a month and lived with friends or in his car. He never gave me a reason for leaving. Now I am afraid I will come home one day and find him gone like last time. If he leaves again, I'm not taking him back. -- Tracy

Tracy, it sounds as though you expect this relationship to end and you don't want to be surprised when he leaves again. Your relationship is past due the time of commitment. Have either of you talked about marriage?

Do you want to be married? Does he? Your son needs a more stable family environment. Your son also needs to be protected legally and financially if his father decides to leave and this relationship ends for good. -- Queenie

♥

Dear Queenie, my husband of 5 years walked out on me and our marriage. After many months of healing and therapy, I have been able to move on and accept what has happened. I am in my thirties. Two months ago, I met a wonderful person that I could fall in love with if things continue to grow. He is mid-thirties, single, and has never been married.

He told me that he doesn't want a serious relationship now and he also feels I'm not ready for one either. He thinks this is a rebound relationship although I've been in a couple of other relationships.

When he talks to me about his feelings he can be confusing at times. He tells me that I am a very special person and that I'm a sweetheart almost every time we are together. Other times he says he's not ready for a serious relationship but again tells me that I'm a special person.

I care a lot for him and don't want to do anything to jeopardize the relationship. What do I do to keep him interested but not push him away? -- Kaye

Kaye, a guy who has been able to avoid commitment this long is not likely to change his ways. He says he doesn't want a serious relationship and he's making excuses why there shouldn't be one. Believe him. He won't change his mind, he likes his life the way it is.

If you want to develop a relationship with the potential for a committed future, look elsewhere. Guys like this make wonderful friends, the kind you can tell your troubles to and ask their advice. He is a jewel as he is, don't try to change him into something he's not. -- Queenie

♥

Dear Queenie, I just met a attractive, single woman from my office and want to ask her out for a date. Trouble is that because of her work demands, she doesn't have much free time to herself even on the weekends but I fully understand her high work commitment and dedication to her boss. Should I continue to ask her out? To my knowledge she's not going out with anyone at the moment. Besides her, I am also seeing other women. -- Tab

Tab, if you've already asked her out and she has turned you down, you should back off. Regardless of whether or not she is dating someone, she is under no obligation to date everyone who asks her out.

It sounds as though the lady is trying to keep her personal life separate from her career. She may not want to date co-workers. Respect her wishes. -- Queenie

♥

Dear Queenie, I have been dating a younger man, he is 32, I am 41. Needless to say our life experiences are quite different. I have three children and my own house, he has never been married and still lives at home with

his mother! I have serious concerns that this relationship will not work. What is your opinion? -- Fran

Fran, the age difference doesn't have to be an issue, the life experiences could be. It really depends whether the two of you can get past the age difference and whether you let the younger man/ older woman scenario put too much stress on how you relate to each other. He could be just what you need to be very happy, and apparently he believes you are the person he needs in his life.

How do you and his mother get along? Is she dependent upon him or would she like to see him have a home and family of his own? How does he relate to your children? What type of career and earning capabilities does he have in comparison with yours? Do you enjoy being with him? Does he make you laugh? Does he make you feel good about yourself? -- Queenie

♥

Dear Queenie, I am 21-years old and have been dating a man who is almost 30 for the past 3 months. I think I love him though I am not sure. Things go really well between us but then go bad. He lies to me sometimes and whenever I try to talk to him about it he just laughs it off.

He has two children from a previous relationship and is of another culture, which I think will be obstacles if in the future if we ever wanted to get serious. I don't know what he wants for us and I can't ask him without sounding like I'm asking for a serious commitment!

Should I take the advice of friends who say don't get bogged down with a pre-made family and cultural differances or should I stay with this man who makes me happy? Or get out before I am totally in love and have invested time and effort in a relationship? -- Wynonna

Wynonna, you have to decide what you want from life. Your friends can give advice but ultimately you have to decide what's best for you.

There are a lot of things to overcome here which might be worth it if he truly, truly was the most wonderful man in the world. Is he? It's your life and your decision. Since you aren't really certain, I think there may be a little too much to overcome. -- Queenie

♥

Dear Queenie, I met and fell deeply in love with a man who had just been divorced after 20 years of marriage. After dating for 5 months he asked me to move in with him which I did. After a year he said he needed space and freedom and I moved out.

I was devastated when he started dating other women. Ultimately, I learned through books and tapes how to pull myself together, but that incredible pain took a lot out of me, and to top it off, I never stopped loving him.

Early this year, after breaking up with the woman he was living with, contacted me. We had a nice date and talked a lot, with a lot of tears and apologies on his part. He asked if we could renew our friendship, but emphasized that he wasn't looking for a serious relationship. The physical chemistry is stronger than ever, and he can't seem to get enough affection from me. He behaves as if he still loves me, but he won't say it.

He has bought a house, which he says is big enough only for him, and he lives alone but he tells me of home-booked meals that this "friend" and that one made for him. Well, excuse me, but any woman who will put on a lobster and a shrimp dinner for a man is seriously on the make, in my opinion.

I'm just waiting, yet again, for the call saying that he doesn't want to date two women at the same time and getting dumped again. I'm wondering if all this has to do with a mid-life crisis, and if I should just stand by him as he gets all this out of his system. I've been loving this man for four years; am I wasting my time? -- April

April, he currently has the pleasures of commitment without the responsibilities that come with it. Certainly it could be a part of his reinventing himself as a result of mid-life crisis, but what happens when he has found the person within himself that he wants to be and that person doesn't need you as much as you need him?

He has told you he isn't ready for commitment. You can continue this one-sided commitment and worry about the next dumping or you can rethink your involvement with him and maybe save yourself some heartache.

Men aren't the only ones who can play the "I'm happy with things the way they are" game. Can you become independent and not always available when he calls? If he truly enjoys your company and believes you're the woman for him, your change of habit and heart may make him take a second, longer look at the relationship.

If he doesn't care whether you date others and doesn't object to your being busy when he calls, then he isn't into this relationship too deeply and you haven't lost a lot except the time and tears.

Four years is not your lifetime. It's a lot of good memories which can be pasted into your heart's scrapbook with all the other good memories from the past. Today begins the rest of your life. If you're emotionally involved with him when the right man comes along, look how much you could lose. If your friend is the right man, he'll let you know. -- Queenie

♥

Hi Queenie, last month I answered a personals ad and met a nice, polite, seemingly sincere man. For the first 3 weeks he was attentive, affectionate, and constantly wanted to be in my company. He even asked if I wanted us to see each other a lot and on a long-term basis, to which I said yes. He introduced me to his daughters, his friends, almost everyone he knows. He wanted me to stay over at his place every night, or he would come and stay with me.

Then I decided to stay home alone a couple of nights and told him I would be over for the weekend. All went well during the weekend until Sunday afternoon when he got into a terrible mood and was really grouchy. I told him that to avoid an argument, I was going to go home for the rest of the day and I would talk to him the next day. Since that time he has completely shut down.

I have tried to talk with him, but I am aware of some financial problems he is having, along with the fact that he is unemployed and doing "odd jobs" till he can get back on his feet. He says that since he cannot afford to take me out or spend any money on me that he has put the relationship "on hold." He doesn't call when he says he will and if I call him he won't admit that anything is wrong.

Is he afraid I will dump him over his financial situation, or is he playing games with me? Oh, yeah, he has a female roommate that I think is making problems, too. I think she doesn't want him to have a relationship because it would threaten her living arrangements there.

What should I do? One of the stipulations in his ad was that he didn't want to meet any woman who played games, yet isn't that what he's doing? Should I write this off? -- Valerie

Men think their value is directly in proportion to their earning capability. He is unemployed so he may feel that he is not "good enough" for you and even if he does like you and like being with you, he may be trying to pull back so that he doesn't get hurt if and when you leave him, which he might expect you to do.

It has been a month since you met this man which is not long enough to develop a strong relationship, particularly when he's dealing with other life crises at the same time.

Your strength (leaving early, taking some nights for yourself) may be very intimidating to him, again, particularly now when he may be feeling less than secure.

You cannot let his insecurities undermine you, but you can try to empathize with his situation. Don't write him off too quickly but trust your instincts if the situation, particularly the female roommate, doesn't feel right to you. -- Queenie

♥

Dear Queenie, how can it work? I am young 50 male dating a 25-year old female. I have told a couple people and yeah, great for me, ego building, flattering, envy, and above all, I have come alive again since my divorce 5 years ago. I've got it made, but the guilt!

She works for me. She likes me, but, she can't tell her friends, family or co-workers. It is wrong, there's nowhere to go for her, no future for her, and we both know she will be gone someday when HE comes along, but for the meantime, how do you justify? The feeling is so good. This relationship is not based on sex. That old song applies "Until It's Time For You To Go."

How about all the songs about older guys, younger women? How about all the movies about older guys, younger women? I don't need Lolita type responses. Help, please, and, thank you! -- Hal

Hal, if you were 75 and she were 50, would it be such a big deal? Would you feel so guilty? Why can't she tell anyone about this relationship? Is she having a problem with the age difference? Does she expect her family and friends to give her grief if they find out she's dating someone twice her age? Or is there something else? Is she your daughter's age? Is that the guilt you're feeling?

You didn't ask but I think it's risky dating someone who works for you. There are any number of high profile lawsuits that will bear this out because of work relationships that have gone wrong. Why risk everything for a relationship that doesn't appear to have a future? -- Queenie

♥

Dear Queenie, I am currently involved with my boss, who is 20 years my senior. I know, very taboo, right? We have been casualy dating now for 5 months and the other night I mentioned to him that it was common knowledge at work that we are involved. He seemed to be quite disturbed at this, although it was he who told many of his male employees, so I felt why should I hide or deny it. We do not flirt at work and it is business as usual.

The reason I am asking for advice is that he commented that if it became public knowledge things would end. It has been public knowledge for weeks now and I am wondering how I could know this and he didn't. If he should break things off how should I handle the situation? -- Jan

Jan, you're in a very bad spot. You like the guy and when it's over, you either have to find another place to work or learn how to handle a broken heart while you still work for him.

Since you're "casually dating" why don't you, nicely and politely, tell him that you think it best for you, him and the business, that the two of you don't date any more. In other words, save face, get out while you still can without causing problems in your working relationship. It, and you, can't be too important to him, if he will end the relationship if it becomes public knowledge.

Incidentally, is he married? -- Queenie

♥

Dear Queenie, I met a sweet and wonderful man 2 months ago. He's 38 and I'm 41. We both felt an attraction and chemistry and have been dating. Now, he feels that we have reached the crossroads in our relationship.

He feels that if we continue to see each other it's a natural course that will lead to romance with the goal of marriage and he's not ready for a full-blown relationship at this time. I don't want a casual relationship.

I've been there before and feel I deserve a man who will love me and who I can love in return. I am also a one-man woman and I don't feel I will have my needs satisfied in a casual relationship.

We ended our discussion with no decision made and he is supposed to call me soon. I don't know what it is I'm waiting for him to tell me and although he has many of the qualities I am looking for in a potential mate, I feel that if he's not ready, he's wasting my time. What should I do? -- Petula

Petula, two months is a little early for any relationship to be at a crossroads. Some don't get there for years. If I can take a guess, he wants to get physical and you're saying "not without a commitment I won't."

There is absolutely nothing wrong with waiting until the right person comes along to become sexually intimate but if you're expecting him to commit to a full-blown relationship when you start having sex, I think you're going to be disappointed with his response.

Attraction and chemistry are important within a relationship. Without it, why bother? But if his needs are purely physical and your needs are security and commitment, then you're on opposite paths. Even if he were to agree to a commitment in order to get you to relax and get physical, how long do you think he would remain in the relationship after the attraction and the chemistry abated?

Rethink what you absolutely must have in a relationship and understand that when you meet someone it takes time to really get to know them. Relationships that are meant for a lifetime need more than two months to develop. -- Queenie

♥

Dear Queenie, my guy, 54, and I, 45, love each other, but he has been married 3 times and is commitment-phobic. We've been together more than a year. He keep's saying if we're "meant" to be together, it will happen.

The other day, I jokingly told him not to buy a toaster oven since we'd be living together someday and I already had one. He acted incredulous, as if the idea of us living together had never entered his mind.

How do I handle the situation? I do love him very much and have never been so happy. But how long should I wait to have a commitment?

He is very open about being attracted to other women, but I don't have a problem with that — it's only human. But is it normal for a guy to tell his girlfriend when he dreams about having sex with other women? It makes me feel somewhat insecure. -- Mickey

Mickey, not the old "meant to be" ploy again! That response works well unless the other person responds that in order for things to happen, they require some sort of action. In this case, it's going to take action from you to get some response from him.

First, because you're asking for advice, I doubt you're as happy with the situation as you say you are. I can understand that since he isn't exactly making you feel special. Actually, I wonder how special he would feel if you told him about your dreams of having sex with other men. Couldn't tell him such a thing? Why? Because you love him and wouldn't want to hurt him? Do you ever wonder why he doesn't love (or respect) you as much?

You have some tough decisions to make. It's up to you as to how long you take to make them. I think if it were me, I think I'd buy him a toaster oven and tell him goodbye. -- Queenie

♥

Dear Queenie, I am a very jealous person and I do not trust my boyfriend because of certain situations. I have tried everything from therapy to antidepressants and I am almost to the end of the line.

My boyfriend and I fight constantly and I'm afraid our relationship will come to a bitter end. Do you have any ideas on how to help me get through my jealousy and untrust? -- Shirley

Shirley, if those "certain situations" mean he has cheated or is cheating, then perhaps he isn't worthy of trust. If you mean that he has cheated in the past but says it's over, then, unless you have some very strong evidence that he isn't to be trusted now, you should forgive and forget.

Which hurts worse? The pain from trusting and finding that trust was misplaced? Or the pain of not trusting and losing his love forever? If you trust, you have a chance of getting hurt, but you also have the chance of a good relationship with him.

I think the risk of a broken heart is a small price to pay for trusting someone you truly love although it shouldn't take therapy and antidepressants to keep a relationship together. -- Queenie

♥

Hi Queenie, I have been casually seeing this man for about two years. He is divorced and older than I am. At the beginning of the year I asked what kind of relationship he was seeking with me and his answer was that he enjoyed our outings but did not want to give up his independence yet. I never have asked him to do so.

I really care for this guy, more than I expected to and more than I have for anyone else I've had a relationship with. During another conversation he told me that he has been seeing other women and was concerned how I might react if I heard or saw him with someone else. I told him that I realized our relationship was not exclusive and that I didn't feel he expected me to not see other men. I also told that while I had been asked out I haven't wanted to go out with anyone else. Now though I do want a closer relationship.

My problem is that while I care for him, I'm still unsure about what I want. I am turning forty this year but I have always valued my independence. It is very hard for me to rely on other people. I want to be closer to this man, but I'm very much afraid of rejection. This all may be moot anyway, because he may not be interested in a closer relationship. To get to the point should I tell him how I feel and be honest about what I what? -- Marla

Marla, I don't think that good relationships can survive without communication and honesty. You two seem to be able to talk about some aspects of your relationship with ease, so why not continue by telling him how you truly feel. As you said, the point may be moot, but why not find out? -- Queenie

♥

Other books published by Home & Leisure Publishing, Inc.

Advice for an Imperfect Single World: Wisdom and Wit from Friends & Lovers' Queen of Hearts
The opinioned online columnist for Friends & Lovers the Relationships Guide tackles the problems of singles and the dating world.
September 2004

Midnight Confessions: True Stories of Adultery
First person accounts of adultery by the betrayers, the betrayed, and the other man or other woman.
February 2005

Also written by Pat Gaudette and Gay Courter:

How to Survive Your Husband's Midlife Crisis: Strategies and Stories from The Midlife Wives Club by Gay Courter and Pat Gaudette. Published by Perigee Books; 1st edition May 6, 2003; ISBN: 0-399-52882-2. Available at Amazon.com and most booksellers.

Their marriages crumbling, their lives in chaos, they went online in a desperate search for answers. They found a sisterhood of survivors... The Midlife Wives Club.

From Chapter 1: Rude Awakenings: First Signs of Trouble

Many members of the Midlife Wives Club recall with excruciating accuracy the precise moment they knew their lives would never be the same. Grace had a premonition. Her husband, Roger, had returned to England from a trip overseas. After sleeping late, he said he wanted to take a walk to get some fresh air and buy a paper. Grace was anxious to hear about his trip and watched the clock. He seemed to be taking much longer than expected. She began to pace the house, which was tidy and clean. She had stayed up into the early hours making everything perfect for him, because before the trip, he complained about the children's messes and how he yearned for "clean spaces." "The fact that I was trying so hard to please him while he was planning to leave me chokes me to this day."

Then, she saw his briefcase by the front door, where the children's backpacks usually littered the hallway. She picked it up to keep the area neat, but for some reason, she popped open the clasp and noticed a packet of condoms. "My heart was thudding, but I felt incredibly calm," Grace said, "even though I knew from that moment my life would never be the same again."

But it hadn't been a bolt out of the blue. Grace had known for a long time Roger was unhappy with his life. He had become depressed the previous year and was taking antidepressants. He was losing his hair, which bothered him. Plus he lost his parents within a short duration of each other and felt guilty that he hadn't spent more time with them in recent years. He felt pressure at work and at home, and he looked forward to the business trip because he said it might help give him some "needed space."

As Grace walked slowly down the street to meet him, she noticed a guarded look in his eyes. She spoke in the calmest voice she could muster. "Do you have anything to tell me?" He said no and she repeated the question. Roger appeared flustered and shook his head. "Are you having an affair?" Grace asked.

Again Roger denied it, but Grace asked once more. This time he admitted it. "I felt as if I had been punched in the stomach," she said, "yet I couldn't stop asking the questions that would hurt me more: how long it had been going on, how old she was—twenty years younger than me!—and if he was still seeing her. Roger told me the affair started six months earlier and reminded me of the day he called in a panic when he learned there had been a takeover bid for his company and they were talking about who might be redundant. I remember thinking that was such a harsh word for someone who had given ten years to his job, and how my heart had gone out to him. He said he had to work late, which I understood, but instead he went out with her. I kept up the interrogation until he confessed that he loved her. From that moment, my marriage of 18 years was over."

Another woman, Annie*, could barely bring herself to recall the moment she faced the truth. It was especially painful for her because as a reporter in Nashville, she was used to uncovering other people's dirty secrets, but chose to ignore her husband Larry's unexplained absences. One day, on a whim, she opened the accounting files. "He paid the bills and dealt with the taxes—chores I hated—so he hadn't hidden the receipts for jewelry and lingerie. But there they were: the proof my marriage was a lie. Up until then, I had a starry-eyed naiveté about love that made my heart turn over every time I saw Larry walk in the door. To think I felt that way even though he had been with another woman!"

Like Annie, Lee* avoided all the signs. "I had been out of town for my father-in-law's funeral and stayed a few extra days to help my mother-in-law. The children went home to Wisconsin with my husband. A neighbor agreed to take care of the children after school until their father got home from work. They were at her house when I got back in town, so I went over to pick them up." Lee wanted to hurry home to unpack, but the neighbor asked her to come into the kitchen for a cup of coffee.

" 'There's something I have to tell you about,' she said, then told me how she had seen James with another woman at a local park. I was about to say it could have been someone from work and she shouldn't jump to conclusions when she said they were kissing. I looked straight at her and said, 'Not my James, he wouldn't do that, there is no way he would ever do anything like that!' I asked if she could feed the kids supper, then went home and confronted James when he walked in the door." James began to cry and begged Lee to believe he had needed to talk to someone who'd experienced the loss of a father. Lee asked him about the kiss, and he swore the neighbor had been exaggerating a friendly peck on the cheek. Still Lee suspected there was more to it.

All these women were blindsided by revelations that their marriages were far rockier than they had imagined. Why? Was it something they had done? Had their spouses been tempted by another woman? Had their husbands changed over time, and they had failed to notice the signs?

*Find out the current status of Annie's relationship in Chapter 10. Other members whose names are marked with an asterisk at first mention are also updated in Chapter 10.

www.ingramcontent.com/pod-product-compliance
Lightning Source LLC
Chambersburg PA
CBHW031502270326
41930CB00006B/214